AF385784

TWENTIETH
CENTURY
COP

For Pam. Together we made it happen.

BARRY APPLETON

TWENTIETH CENTURY COP

THE FLYING SQUAD DETECTIVE WHO WROTE 'THE BILL'

with
OLIVER CROCKER

First published in Great Britain in 2026 by
PEN AND SWORD TRUE CRIME
An imprint of
Pen & Sword Books Limited
Yorkshire – Philadelphia

ISBN 978 1 03619 951 7

Typeset in Times New Roman 11/15 by SJmagic DESIGN SERVICES, India.
Printed and bound in the UK by CPI Group (UK) Ltd.

The Publisher's authorised representative in the EU for product safety is Authorised
Rep Compliance Ltd., Ground Floor, 71 Lower Baggot Street,
Dublin D02 P593, Ireland.
www.arccompliance.com

For a complete list of Pen & Sword titles please contact
PEN & SWORD BOOKS LIMITED
George House, Units 12 & 13, Beevor Street, Off Pontefract Road,
Barnsley, South Yorkshire, S71 1HN, England
E-mail: enquiries@pen-and-sword.co.uk
Website: www.pen-and-sword.co.uk

or

PEN AND SWORD BOOKS
1950 Lawrence Rd, Havertown, PA 19083, USA
E-mail: uspen-and-sword@casematepublishers.com
Website: www.penandswordbooks.com

CONTENTS

PROLOGUE

WELCOME TO MY WORLD

The unsuspecting pedestrians on Wood Green High Road were enjoying what appeared on the surface to be a pleasant summer's day. But lurking just around the corner were several armed robbers. Their target was the delivery yard at the rear of a thriving department store. The driver at the wheel of the stolen Ford Transit smoked another fag, waiting in eager anticipation for what he hoped would be the biggest payday of his career so far.

But what he had no way of knowing was that the van parked a little further down the road, with 'Fresh Farm Eggs' written on the sides, contained five Flying Squad officers. On top of our van was a small, encased fan, making it look like our advertised goods were refrigerated. In fact, this concealed a periscope, meaning we could see the sweat on the driver's brow in such detail that we could have been sat next to him. We were his shadow and his worst nightmare.

Five Squad had received a tip-off from a reliable source that a security van was going to be hit whilst collecting the takings from the store. Our information was that the robbers would reverse their Transit in behind the security van, as if they were about to make a delivery. Then as the guards returned from the store with the takings… boom!

Weeks of patient surveillance had led to this moment. For now, all we could do was sit tight and wait for events to unfold. The tension was palpable. After about twenty minutes, the security van came down the road and turned into the yard. The driver of the Transit put on a balaclava. I took a deep breath. This is what I was trained for. After what felt like an age, the Transit started to slowly creep in behind the security van…

We made our move.

Two of our officers immediately apprehended the driver whilst he was reversing. Armed with my Smith & Wesson, I ran to the back of the van with another officer, ready to arrest the rest of the gang as they got out. But something was wrong. The doors were already open and the back was empty. I spun around to discover one of the robbers facing me. Dressed in baggy overalls and wearing a balaclava hood, he was holding a sawn-off shotgun, which he began to point at me. Using a standard two-handed grip, I fired…

Then all hell broke loose.

CHAPTER 1

YOU'RE ON YOUR OWN, KID

My journey to the Met began in January 1957, when I boarded the famous Red Dragon steam train at Newport. As the powerful locomotive began to chug its way towards London, I stared out of the window and glimpsed the picturesque Welsh valleys disappear behind thick plumes of grey smoke. As my past faded away before my eyes, I found myself thinking about the life I had left behind.

I was born in the market town of Monmouth on 14 March 1939, and grew up living with my maternal grandparents, Thomas and Ivy Cummings. My granddad's Scottish roots earned him the nickname 'Jock', a very proud man and a true gentleman who gave me a lot of time as a child. He was a signwriter by trade and later died with his boots on whilst painting a name on the side of a freight truck at Chepstow railway station. I loved the guy.

Jock and Ivy's house at 119 Monnow Street was rather dilapidated and tended to get flooded every winter by the wild river Monnow, which would fill up over the banks, in through their home and out onto the street. As they had no electricity, the house was lit only by gas mantles. Saturday evenings were a big occasion; a tin bath would be placed in front of the fire and filled with water heated from a kettle. Everyone in the house would then use the bath in turn. I was usually the last to go in, meaning I could stay in for longer. Simple pleasures.

This was the time of the ration book and there was not much food to go around. Fortunately, my grandparents kept chickens, meaning we wouldn't starve in wartime. We never ate our chickens, as they were too valuable for laying eggs, and cleaning out their runs was one of my chores. We got to enjoy one big meal a week for Sunday dinner, which was always rabbit.

One of my earliest memories is looking out of the house at night and gazing in wonder as the whole sky lit up in the distance. As a kid, I didn't fully comprehend the reason behind this exciting spectacle. I knew we were at war, but it never occurred to my young mind that with every flash above, many innocent people were losing their lives on the ground below.

To help prepare me in case of invasion, I had to wear a gas mask to school. Some sported a picture of Mickey Mouse on theirs, an attempt by their parents to make it seem more fun and less frightening. On my way to school I would pass a painting of the 'Squander Bug', the famous propaganda character created to discourage waste. There were always soldiers training in the street, rehearsing how they would defend the town from an attack. An armed guard was permanently posted on Monnow Bridge, an ancient structure which was then a vital link for traffic going to and from the local cattle market. I also recall going on protest marches at night, where hundreds carried lighted torches and burnt effigies of Hitler on a large bonfire.

The war was the reason I spent the first six years of my life growing up without my parents. My dad, John 'Jack' Appleton, was enlisted and served with the Royal Engineers. My mum, Mildred 'Millie' Cummings, worked at a munitions factory near Abergavenny, later becoming a conductor on the buses travelling there. While my parents were contributing to the war effort, I had to quickly learn how to look after myself. Like so many other kids at this time, I was on my own – it was just the way it was.

I became a lone wolf and spent a lot of time by myself, either kicking a football against the garage door or going scrumping. I also enjoyed a game called 'eel stabbing', where along a patch of the river that was just ankle deep, armed with a fork, I would carefully lift a stone up and at the first sign of movement, boom!

I also used to mess around on the railway tracks, where one of my favourite games was to put a coin on the track about halfway along the railway bridge and hide. I'd then wait for the steam train to come booming along on its approach to the railway station, which was just around the corner. I'm not sure what damage I expected my coin to do, but on one occasion the train stopped before it got to the bridge. I had been spotted!

The crew climbed out and chased me as I ran away. I was too quick for them though and I made my daring escape by jumping in the river and swimming across to the other side. But when I got home, the police were at the house, knocking on the front door, so I fled again. Little did I know that a couple of decades later, I would be the one in uniform doing the knocking!

It wasn't until after the war that I started to get to know my parents. I can't ever remember seeing any real affection between them, though I think that was more to do with how couples behaved in front of their children in those days. When my much younger sister Susan came along a few years later, my mum and dad got a chance to enjoy parenthood in a way they had not been able to do during the war. As such, I suspect Susan probably had a much happier childhood than I did.

This was not a good time for me, mainly because I hated my secondary modern schooling. I wasn't a very good pupil and was always in trouble, usually for fighting. There was very little about my education that interested me outside of doing sports. But I discovered the benefits of working hard from a very young age, getting my first job doing the local paper round.

I had to be at the newsagents by 8am on my bicycle and have all the papers delivered before I started school at 9am. There were two more paper rounds in Monmouth and, when one of the other kids dropped out, I asked if I could take over and do a second one to make extra money for Christmas. This was when I discovered that I could make things happen for myself by applying a little effort and determination.

After somehow passing all my school exams, I got a job as a trainee mechanic at George Mann's St James Garage in Monmouth. A specialist automobile engineer, Mr. Mann was also an agent for Morris and Austin cars, displaying a shiny selection of vehicles in a very upmarket showroom. Mr. Mann was always immaculately presented, wearing a pinstripe suit and waistcoat, complete with gold fob watch and chain. At the end of each day, I had to clean all the tools and put them back in their correct place. Once, Mr. Mann came into the workshop and, on discovering I was still there working after all the other staff had gone home, gave me half a crown. He was a great boss.

At lunchtimes, when the old boy who worked the petrol pumps took his hour break, I would take over the pumps, which were hand-operated by levers. When the Suez crisis kicked off in 1956, petrol was placed on ration and I earned lots of tips for being overly generous with fuel!

I shadowed two of the mechanics, Tom Ebborn and Jack Williams, both seasoned professionals who had worked at the garage all their adult lives. These two great guys showed me the ropes, teaching me how to repair punctures, adjust thermostats and replace fan belts. They also taught me how to drive a car and thanks to them I passed my test first time.

I had a terrific time working at the garage, but as much as I enjoyed training to be a mechanic, I was nearly 18 and the threat of National Service loomed. I didn't mind the idea of doing my bit for the nation, but my dad said it would be a waste of time going in the Army and insisted I find an alternative. With time ticking away, I needed to come up with a plan.

David Edwards, an older Monmouth boy who also grew up on Monnow Street, had recently joined the Metropolitan Police as a constable. He told me that it had been a great move, giving him lots of opportunities to play sport and have plenty of fun in the big city. He tipped me off that if I joined as a senior cadet before I was 18, I wouldn't have to go in the Army.

I had applied initially to be a cadet with the British South Africa Police, which would have meant being posted to Southern Rhodesia. I was accepted by them, but as the next posting wasn't until the following March, I would have been called up before then. However, if I could get accepted as a cadet with the Met, I would remain exempt from National Service as long as I didn't leave the force before the age of 26. Result!

An advertisement for police cadet recruitment running in the *Sunday Mirror* at the time promised:

> The training's exciting, with plenty of companionship and sport. And there's no more worthwhile job.

While another warned that:

> Police standards are high — but if you think you're good enough, here's a career for you.

As I was taller than the minimum height requirement of 5 ft 8 in., all I had to do was write to the Metropolitan Police Recruiting Centre in Beak Street and request an application form. A week or so later, the Met sent a reply to our local police station and a uniformed sergeant arranged to come over to our house and interview me. He alone would decide if I was suitable to be a cadet. Thankfully, he hadn't been one of the coppers sent to investigate my childhood escapades on the train track and I was accepted to train as a cadet at Hendon.

I would be paid £5.11.2d a week as a cadet and, subject to passing all my exams, I would then be posted to a police division on attachment for practical experience. The aim would then be to become a fully fledged constable when I turned 19, earning a salary of £490 – roughly the equivalent of £15,000 today. It would have been practically impossible for me to earn that amount in Monmouth.

I can't recall feeling nervous about moving 150 miles away from home, perhaps thanks to how self-reliant I had felt from a young age. Before I knew it, the Red Dragon had roared its way to Paddington station. Welcome to the Metropolis. My first mission was to make my way down onto the London Underground, which was a whole new world for me. I'd done my homework and knew I had to get the appropriately named Metropolitan line over to Aldersgate station, renamed Barbican in 1968. From there, a short walk led me to Beech Street, where the Metropolitan Police had an office for all the new intake to report to before being transported by bus to our new home in Hendon.

The Metropolitan Police Training School first opened in 1934, making use of the old airfield on Aerodrome Road used during the First World War. An important figure in the development of the school was Lord Trenchard, who served as Metropolitan Police Commissioner between 1931 and 1935. Prior to this, he had commanded the Royal Flying Corps' Central Flying School. Many of the leftover vehicles from the Royal Flying Corps were later refurbished and deployed to the Flying Squad, which many believe is how the squad earned its famous nickname.

Aerodrome Road has been significantly redeveloped in recent years and the area is now totally unrecognisable to me. The Hendon Country Club building that we all reported to in 1957 has long since been demolished and today the Metropolitan Police Academy operates from a brand-new purpose-built site. Times have changed. While today's intake is housed in modern apartment blocks and all the comforts of home, my initial accommodation was an old Nissen hut, shared with thirty other cadets. A hangover from the war, the hut was fitted with a lone cast-iron stove to try and keep us warm in the depths of winter.

We were assured that this was only a temporary measure, as our proper accommodation was still full of outgoing cadets who hadn't been posted to Division yet. I'd experienced much tougher conditions growing up on Monnow Street, so I didn't find the huts too bad. I immediately felt a great sense of camaraderie between all of us young lads, many of whom had travelled from all across the country to get out of doing National Service. Or so we thought…

On the first day of our thirteen-week course, we were met by two uniformed sergeants, both reportedly former military policemen from Aldershot, who informed us of what we had in store… 'If you 'orrible lot think you've wormed your way out of National Service, you are in for a big surprise!' The morning began with us all getting our hair scalped and then falling in to be trained in the art of marching and parading.

In the early hours of the morning, we were woken up and ordered to stand to attention. We then had to remake our beds, again and again, until those two thugs were happy. At dawn, six of us were given tins of white paint with brushes and ordered to paint decorative stones placed around the Nissen huts. These dastardly sergeants paced around, watching our every move. I suddenly stopped painting, put my paintbrush down and stood up. I turned to face the morning sun and saw the silhouette of one the Aldershot bullies marching towards me…

```
DISSOLVE TO:
EXT. METROPOLITAN POLICE TRAINING YARD. 1957. 0645.
SERGEANT CROSSLAND, 40s, tall, hard-nosed, square-jawed,
marches over exuding an air of pomposity and a gleam of
perverse pleasure.
                    CROSSLAND
          Why have you stopped painting, Appleton?
                    BARRY
          Why are we doing this?
                    CROSSLAND
          Discipline, lad. Discipline.
```

```
          BARRY
Because we were drinking and singing last night?
          CROSSLAND
You're a fucking Welshman and you call that
singing?! You woke up half the Borough with that
noise. Luckily for the people of Hendon, you lot
will be moving into your shiny new accommodation
later today and we can all get some peace and
quiet.
          BARRY
Does that mean we won't be seeing you guys anymore?
          CROSSLAND
Oh don't you worry, Boyo. We'll be teaching you lot
self-defence next week. And guess what, Appleton?
You just volunteered to be the first in line. Be
prepared to have the shit kicked out of you.


CROSSLAND walks away laughing to himself, not noticing
BARRY giving him a two-finger salute.
```

Within a few days, we were issued with our uniforms. I remember trying mine on for the first time and I must confess that I felt quite good wearing it. I was lucky that mine fit me, whereas some of the other lads got lost in their tunics or had their caps down over their eyes! We would have to wait for the famous helmet, which you didn't get until you had finished being a cadet.

The uniform was made up of a dark blue serge tunic, with matching trousers and tie, along with two blue shirts, which came with two or three separate collars. You had to place a metal stud in the neck of the shirt and another at the front, which was bloody awkward if you were in a rush! I remember being in such a hurry to get changed and ready for parade sometimes that I used to clean my teeth whilst taking a shower to save time, a habit I still occasionally repeat all these years later.

We were all responsible for keeping our uniforms neat and tidy, washing and brushing them by hand. We were also given a pair of boots, but these were horribly uncomfortable, so we all went out and bought our own. We had to polish these every day from top to bottom, even underneath! I didn't mind at all; I just embraced the routine and saw it all as part of the great adventure.

I used to write home to my parents and let them know how I was getting on. I never felt homesick and I don't recall any of my mates saying so either. I think we all felt the same excitement about getting away and starting a new chapter of our lives. Thinking back, we were an incredible bunch of misfits and unlikely law enforcers. Some of the cadets were very talented musicians, who should have been destined for stardom. Once we moved into our proper accommodation, a few of us formed a skiffle group, playing on washboards and any other appliances we could lay our hands on that could make a useful sound.

Once our training got underway, we spent most days studying law and attending lectures. We also took part in mock trials, giving evidence in court and being put in the witness stand to see how we would react to having our statements cross-examined. That was my first taste of drama, as it was effectively acting and role play, though it never crossed my mind that I might one day write my own dramatic courtroom scenes for television.

In 1957, British Pathé produced a training film at Hendon, capturing rows of young police officers sitting at desks, having lessons in how to use a typewriter. The voiceover on the film enthusiastically claimed that 'the first steps of typing will often lead to the criminal investigation branches…' Well, having trained there that very same year, this expert witness can confirm that such typing lessons never happened during the months I was at Hendon. That whole sequence was pure PR, staged to encourage recruitment, though with my screenwriter hat on, I understand now why some creative licence was used to engage the audience.

Despite the threat I had received for downing my paintbrush, the classes I most enjoyed at Hendon were the self-defence lessons, where we were taught jujitsu. This included learning how to spin an opponent around, take their feet off the ground and hold them over your back until they passed out. We also learned how to apply a hammer lock, a very solid defensive technique that makes it very hard for your attacker to move. Instead of the two thugs from Aldershot, we received our tuition from a selection of highly skilled instructors, who would call one of us young upstarts out and challenge us to have a go at them. Sure enough, they used to throw us all over the place. Great fun!

We also had brilliant sports facilities. I loved playing football, especially as I had never been able to play properly as a kid. My position was left-back, though I would volunteer to play any position in order to get a game. Whenever I had time off, I would go to Hackney Marshes, where there were many pitches and I'd always be able to find at least one team that was short of a player. Great days.

It wasn't all play though, as we had lots of studying to do to make sure we passed our regular exams. We all used to help each other revise in the evenings and, as we didn't have much money, we would study over the weekend too, testing each other on aspects of the law and the constitution.

Our treat after a lengthy revision session was walking down to a nice coffee bar in Hendon Central called 'La Fiesta'. We didn't eat there, as all our food back at Hendon was on the house, but we used to play on the jukebox and listen to all the latest singles from American musicians like Elvis Presley, Del Shannon and Buddy Holly, plus Scotland's 'King of the Skiffle', Lonnie Donegan. That coffee bar was really special, especially for those of us who had never had anything like that back in our hometowns. This was where we could meet girls too, as female cadets were not trained at Hendon. We didn't get much interest from them though and we couldn't have afforded to buy them drinks anyway!

Those three months at Hendon went by like a blur and before I knew it my training was over, passing with a score of 93 out of 120. Not everyone made it through; one of the guys was thrown out after he was caught cheating at cards. I never saw him again. Plenty of others dropped out along the way as well, but those of us who went the distance got a few beers in to celebrate when we eventually passed all our exams.

In April 1957, I was posted to G Division. At this point I was also issued with a ceremonial uniform, complete with capes that were very Victorian in style. I also got my all-important warrant card, a folded piece of card bearing my warrant number, which I still remember to this day, followed by my name and signature. There was no photograph as these weren't added until much later.

My reward for passing my exams and joining the force was to live in a dormitory behind Aldgate Police Station that was like something straight out of a Charles Dickens novel. Twenty young officers had to live in each room, sharing only one toilet and shower between us. It didn't feel like much of a welcome to the Met and even some of the hardships I had experienced growing up during the Second World War felt like luxury by comparison.

There was nowhere to hang your clothes, so I had to keep all my belongings in a suitcase under my bed. One night, I decided I was going to hit the town. I laid out my nicest outfit on the bed, ready to take the West End by storm… When I came back from the shower, all my clothes had vanished. It turned out that one of the other coppers had helped themselves to my best shirt and trousers and gone out wearing them!

Thankfully my spell in that awful place didn't last long and soon I moved to a brand-new section house in a posh area of Islington. Surrounded by vast gardens, Olive House was a beautiful place at 22–36 Canonbury Park South, accommodating about 600 single officers of all ranks. I was given my own room on the ground floor, with my own shower and toilet. Our money went up once we joined a division, as we no longer had the complimentary meals provided to us at Hendon.

There was a canteen at Olive House with kitchen staff serving up cooked meals, while on the other side of the room was a gas hob for the gourmets among us who preferred to cook their own meals. There were lockers where we could keep our own groceries and ingredients. Some coppers would make a stew and spread this out over a day or two to save money. Their saucepans of food would then be stored above these lockers, but as people would often forget about what they had put up there, these concoctions could sit there for days and gradually stink the canteen out! I might have been guilty of committing this crime once or twice…

There was a sergeant permanently on duty at the section house to maintain law and order and keep us all out of mischief. One of them was partial to the odd card game, meaning we could earn his money as well as our own! We also had cleaners who would come in and clean our rooms, but we still had to do our bit, and they would report you if you didn't make your bed! I put up posters of motorbikes and Marilyn Monroe, as well as Airfix models of planes that I made in my spare time.

Olive House was an incredible place to live, fitted with everything you could wish for. That lovely old building was demolished in the 1990s, but it lives on in the memories of many a retired copper. Whilst I made plenty of friends there, when I began my posting at City Road Police Station, I discovered that no one wanted to work with cadet no. 9093. All the established constables seemed to have their own little perks that they didn't want to divulge to a young greenhorn: where they could go for a free bacon and egg breakfast, or places where they could slip away off their beat for a bit. Once again, I was on my own.

When I discussed this with fellow cadets who had been posted to other stations on the division, they too had the same problem. Whilst it was initially a shock to the system for us all, it didn't seem to do us any harm in the long run. I continued to cross paths with a few of these cadets throughout my career; including Dave Dixon, who would later be my partner on the Flying Squad, and Bob Robinson, who would start off in CID, before shrewdly arranging to get transferred back to uniform. Bob worked out that it could take a long time to rise through the ranks in CID, where a detective constable hoping for promotion could often be tagged with wearing dead man's shoes.

I certainly had no thoughts of promotion in 1958; for now all I wanted to do was learn my way around the manor. G Division covered a large area of East London, including Commercial Street, West Smithfield, Angel, Dalston, Old Street, Sadlers Wells, Finsbury Square, Shoreditch and parts of Bethnal Green. No one showed me where all these different beats were – I had to work them out on my own. In fact, nobody at the nick seemed especially worried about me at all; I imagine they were just glad I was out of their way. I could have probably vanished for a week and not a soul would have noticed.

I loved exploring the great city in all its glory, which seemed so modern, futuristic and alive in comparison with the relative wilderness of the Welsh Valleys. If we were on Early shift, a few of us cadets from different divisions would meet up in the afternoon and go to the cinema. *South Pacific* was the first film I ever saw in the West End. Before the beginning of the film, a trailer showed a skier going down a slalom, shot on a Panavision camera. I couldn't believe how good this incredible footage looked on a massive screen; it was certainly a huge leap from the crackly old saturday morning pictures I had seen back in Monmouth as a kid.

Another highlight of living in London was discovering the many historic churches that the city had to offer. Growing up in Monmouth inspired a lifelong appreciation of church architecture, thanks to its two contrasting places of worship. The town is overlooked by the impressive medieval spire of St Mary's Priory Church, while over the Monnow Bridge is St Thomas', built in gorgeous old red sandstone that glistens in the sun.

St Thomas' is a very clean church today, but as a kid I was always struck by how dusty it was and how very old it smelled. I used to love looking at the ragged and timeworn flags hanging from the pillars, each commemorating different wars from history. I joined the choir, where all the boys delighted in singing hymns, which was second nature to us all, as we used to start every day with prayers at school, followed by a religious hour where we would read the Bible. I then started earning extra pocket money on a Sunday by pumping air into the bellows of the grand old organ, which lifted me off my feet most of the time.

The closest church to City Road Police Station was St Helen's in Bishopsgate, which has stood proudly in London since the thirteenth century, surviving the devastations of both the Great Fire of London and the Blitz. There was still plenty of damage on many of the churches and buildings in London from the air raids. Seeing these tangible reminders of the pain and suffering that affected so many during the war made me very emotional and appreciate how lucky I had been to grow up in a town that was not a major target for the Luftwaffe.

Throughout my police career, I sometimes felt like I was living a dual life as two different characters slightly at odds with each other: the copper who in another life might have studied theology and become a parish priest. Whenever I had a chance on my beat, I would go into a church, sit down and pray. From the moment I landed on G Division, I knew that God would be by my side every time I put on the uniform and walked the beat. I was no longer on my own and I was ready to start tackling crime.

CHAPTER 2

ON THE COBBLES

After serving as a senior cadet for a year, I was looking forward to becoming a fully fledged uniformed police constable. I had already started to feel like the real deal, performing the same duties as a regular bobby. On 7 March 1958, I reported to Lambeth nick to be officially sworn in. I was issued with my new uniform, which was very similar to the cadet version, though now I would be allowed to wear the famous helmet. Trying mine on for the first time was a wonderful experience – I now felt like I'd really made it! I was also issued with a pair of handcuffs, a baton, a torch and a whistle, which I still have in a box somewhere.

It wasn't always the case that a PC would remain at the same station they had served at as a cadet, but luckily for me I got to stay at City Road. Almost as soon as I walked back through the doors, everybody at the station treated me differently now I was a 'proper' PC. Each team, or 'relief', working a specific shift would report to a sergeant, and the best at G Division was a terrific guy called Bob Haughin. He in turn reported to the station inspector, though I don't recall ours ever doing much. I mainly saw him behind his desk waiting for his bacon and eggs every morning. This would be one of the many 'odd job' responsibilities around the nick for the station's van driver, whenever they weren't out transporting prisoners. The popularity of the inspector would impact the quality of their breakfast and it wasn't uncommon for drivers to add an extract of phlegm if they didn't like the guv'nor in question…

At the end of each week, we were paid in cash. I would have to stand to attention and salute the wages clerk, who would then hand me a brown envelope containing my 'readies', which began at £9.7.10d. I would hopefully get another pay rise if I passed my probationary period and my performance would now be regularly assessed over the next two years. For my first couple of weeks, I was paired up with a more senior PC, even though I had got to know the area very well by then. I still found this interesting, as I would often be with a different officer each shift – whoever was judged least likely to teach me any bad habits. After that first fortnight, I was out on my own once again.

Early into my probation, I got to spend two weeks back at Hendon, this time at the driving school. I had only spent one day in a police car during my cadet training, where to mark the occasion, I had a photograph taken standing in front of the car in my senior cadet uniform, looking the business. Now I was the real deal, I would be taught basic car mechanics before taking exams, where I had to complete drawings of car components and describe their common faults. Fortunately, this came quite easy to me, thanks to my time working as a trainee mechanic at Mann's Garage.

One of the highlights of my time at Mann's was watching Tom Ebborn and Jack Williams taking it in turns on their lunchbreak to rebuild the engine of a 1932 Standard. This vintage car had been abandoned during the war and was taking up valuable space in an outbuilding at the back of the garage. Mr. Mann had decided the time had come to have this lovely old car scrapped, until Tom and Jack volunteered to repair it in their spare time. After I passed my test, they presented the car to me as a gift. I couldn't believe their generosity and kindness.

This meant that I knew my way around a motor when it came to spending a few mad hours on the famous Hendon skid pan, where we got to chase a 'bandit' car. All of us took it in turns to make fools of ourselves in a battle-scarred Hillman Minx, skidding and screeching all over the place. The instructors then showed us how it was really done, sliding to within a few inches of each other as they waltzed around us in circles. These guys were classy drivers who performed this party piece on an almost daily basis in front of visiting guests or for exhibitions.

Once playtime was over, and after we had reached a certain standard, we were let loose on the open road, initially in a Wolseley 6/90 six-cylinder saloon. Then in the afternoon, we would take over the wheel of a Riley Pathfinder, a four-cylinder saloon. Compared to today's cars, these were slow and cumbersome machines. The Riley was unique, as the gear lever was on the driver-side between you and the door, meaning you had to change gear with your right hand. It took some getting used to, but it wasn't a problem. The last few days of training were spent driving police vans and we had to wash and vacuum each vehicle after use until they were spotless.

After a fun fortnight behind the wheel, it was time to get my feet firmly back on the cobbles of G Division. Every Wednesday afternoon, all newly sworn in constables had to report to Commercial Street Police Station and attend a briefing held by an inspector, who would keep us up to date on what was happening in the law and any changes to regulations. It was whilst I was on my way to one of these briefings that I made my first arrest…

I used to take the bus to Commercial Street, as the Met had an arrangement with the London Transport Executive, the organisation responsible for public transport in Greater London until 1962, that police officers could travel for free. In return, we would make ourselves available to assist the conductor, should there ever be any trouble on the vehicle we were travelling on.

One Wednesday afternoon I was on the bus, watching the world go by as we passed a row of shops, one of which had rugs and carpets for sale, all rolled up outside. I watched as a guy casually walked by the shop, picked up one of these big rolled up rugs and continued down the road, without going inside to pay for it. When the bus pulled in at the next stop, I jumped off and the thief literally walked straight into my arms. Boom! I was on the board, which gave me plenty of confidence.

I got an opportunity to add to my tally later that month, whilst on night duty. Towards the end of my shift, as I walked back to the station to hand over to the early turn, I checked all the parked cars down a street, making sure that all the licence plates matched the information on the tax discs. I came across a Ford Consul with identification that didn't match. I had found a stolen car, known in the trade as a 'ringer'. A big result for this young greenhorn.

These were the days before police radios and as there was no phone box on the street, I went back to the station and told one of the PCs that I was going to go back and keep an eye on the car. I asked that they send the early turn to assist me once they came on duty. I swapped my tunic for a civilian jacket and returned to my own private surveillance, observing from a discreet distance.

Whilst I waited for back-up, three guys came out of a house opposite and headed straight for the Consul. They got in and started the engine. I ran over, pulled the driver's door open and removed the ignition key. I asked them all to leave the vehicle and step onto the pavement. As they got out, they assured me that I'd made a mistake, before they suddenly made a run for it. Without hesitation, I jumped in their car, started her up and drove after them down the centre of the street. I was gaining on them, but at the end of the road they jumped over a wall and into the labyrinth of a nearby council estate shrouded in darkness. Too risky.

Despite not making an arrest, I did at least have the car as evidence. I drove it back to the station and parked it in the only available space, which had white letters painted in front of it reading CHIEF SUPT. Later that morning, after filling out all the associated paperwork to report this stolen vehicle, I was called up to see the chief super. As I walked upstairs, I imagined the positive feedback I would get for how I had used my initiative. But inside his office, the first thing he did was give me a severe dressing down for parking in his bay!

A few weeks later, I was standing at the corner of East Road and City Road, just before Old Street, directing traffic on point duty during rush hour. This was part of my usual duties, as opposed to any punishment handed down for my recent choice of parking space. Within a long queue of oncoming traffic, I spotted another Ford Consul with three familiar faces inside…

As these guys had never seen me in my uniform, they didn't recognise me under my helmet. I calmly walked up to the car, opened the driver's door and said, 'You're nicked.' The two in the back made a run for it, but I arrested the driver and walked him back to the station, leaving the Consul abandoned in the road and no doubt making the traffic even worse!

Back at the station, Sergeant Haughin charged the driver, who was then taken up to CID to have his fingerprints taken while all the paperwork was filled out. After a while, I went up to take my prisoner back to his cell and I couldn't believe my eyes… There he was, sitting down with two detectives, drinking whiskey with them in their office! It turned out this driver was a well-known villain and CID were obviously trying to keep him sweet. When I told Bob Haughin what was happening, he stormed up there, dragged the prisoner by his collar down the stairs and threw him in a cell. Bob was a hard man and a straight copper, who many years later I always had at the back of my mind whenever I wrote dialogue for Eric Richard's similarly stalwart Sgt Bob Cryer in *The Bill*.

It turned out that the driver and his brothers had been planning a robbery and I'd managed to catch them in not one but two of their getaway cars. For some villains, getting arrested wasn't enough of a deterrent and this wouldn't be the last time I investigated these guys in connection with a robbery. But that was all to come, for now I was pleased to get my first major result.

Earning a decent salary for the first time in my life, I decided to treat myself to a motorbike. I had inherited a love for whizzing around on two wheels from my dad, who was mad about motorbikes. A very gifted mechanical engineer, he and his brothers had made up two Indian motorcycles using spare parts that had been discarded by American dispatch riders during the war.

For my 14th birthday, they built me my first motorbike: a flat tank side-valve 500cc Norton, with a converted foot gear change. Early on a Sunday morning, they let me loose on a large cinder car park outside the local sports ground, where I emulated the famous speedway bikers of the day, riding with my foot out. I even had a go at 'scrambling', known today as motocross, but my old rattler wasn't built for competition.

Thanks to making it as a bona fide beat bobby, there was only one bike I wanted: a Douglas Dragonfly. This great machine had launched a few years earlier at the London Earls Court Show. Mine was yellow and had Reynolds-Earles long leading-link forks, different to the usual telescopic ones. Because the engine was so low, it was great at cornering. I used to park this gorgeous bike in the car park at the front of the section house, which was right next to a row of lovely old Georgian houses. The first house was owned by the infamous Labour MP John Stonehouse, who complained all the time about the noise made early in the morning by all us bobbies revving up our motorbikes.

On our weekends off, a few of us would hop on our bikes and ride down to Southend for a day at the seaside. Coming back from one of these trips, there were five of us riding along the New North Road. It was just after midnight and we were almost back at the section house when, out of nowhere, a car pulled out in front of me and BANG!

There was no time to slow down and I hit the car head on at speed. I was thrown off the bike and landed on my arm, breaking it in three places on impact. I was very lucky I hadn't been killed. I was wearing an all-in-one Arctic suit, which I had only just bought from Gamages. When I was taken to St. Barts Hospital, the first thing the doctor did was put a pair of scissors straight up my brand-new gear to cut me out and assess my injuries. They did the same to my boots, at which point one of the boys at the end of the stretcher joked, 'I thought you was gonna die with ya boots on?'

The driver got done for dangerous driving, while sadly my beautiful Dragonfly was wrecked beyond repair. Of course, it could have been so much worse. Thank you, God. The Met was very supportive and I was given a month off on full pay to recover. I spent some time recuperating at the section house, where they had a television, which was still a novelty to me.

After a spell on light duties, I was fighting fit and back walking the beat, which was always an incredible experience. There were many good times out on the streets, where people would shake my hand and thank me for my help or assistance. Those lovely moments made the occasional encounter with troublemakers all worthwhile. Uniform coppers weren't dealing with major crimes every day of the week in those days. As well as doing a spell on point duty, I might find myself dealing with domestic disputes, though I did my best to stay out of these situations, as it wasn't unknown for the people attacking each other to suddenly join forces and turn on you!

If I needed to contact the station on my beat, I had to use a police telephone box. There was only one on G Division, standing on Goswell Road, almost right opposite the old Gordon's gin distillery. At a certain time, I had to phone the station to confirm my position. These tall, concrete navy blue phone boxes were also very handy if I wanted to sneak out of sight for a crafty smoke! If I wasn't near a TARDIS and needed assistance, I would ask a member of the public if I could use their landline. Though in most cases, when things were getting out of hand, someone would have already dialled 999 and help would be on its way.

Now fully recovered from my accident, I soon started to build up my arrest tally. As these increased, I also began to make a name for myself in the press. My first mention in print came in *The East End News and*

London Shipping Chronicle on 5 September 1960, when they reported that I was called to an office to deal with an accountant who had lost his temper. I asked him to leave the premises twice, but both times he refused. Then when I escorted him from the building, he became very excited in the street outside, shouting 'You should respect me and not treat me like a Communist.' I then arrested him for causing a breach of the peace and using 'insulting words'. I'm sure not a patch on what officers are called today!

I was back in the paper on 22 December 1960, this time giving evidence at Old Street Court against a man I had arrested at St. Bartholomew's Square for wilfully obstructing me in the execution of my duty. The report details that the suspect had pleaded guilty to signalling to a street bookmaker in an attempt to prevent me from arresting him. Speaking from the dock, the accused told the judge, 'The constable was too alert.' He was fined £5, the equivalent of over £100 in today's money. If he didn't pay within a fourteen-day deadline, he would have been jailed for a month by default. I hope for his sake that he paid.

Every year, G Division ran what they called a 'bookmakers' initiative' for about two weeks, where the aim was to catch guys on the streets illegally taking betting slips. It was a very theatrical set-up, as the bookmakers used to put up a 'dummy' guy, who you would nick with the betting slips, which turned out to be for fake bets. Because this dummy guy would never have had a previous conviction, he'd only get a comparatively small fine at court. Next time, they'd use a new guy and the merry-go-round would start again. It was a cheap way for this outfit to operate and we all knew what was going on. Proving it was another matter.

Leading one of these bookmakers' initiatives was a very unpopular sergeant who, for many reasons, had earned the nickname 'the Dog Turd'. He picked me out on parade and assigned me to drive an unmarked van to take him over to the bookmakers. Wearing plain clothes, the Dog Turd hoped to be able to collar some of the guys on his hit list. One suspect was operating outside a pub, where he had a little box with a slit on top for people to put their illegal bets inside. We got into position and waited.

As soon as the first person placed a bet in this guy's box, the Dog Turd ran over like a possessed pit bull terrier, grabbed the man at the box and held him against a wall. After dishing out a rehearsed 'you boys never learn' speech he had obviously recited throughout his unremarkable career, Sgt D.T. barked at me, 'Get the van!' As I started the engine, from behind the wheel I saw the cellar flap of the pub behind the box open. Out came a hand, which quickly whisked the incriminating box away, before slamming the flap back down.

On hearing the metal clank, the Dog Turd did a fabulous double take to discover his evidence had vanished into thin air. There might not have been a puff of smoke, but a red mist emanated from my now apoplectic sergeant! In the absence of any evidence, he had to let his guy go and return to a chorus of 'Nice one, Sarge' and 'Give the dog a bone' jokes back at the station.

In September 1961, I was back in the papers, this time featured in a report under the rather exciting headline 'THE MAN IN THE TYROLEAN HAT ACCUSED OF WAGES SNATCH.' The titular hat-wearer was suspected of snatching £500 of wages from a cashier of an Islington firm. When I arrested him and explained that he matched the description of a wanted man, he simply replied, 'All right by me.' Not only was he sporting his distinctive green hat, but he had parked his own bright blue car, the licence plate of which we had on record, right outside the firm he was robbing… He was refused bail.

In the early 1960s, I made a string of arrests concerning the possession of Indian hemp, better known today as cannabis. Whilst this is now considered a minor offence, back then possession of this substance was in direct contradiction of the Dangerous Drugs Regulations and carried a significant penalty. On 16 March 1962, I searched a young Maltese man at a Brick Lane café who I believed to be in possession of hemp. Rather than deny this, he casually suggested that it was only a small amount. I found six packets on him, concealed in a cigarette packet. He pleaded guilty and was jailed for six months, which might seem harsh, but his previous conviction for theft didn't help his cause.

Later in the year, I found six packets of hemp hidden under a carpet in the home of a young unemployed woman in Bethnal Green. The Maltese seaman she had got herself mixed up with was a repeat offender and had a seventh packet on his person. He was jailed for three months, while she was let off with a caution. Hemp was again the order of the day when I was part of a twelve-man raid on a house in Whitechapel. I searched a man's bedroom and found eight packets of the stuff hidden in a pair of his socks. Upstairs, a woman was found in bed reading the Bible. She denied that there was any hemp in the room, but when she was asked to get out of bed, the officers found two dozen packets between the sheets! As for the Bible she kept clutched to her chest, this was in fact hollow, with more packets hidden inside. No wonder she kept it close!

One of the most memorable incidents from my time as a PC happened one evening when I was on a late turn. It was getting close to 10pm, when I would be booking off duty. Ideally you wanted to avoid any trouble that close to the end of your shift, as making an arrest involved a lot of paperwork. If I timed it right, I could enjoy a very pleasant stroll back to the station via Rosebery Avenue and take in all its architectural splendour.

As I passed Sadlers Wells Theatre, the elderly owner of a very elegant Italian restaurant opposite came rushing out. He was very upset and pleaded for my assistance. 'I have a man inside making trouble and he won't pay his bill. He's turning away customers. Can you do something please, officer?' I followed the gentleman into his restaurant. I felt like I was walking into a Western saloon, as the few customers who had chosen to brave it out were all sat in awkward silence. You could cut the atmosphere with a knife.

All eyes were on me as I approached the guy in question. In his 50s, the troublemaker was aloof, arrogant and wearing a threadbare tuxedo that was badly stained. I didn't muck about: 'You have a choice. Pay the bill or get your collar felt.' As he grudgingly paid the bill, he threatened that he knew several senior police officers personally and assured me that my career would soon come to an end. After I escorted him from the premises, the owner thanked me profusely, shaking my hand several times. He invited me for a meal with his family when I came off duty. As I'd never had a proper Italian meal before, I thought 'Why not?'

After the rest of the customers had finished their meals in peace, the door of the restaurant was closed, the open sign turned over and all the curtains drawn. I was invited to take my seat, surrounded by this Italian family who all welcomed me like an old friend. A white starched tablecloth was spread diagonally across two tables that were pulled together to accommodate their special guest. Each member of the family then took turns in bringing dishes out from the kitchen. Any Italian food I had eaten previously had probably come out of a tin, so I didn't know what to expect.

The cuisine served up by this classy restaurant was an education. Every dish was exceptionally delicious, blending a mixture of flavours that I'd never before had the pleasure of tasting. I washed this sumptuous feast down with a seemingly never-ending combination of Chianti and Caruso. This was a completely new world to me and I felt extremely privileged. I'm sure that even a connoisseur like Stanley Tucci would have been humbly frothing at the mouth at the glorious spread presented to me. Buon Appetito!

With plenty of arrests under my belt, I was now enjoying a weekly wage of £15.0.11d, which had risen annually since I'd passed my two-year probation. I couldn't resist the urge to get back on two wheels again and bought myself a two-tone green BSA A7 Shooting Star 500cc. This twin-engine bike was the business – it handled beautifully and was a pleasure to ride.

In 1963, I rode the Shooting Star up to visit my parents in their new home. Jack and Millie had decided to leave Monmouth behind them and buy a house in Gloucester. Their very nice semi-detached house on Newark Road had three bedrooms, one for them, one for my sister Susan and a third for guests. This was a world away from their humble beginnings back at Monnow Street.

The only snag was that their next-door neighbours were both deaf and could often be heard shouting at each other very loudly through the living room wall! Despite this, my parents and sister were really happy in Gloucester. The house came with a lovely garden that Jack enjoyed tending to, which was also big enough for him to ride his little Honda motorbike around in. He had got himself a maintenance job in a warehouse down on the docks, which he enjoyed. It was nice to see them all doing well.

After my visit, I set off early in the morning to get back to London in good time to go on duty at 2pm. It was the middle of winter and while going downhill through the picturesque Forest of Dean, disaster struck once more. Skidding over a patch of ice on the road, the bike suddenly went from underneath me. This time, I was still holding on as the machine spun out of control, around and around, until it smashed into a wall. Lights out.

I don't know how long I laid unconscious. Eventually, through blurred vision, I saw a pair of headlights approaching me. I was unable to move to attract attention, but thankfully the car stopped and a young couple took me to hospital. It turned out that the tyres had hit the wall first; another half-rotation and I would have been crushed to death. My Shooting Star might have been wrecked beyond repair, but I walked out of hospital the same morning.

I got a train back to London and, feeling I was fit enough to do so, reported for night duty and told no-one about my near miss. However, a few hours into my shift I collapsed, suffering from delayed shock and concussion. For the second time in my short career, I was put back on light duties. Reflecting on the crash, it was a miracle that I hadn't been killed. In moments like that, your faith in God can only intensify. It was a long time before I mounted another bike. Perhaps through missing the speed and excitement on the road, I sought a chance to tackle new danger on the streets…

CHAPTER 3

CHANGING GEAR

The 1960s were an incredible time. The way everything changed from the previous decade was almost impossible to comprehend. Places like Carnaby Street and Oxford Street transformed overnight to reflect the new fashions and trends of the Swinging Sixties. Young women were now wearing miniskirts, instead of hand-me-down twin sets inherited from their mothers.

Meanwhile, us bobbies on the beat benefited when the Met introduced a new summer uniform, meaning we could wear a short-sleeved shirt instead of sweating out our shifts in heavy serge. The sun always seemed to be shining in the Sixties and by the middle of the decade, the Beatles were top of the pops and James Bond was making a killing at the box office.

Britain really was Great then; it felt like we could do nothing wrong. We were a nation respected by foreign powers, our industries were thriving, and London was the place to be. There was a saying in the Sixties, 'If you want to be a brain surgeon, you can become a brain surgeon.' Anything was possible and we all felt empowered that we could be whoever we wanted to be. For me, my ambition was clear: I wanted to be a detective.

The guv'nor at City Road CID was Detective Inspector (DI) Fred Gerrard; a great man, whose reputation as a solid thief catcher preceded him. He would later rise to the rank of commander and be awarded an MBE. I'll never forget our first meeting at the bus stop near Olive House, where Fred lived with his wife in their married quarters.

```
DISSOLVE TO:
EXT. BUS STOP, CANONBURY ROAD. 1964.

PC BARRY APPLETON arrives at the bus stop. Already
standing in the queue is DETECTIVE INSPECTOR FRED
```

CHANGING GEAR

GERRARD, 40s, a square-jawed, smartly dressed, seasoned copper.

>   FRED
> Barry Appleton?

>   BARRY
> Good morning, sir.

>   FRED
> You're making a name for yourself, my son. I've had a look in the crime book, you've got some good collars under your belt.

>   BARRY
> Thank you, sir.

>   FRED
> I could do with someone like you on my team. If you apply to be an aide, I'll put a word in for you.

>   BARRY
> That would be great, sir!

>   FRED
> You can cut out the sir, I ain't got my letter from the palace just yet. You think about it.

FRED leans in and gives BARRY an encouraging pat on the shoulder.

>   FRED
> You wanna know what your greatest asset is, my son?

BARRY shrugs as the bus pulls in behind him. FRED leans in with a wry smile.

>   FRED
>   (whispering)
> You don't look like a copper. In fact, you look like a fucking villain!

Joining the CID wasn't easy, but thanks to Fred's encouragement and the word in the right ear, I got accepted as an aide on my first attempt. All of a sudden, I was out of uniform and had to swap my long baton for a short one, which I found odd. Were the villains that CID dealt with going to be smaller than those I'd encountered on the beat?

G Division had a crime squad formed of twenty very keen trainee detectives, known then as aides, overseen by an experienced detective sergeant. Operating out of City Road station, we had our own little office, with a dedicated typist working for us. Known as 'the aide squad', we were dedicated to going out every single day with one objective: to nick villains, usually thieves or handlers of stolen goods. Unless we already had a job lined up, we'd start the day by grabbing a coffee and deciding what area we were going to focus on that day. We were tasked with policing the whole division, including Aldgate, Chapel Market, Commercial Street, Finsbury Square, Highbury and Kings Cross. A lot of ground to cover.

I was shown the ropes by John Collier, a nice guy who was still working as an aide despite being an experienced officer. Every Sunday morning, we all had to monitor Petticoat Lane, where there was always a load of stolen gear to be found. John would pass the time by rummaging through all the LPs, on the hunt for old jazz records. He recommended I listen to the American saxophonist John Coltrane, which sparked my lifelong love of jazz. As well as an ear for music, John had a good nose for crime and he taught me a lot about my new life in CID.

We would spend every day scouring the streets, either on foot or driving around, literally looking for suspicious characters. We only had to walk around Liverpool Street or Chapel Market for a few minutes before we'd suss out a villain up to no good. The ones that stood out were young men who didn't appear to be working, just wandering aimlessly around. If they veered away from the market and snuck down a side street, chances were that we'd find them trying car doors. I quickly learned that it was a case of being patient and waiting to catch them in the act.

The roughest patch on our ground was Hoxton. Nowadays Shoreditch is considered a trendy place to live, but back then it was a dodgy area, populated by a hive of villainy, with a litany of stolen motors hidden around the local council estates. As coppers, we were judged on how many arrests we made. If my crime figures were down and I needed a few collars, Hoxton was the perfect hunting ground for criminals. You could pick anybody up and, more often than not, they would have something on them.

If we suspected someone, we used Section 4 of the Vagrancy Act to perform a stop and search. If they were clean, we'd let them go, but they'd know we'd be watching them. If they had something on them, drugs or a weapon, we'd bring them in. It was an example of proactive and preventative policing.

One Friday morning, I was driving a nondescript van when I spotted a green Austin Westminster being driven very slowly around the back streets of Dalston. With me were fellow aides Dave Dixon, who I had been a cadet with, and Peter Mutton. We'd already been in a few scrapes together and it soon became clear to us all that the drivers of the Austin were looking for a vehicle to steal. The Austin stopped and out stepped William McGuire, a known face on the manor, wearing a long raincoat. Immediately, he tried to open the door of a parked vehicle. Boom!

Dave and Peter jumped out and grabbed McGuire, while I drove in pursuit of the Austin. The driver, Ernest Page, pulled over and I arrested him without any trouble. As Dave and Peter walked over with their suspect, I noticed that McGuire had his hands buried deep in his raincoat pockets. He was smiling. I wasn't. By the van, I told McGuire to take his hands out of his pockets very, very slowly. As he did so, I saw the butt of a gun sticking out of his right-hand pocket. It paid to be suspicious. I quickly grabbed the gun. 'It's only a toy! You can't nick me for that.' It was a loaded air pistol. Back at the station, as both men were being searched in the charge room, McGuire punched me in the face and made a run for it. Within seconds, Dave and Peter had him in a cell.

Despite the odd skirmish, I was really enjoying CID work and found that once I started spotting villains, I became quite proficient at it. Even on a night out, I would walk by someone and think 'He's got a burglar's head!' The aide squad built up quite a reputation and became so successful at taking down robbers and foiling wage snatches that some of the smarter villains avoided crossing G Division for fear of getting nicked. But there were still plenty who never believed they'd get caught.

When pickpockets started working our ground, targeting bus stops, we decided to monitor one on City Road. The perfect observation point came from the Leysian Mission, and with another aide called Terry Brown, I ventured all the way to the top of the building, where we had a great view through the huge windows high above. We hadn't been there long when suddenly we saw a group of five pickpockets at work: two women and three guys. We had to hand it to them, they were very good.

One of the girls would attract a commuter who was waiting at the bus stop and while she distracted him, one of her partners in crime would pick his pocket. The two couples did this in rotation, with the fifth gang member on look out. Once we'd seen enough, Terry and I ran down. They sussed us pretty quickly and made a run for it. We managed to catch two of the pickpockets, who were both Italian, and walked them up the road to the station. We didn't have handcuffs; we would just put their arms behind their back and keep a firm grip on them. There was no need to manhandle them, as they usually tried to talk themselves out of trouble. In the end, we got their three accomplices too.

One of my regular haunts in Hoxton was a pub called The Kings Arms, a popular drinking hole for cops and robbers alike. The regulars all knew we were coppers and the villains who wanted to keep us onside were keen to discreetly pass on any information about bigger fish operating on their patch. In return for useful tip-offs, we would 'befriend' these people, to a point, so they felt they could talk to us. One of our regular beermat informants, a guy called Stan, soon found himself in the frame when another local villain was murdered...

DISSOLVE TO:
EXT. TERRACED HOUSE. HOXTON STREET. 1964.

BARRY is with DETECTIVE SERGEANT PETER WAGNER, mid-30s, looks older. He is tall, very thin and smokes a lot. Not a healthy-looking man. They are followed by DETECTIVE CONSTABLE TERRY BROWN, early 20s, overweight, short brown hair. A drinker and a good interrogator.

BARRY knocks on a front door that is long overdue a fresh lick of paint. The door is opened by STAN, 60s, cockney, short, bald, wearing a tatty moth-eaten sweater. Always has a cigarette on the go.

        STAN
I thought you'd come. You think I did it, don't ya?
        BARRY
No Stan, not at all, we just want to see if you
knew anything and check where you were, you know
the S.P.
        STAN
Bleedin' marvellous innit. After all the
information I've given you lot over the years.
I suppose you'd better come in.

DISSOLVE TO:
INT. TERRACED HOUSE. LIVING ROOM. LATER.

The house is crammed with Fifties furniture and an
old upright piano. BARRY and WAGNER search through
drawers. Playing it cool, STAN helps himself to a large
scotch from a drinks tray. TERRY returns from upstairs
and shakes his head at WAGNER.

        STAN
What did I tell you? Would I keep a gun if I'd
done the dirty deed?
        BARRY
He was screwing your wife. You have a bloody big
motive, Stan.
        STAN
He'd been doing her for at least ten years. Why
haven't I taken him out before now then, eh?
        TERRY
Because you'd been into villainy with him. D'you
think we didn't know?
        WAGNER
There's no other suspects, Stan. Just you.

TERRY lifts the lid covering the piano keys.
        STAN
I've lost count of how many times I've helped
you guys out. Why are you lot doing this to me,
Mr. Wagner?

TERRY starts to play the piano with one finger. All of a
sudden, there is a strange clunking sound when he tries
to play the higher notes. Everyone stops talking and
turns to TERRY.

        TERRY
   (joking with excitement)
What do you know? I've found the lost chord!

Suspicious, BARRY walks over to the piano.

        STAN
It's nothin'. Just needs tuning.

BARRY lifts the lid of the piano and peeps inside. He
turns to the others and smiles.

        BARRY
It's not the piano that needs tuning, Stan. It's you!

BARRY picks up a nearby wire coat hanger and uses this
to lift a revolver out of the piano. STAN awkwardly
looks around the room.

        STAN
Have I got time for another scotch?

        WAGNER
Terry, get that bagged up and take it to ballistics
first thing in the morning. In the meantime, get
it printed. Do the honours, Barry.

BARRY takes a resigned STAN by the arm.

        BARRY
This way, Liberace.

Occasions such as this taught me that, sometimes, getting a result was
purely down to fate.

    I was enjoying my time with the aide squad and my arrest rate continued
to impress. But even when posted to CID, some occasions required all
officers in the Met to dig out their ceremonial uniforms from the back
of the wardrobe. One of the more solemn occasions that required me to
get back into uniform was the state funeral of Sir Winston Churchill on

30 January 1965. We were briefed in the morning by an inspector from another division, who told us precisely where each of us were going to be positioned and how many paces apart we would stand from one another.

I was positioned in a line of officers near Westminster Cathedral, standing well into the road because of the vast number of people wanting to pay their respect. This was a showing of homage and sorrow on an unprecedented scale. It was typically dismal weather for a funeral, and I stood in the rain on that cold morning for hours. The only trouble for any copper in that situation is if you need to pee, you've got to hold it in for the duration.

The funeral began at 9:45am, with the chiming of Big Ben, after which the clock remained silent for the rest of the day. In Hyde Park, a ninety-gun salute was fired, marking each year of the great man's life. I shall never forget the coffin, draped with the Union Flag, passing in silence within a couple of yards from me as part of a military procession on its journey to St Paul's Cathedral. I saluted and shed a tear like everyone else. I had huge affection and respect for this extraordinary leader, who had brought the nation together in their darkest hour.

Another fateful date every copper in the force at that time will never forget was 12 August 1966. I was in the yard at City Road when I heard an urgent call for assistance over the radio. Shots had been fired at Braybrook Street, a residential area not far from Wormwood Scrubs. Three police officers, DS Christopher Head, DC David Wombwell and PC Geoffrey Fox, were driving an unmarked car when they spotted three men sitting in a car with no tax disc on display. Was this a getaway vehicle for a prison escape?

The occupants, Jack Witney, John Duddy and Harry Roberts, all had form, ranging from petty theft to robbery with violence. But not murder. Within moments of being challenged, those men each became killers and all three police officers lost their lives in brutal and horrific circumstances. The subsequent reports about this massacre caused widespread outrage from an angry public, with many calling for the death penalty to be reinstated.

With all three of these callous men now on the run, many aides were drafted in for the manhunt. I was one of the officers tasked with tracking down Harry Roberts, a former soldier who we eventually found living in a makeshift tent in Epping Forest. The judge who sentenced those three killers to life imprisonment described the murders as 'the most heinous crime to have been committed in this country for a generation or more'.

Those shocking murders were a reminder of what could happen to any of us on the force. I'm sure an incident like that would have made many a copper rethink their career and, being truthful, perhaps there were times when I wondered 'Maybe I should do something else?' However, my faith gave me strength to take on whatever life threw at me, no matter the consequences. I never lost any sleep over the job, nor did I ever dread getting out of bed in the morning. In fact, I was often excited to get to work.

Whilst our main objective was tackling street crime, the beauty of being on the aide squad was that we could all be called in at any moment to assist with a big operation. This is what we were expecting one Monday morning, when we received word that we all had to report to DI Bert Wickstead at Stoke Newington station for a 10:00 briefing. We all thought 'Something's going down…'

As we walked into the CID office on the ground floor, armed with eager anticipation as to what job the DI had in store for us, Bert Wickstead was in his office on the phone. Sitting outside was Jean Simonette, a young typist who had worked there since leaving school. Jean continued typing away when Bert came out of his office and revealed why we had all been summoned…

'Right, you lot, I've called you in here to tell you that I have asked Jean to marry me. I'm telling you this now because I don't want anything said behind my back. I also wanted to give you all this chance… Do any of you present have any objection to me marrying her?' The room quickly filled with a heady mix of astonishment, embarrassment and mild hysteria. One of the jokers in the pack wisecracked, 'Are we getting an invite to the wedding, Guv?' An irritated Bert quickly blurted, 'No! I don't want you lot anywhere near it!'

I hope the above memory justifies why I thought Bert was a rather strange man. He referred to himself as 'the old grey fox' and seemed to be a real loner, though as he later headed the Met's Serious Crime Squad, eventually becoming a Commander, perhaps he preferred his friends in higher places than us lowly aides. Bert courted a lot of publicity and after retiring from the Met, he even got a job working for the *News of the World.*

Aside from that rather extraordinary 'briefing', usually when we were drafted onto cases at the last minute it was for something serious. That proved to be the case on 9 August 1967, when I was one of the officers called to the top-floor flat of 25 Noel Road, a residential street in Islington running parallel with Regent's Canal. After hearing a disturbance from the flat above, a concerned neighbour had failed to get an answer. After looking through the flat's letterbox, she had called the police.

At the time, I hadn't yet caught the writing bug myself, so the name Joe Orton didn't initially mean anything to me. I soon learned that I had been called to the home of a renowned playwright, whose many plays are still being staged around the world to this day. Orton shared this top-floor flat with his lover, Ken Halliwell. Sadly, when we forced entry into the flat, we found both men dead.

It was a weird crime scene. Halliwell's body was naked, while Orton was undressed from the waist down, wearing only a pyjama jacket. Orton's corpse was covered in blood. I attended so many crime scenes with bodies, not always murder cases, but also suicides and accidental deaths. The one constant was the grisly smell of death, which is overpowering. Sadly, it is one of the things that police officers have to learn to get used to on the job.

If there had been only one body after the reported disturbance, and the alleged attacker had gone missing, then the whole case would have been different and the aide squad would have been out searching other addresses looking for him. In this instance, our job was to help gather as much evidence as we could to establish what had happened. Examining the bodies at the crime scene was Francis Camps, a very smart guy and well-known pathologist from the Home Office. Professor Camps concluded that Halliwell had bludgeoned Orton nine times with a hammer and then, thinking he was dead, took an overdose and killed himself. However, he also determined that Halliwell had died from his overdose prior to Orton succumbing to his injuries. A sad case.

Something from that crime scene has always stuck with me. As we searched the room, I noticed that they had been drinking brown ale at the dinner table, out of wine glasses. Perhaps I should have remembered other more important details from the crime scene, but the image of that beer in those wine glasses, a tragic couple's last drink, has stuck in my mind for all these years.

Once I had amassed several years' experience as an aide, I was posted to the Detective Training School in Chelsea, where I began an intensive six-week advanced criminal law course. Because I struggled at school, I knew I would have to study hard to pass my civil service exam. I started to read newspapers like *The Times* to increase my knowledge of current and international affairs. Despite this, I failed to pass the exam. I kept resitting, as I desperately wanted promotion after a decade in the job. After what proved to be my last attempt at the civil service exam, I had to escort a prisoner to Old Street Magistrates Court…

```
DISSOLVE TO:
INT. OLD STREET MAGISTRATES COURT. CORRIDOR. 1967


A long narrow corridor with no windows. The far door is
the entrance to the magistrate's court, which is now in
session. A long line of officers and their prisoners are
waiting to be called. BARRY stands at the front of the
queue with KEITH SUMMERS, late 20s, a burglar with form as
long as your arm. They wait for their case to be called.
          SUMMERS
     I've got to get out and earn some bread. I can't
     afford to be in clink, man. Did you try my sister?
          BARRY
     She won't stand bail for you. She said 'Never,
     ever again.'
          SUMMERS
     Shit, man!
          BARRY
     It happens.
          SUMMERS
     I'm gonna fight tooth and nail to get outta here.


The door to the court opens and a P.C. reading a clipboard
calls out 'Summers.'
```

CHANGING GEAR

CUT TO:
INT. MAGISTRATES COURT. DAY

SUMMERS is placed in the dock. I walk around to the
witness box and stand just outside. NEIL McELLIGOTT, the
magistrate, is busy writing up the previous case. The
CLERK OF THE COURT stands up and turns to SUMMERS and
reads out the charge.

> CLERK
Do you understand the charge, Mr. Summers?

> SUMMERS
Yeah, man. But…

Without looking up, NEIL McELLIGOTT raises his hand,
which immediately silences SUMMERS.
The CLERK turns to BARRY.

> CLERK
Are you objecting to bail, officer?

BARRY steps into the witness box. Just before he is
about to speak, NEIL McELLIGOTT again raises his hand to
halt proceedings. This time he glances up, looking over
the rim of his spectacles.

> McELLIGOTT
Detective Appleton, I believe you sat your civil
service exam last week. How did you get on?

> BARRY
I think I've done OK. Thank you, sir.

> McELLIGOTT
Splendid. I'm pleased to hear it. You deserve it.

McELLIGOTT nods to the CLERK to continue.

> CLERK
You are objecting to bail?

> BARRY
The defendant is single and of no fixed abode.
I fear if granted bail, he will commit further
offences.

McELLIGOTT sits upright and with an intimidating look,
addresses SUMMERS.

    McELLIGOTT
You heard what detective Appleton has said. Are
you still asking for bail?

A resigned SUMMERS bows his head.

    SUMMERS
No.
McELLIGOTT raises an eyebrow.

    SUMMERS
No, your honour, man.

    McELLIGOTT
You will be remanded in custody for seven days.
Next case.

CUT TO:
INT. CUSTODY AREA. LATER.

SUMMERS stands in front of a CUSTODY SERGEANT filling out
paperwork. BARRY lights a cigarette for SUMMERS.

    BARRY
What happened to fighting tooth and nail?

    SUMMERS
What chance did I have with you being best buddies
with the beak? Shit, man, just send me to Holloway.

    BARRY
Those women would eat you alive. You're going to
Brixton like everyone else.

    SUMMERS
Brixton? No way man, that's a fucking penal colony!

    BARRY
You should have listened to Sammy Davis Jr. 'Don't
do the crime if you can't do the time.'

Neil McElligott was something of a legend in the legal profession; a
formidable magistrate who feared no one. After I became a detective
constable, I once took the great man out in an observation van to show him

around the Brick Lane area, to give him some background to a puzzling case that had been presented before him. He was pleased that I'd passed my civil service exam and I was proud to have finally become eligible for promotion.

Police officers are often associated with having a dark sense of humour, which many draw on as a coping mechanism to help during times of great stress. The banter in CID was especially strong, where we took the mickey out of each other all the time. Soon after joining the ranks of City Road CID, I very quickly learned that our old friend the Dog Turd, now based at another nick, disliked us suit-wearing sleuths immensely.

By this stage of his career, he was more or less permanently confined to his desk, a spent force with no prospects of promotion. He was never the sharpest knife in the drawer, but now the powers that be had decided he shouldn't be let loose on the public anymore. A fellow detective constable, Tony Davenport, had several understandable grievances with the Dog Turd. One night, after a few drinks in the pub, a few of us decided to hatch a plan that would leave the Dog Turd with egg on his face…

Another detective on our team, nicknamed 'Ringo', often visited his British parents who lived and worked in Bahrain. He was always bringing back souvenirs and his most recent purchase was a full sheikh's outfit, along with a dagger. This proved to be the genesis of an idea. The Dog Turd was renowned for panicking whenever prisoners were brought in while he was on custody. Maybe we could use Ringo's gear to play the ultimate wind-up on him? As I was very tanned at the time, they looked at me and smiled… 'No way!' I protested. 'We'll never get away with it!'. "You're perfect for the part', Tony convinced me. We came up with a plan and, after rehearsing it several times, I soon found myself being escorted into a police station dressed as an Arab…

DISSOLVE TO:
INT. CHARGE ROOM. SOMEWHERE IN LONDON. NIGHT.

TONY DAVENPORT, late 20s, handsome, well-dressed, pokes his head around the door of the front office to find THE

DOG TURD, mid-50s, overweight, uncombed thick grey hair, slurping a mug of tea, crumbs from his recently scoffed sandwich all over his desk.

                    TONY
          (urgently)
     Sarge!
Startled, the slouching DOG TURD spills some of his tea as he sits upright.
                    TONY
     Got a prisoner!
                    DOG TURD
          (snarling)
     When I'm ready, Davenport.
                    TONY
     This one won't wait, I'm afraid, sarge.

The DOG TURD pants heavily as he stands up.
                    DOG TURD
     What load of crap have you brought me this time?
                    TONY
          (stifling a laugh)
     How about diplomatic immunity?

As if a rocket has launched up his backside, THE DOG TURD charges around his desk before coming to an abrupt halt. Sat on a bench in front of him is an ARAB, curled up and shaking. A detective, HARRY, 30s, casually dressed, slicked back hair, holds up a jambiya, a short dagger with a curved blade.
                    DOG TURD
     You're kidding?
                    TONY
     An offensive weapon, *per se*.
                    DOG TURD
     Well, what does he *say*?!
                    TONY
     How the hell do I know?

      HARRY
There's loads of different dialects, sarge. Think of all the shit this could get you into, this could lose you promotion forever!

      DOG TURD
You trying to cheer me up?!

      TONY
It's probably written in the stars. I don't envy you one bit, sarge.

THE DOG TURD clicks his fingers.

      DOG TURD
We'll get Special Branch involved! That's it! Let them do the fucking work for a change.

      TONY
They'll only pass him back to you. You're the one who's had eyeballs on him.

      DOG TURD
No thanks to you!

HARRY points down at the ARAB.

      HARRY
Look! He's wet himself.

      DOG TURD
   (barking)
Put him in a cell!

      HARRY
I wouldn't do that, sarge.

      TONY
He's got diplomatic immunity, remember?

      DOG TURD
No! Don't put him in the cell. What the hell am I thinking?
The ARAB starts waving his arms around angrily, speaking loudly in an unknown language. The DOG TURD spins like a top, hands on his head.

                    HARRY
You've upset him now, Sarge.

                    DOG TURD
Me upset him? This is all your fucking fault,
Davenport, you're the one who nicked the bloody
Prince of Persia!

                    TONY
What was I supposed to do, let him wander around
London with a fucking dagger?

                    DOG TURD
Shit! What the hell are we going to do?

                    TONY
We? You're the one with the stripes, sergeant.
This is your problem, not ours.

                    DOG TURD
I'm getting an ulcer. I can feel it.

                    HARRY
Hey! What about Ringo?

                    TONY
Now why didn't I think of that. Ringo, of course!

                    DOG TURD
Ringo? Who the fuck's Ringo?

                    HARRY
One of our lot, Sarge. He speaks the lingo, does
Ringo. I think he's in the canteen…

                    DOG TURD
Get him! Now!!

CUT TO:
INT. CHARGE ROOM. MOMENTS LATER.
RINGO, late 20s, mixed race, handsome with a huge,
friendly smile, arrives on the scene and walks over to
the ARAB.

                    RINGO
This man has wet himself?

                    DOG TURD
For fuck's sake. Do something! For a start ask
him what his bloody name is!

RINGO starts speaking in an unknown language, until the ARAB can contain his hysterics no longer. He bursts into laughter, leaning back to reveal the face of BARRY. TONY, HARRY and RINGO all roar with laughter. THE DOG TURD is panting with fury.

>   DOG TURD
>   (enraged)
>   You bastards! I'm going to get you lot for this!

When I wasn't dressing up as an Arab, I remember desperately trying to locate a pair of white jeans like David Hemmings wore in Antonioni's *Blow-Up*, which never seemed to get dirty despite him rolling all over the floor with two teenage girls. I tried raiding all the trendy boutiques in Carnaby Street and Chelsea, but to no avail. I also loved my mohair suits, when I could afford them, which I got from a little Jewish tailor on Bethnal Green Road. I even bought a hat like Frank Sinatra wore in his movies at that time, to complement the style. But who was I aiming to impress?

CHAPTER 4

CRICKLEWOOD

I was so lucky to be a young person living and working in London during the 1960s. It was such a beautiful time. Whenever I finished an early turn, I went to tea dances at the West End's Café de Paris. This famous cabaret club had played host to many top artists over the years, including Noel Coward, Marlene Dietrich, Judy Garland and Frank Sinatra. Despite this incredible history, the Café de Paris always felt like a bit of a secret to me, as there were never many people in there. This worked for me though, as I knew this would be the place I was most likely to meet very classy women.

I'd first had a girlfriend whilst growing up in Monmouth. Her name was Margaret, a waitress working in the best restaurant at the top end of Monnow Street. Once I started earning a bit of money at Mann's garage, I was able to take Margaret to the cinema or to Rolls Hall, an impressive theatre opposite the garage, where a live band would perform every Saturday night and we would go to dance. During my lunch break at Mann's, I would sneakily select one of the customer's pristine cars and take Margaret for a quick ride around the Wye valley. Good job I never had a crash!

Margaret had an attractive older sister who had won a major beauty contest quite a few times in Ross-on-Wye. The following year, I persuaded Margaret to enter it. The competition was held in a big hall, packed out for the big occasion. Margaret won, beating her sister! I asked my Beauty Queen if she would like to dance and the audience cheered as we took to the floor on our own, while the band played 'Cherry Pink and Apple Blossom White', which Jane Russell had danced to in the movie *Underwater!* in 1955, making it a huge hit. Despite getting off to a great start, Margaret and I split up not long after I joined the police, because of the 150 miles between us.

It was then during one afternoon at the Café de Paris early in my career that my life almost followed a different path altogether. I met a beautiful

Jewish girl called Sandra, who was 18. She was very intelligent and hoping to study as a psychologist. She didn't have a job yet and still lived at home with her family in Hampstead. She was very impressed about me being a police officer. When I explained I hoped to join the CID one day, she nicknamed me Dick Tracy. We quickly fell in love, or at least we thought we had, as you do when you're that age and don't know any better.

Sandra soon invited me home to meet her parents, who were very nice, if a little wary of me as I wasn't Jewish. They soon welcomed me into their family with open arms and even took me on holiday with them to the beautiful seaside city of Blankenberge in Belgium. Sandra's family were soon encouraging us to look for a house to buy, even though I was still on probation as a police constable and certainly couldn't afford a deposit. I didn't like the feeling that my life was being taken out of my hands. It wasn't long before Sandra wanted to get married. She was willing to tie the knot in a registry office, but explained that this would be a problem for her parents, who wanted her wedding to take place in a synagogue. This was when I did something rather naïve…

I wasn't going to have our religions divide us, especially as I felt we were both praying to the same God. I offered to change my religion and become Jewish to please her and her family. This required me to attend a liberal synagogue in Stamford Hill called the School of Instruction. I actually enjoyed the history of the building and embraced all the religious aspects, even volunteering to wear a kippah on the back of my head. I was treated like a celebrity by Sandra's family for doing this and they threw a huge party for me that was quite the occasion.

During this celebration, one of Sandra's elderly relatives came up and talked to me. He was a little old man with a kind face, who revealed that he had been held at one of the concentration camps during the second world war. Whilst he was there, under those unimaginable circumstances, he had kept his copy of the Old Testament hidden from the Nazi officers. He then produced that precious Bible and said that he wanted me to have it, as a gift.

It was at that moment that I realised I was changing my faith for the wrong reasons. I felt like such a fraud. How could I take this man's gift, along with everything that it represented? I was reminded of a piece of wisdom hailing from ancient Greece. Discovered inscribed on the

Temple of Apollo were two words… 'Know thyself.' I knew I shouldn't have been going through with this whole experience and decided to walk away from it all. I still feel very sorry about the unhappiness I brought to Sandra.

By March 1965, I had been serving as a police constable on G Division for seven years. Each year, I had received incremental pay rises and was now earning £18.11.10d, almost double the salary I started on. Earning some real money now, me and a couple of mates from G Division, Bob Andrews and Jock Reynolds, decided to book a cheap holiday to Majorca. The thought of spending time lying in the sun and swimming in the Mediterranean, away from the grimy, crime-ridden streets of Hoxton, was a beautiful one. As I counted down the days to our summer leave, it felt like paradise was on hold, just waiting for me to arrive.

We booked through a Spanish airline called Spantax and discovered when we boarded that we were the only passengers… Perhaps unsurprising as our Constellation plane had three tails at the back, with wobbly wings that flapped like a seagull when we took off! We all shared a great sigh of relief when we landed in one piece at Son Sant Joan international airport on the south coast. Our destination was Ca'n Pastilla, a small purpose-built holiday resort.

On the first night, Bob and Jock seemed to be taking hours to get ready. Itching to explore, I left my mates to groom themselves while I went for a walk to explore. Nowadays Ca'n Pastilla is a popular destination for ex-pats and tourists, but back in 1965 there were just a few bars and a handful of shops. A short walk away was the Sant Antonio de la Playa, a small parish church steeped in the history of old Spain, surrounded by tightly packed streets that led down to the picturesque harbour. I made my way down to the white sandy beach and absorbed the warm glow of the sun as it glistened against the turquoise sea. Paradise, I had arrived.

Just off the beach, I heard the Del Shannon song 'Runaway' blasting out from a very small bar called the Ali Baba. I ventured inside this 'happening' place and manoeuvred my way through the hustle and bustle to the bar. I sat down on a vacant stool and soaked up the carefree ambience that encapsulated the Sixties. As I turned back to face the bar, I saw that sitting beside me was the most strikingly attractive girl I'd ever seen. Deeply tanned, with long blond hair almost down to her waist, she gave me the benefit of a welcome smile as she crossed her long shapely legs. I thought she might have been Swedish...

```
DISSOLVE TO:
INT. ALI BABA BAR, CA'N PASTILLA. 1965.
          BARRY
     (pointing at himself)
   Ba-rry, Shore-ditch.
          PAM
     (pointing at herself)
   Pam-e-la, Crick-le-wood.

They both burst out laughing. BARRY notices that PAM's
glass is almost empty.
          BARRY
   What are you drinking, Pamela?
          PAM
   Cuba Libra, thank you. And you can call me Pam.

BARRY tries to draw the bartender's attention without
success. PAM knows better.
          PAM
   Over here Sam!

BARRY attempts his best BOGART impression.
          BARRY
   Of all the gin joints, in all the world...
          PAM
   Can't you come up with something more original?

SAM comes over and BARRY orders two Cuba Libras.
          BARRY
   Don't you like Casablanca?
          PAM
   I love it. I just don't like Humphrey Bogart.
          BARRY
   You're breaking my heart already.
```

PAM reaches over and touches BARRY's hand.

          PAM

I wouldn't do that.

          BARRY

You flirting with me?

          PAM

Maybe.

          BARRY

Listen. I'm here with two mates, who at any moment are going to come bungling in looking for me. How about showing me around the principality?

          PAM

You want the good news or the bad news?

          BARRY

I always take the bad news first.

          PAM

I was keeping that stool for someone.

BARRY does his best to supress a groan.

          BARRY

And the good news?

          PAM

He's late.

BARRY jumps off his stool and offers his hand.

          BARRY

Best news I've heard all day.

A few moments later, SAM returns with two Cuba Libras and discovers two empty stools.

Pam and I found somewhere quieter to chat and I couldn't believe how much we had in common. We both had similar upbringings, coming from hard-working families who hadn't had things easy. We both enjoyed completing 'painting by numbers' kits and I described my latest masterpiece back at the section house, featuring a Spanish dancer. Incredibly, Pam had just painted the very same one. The more we talked, the more we discovered we had in common.

A couple of years older than me, Pam had done some modelling before training as a colour artist and working for the legendary hairdresser Rose Evansky, who trialled her new 'blow dry' technique on Pam in 1962, becoming the first person to ever sport this famous hairstyle. Pam worked her own magic on many pop stars, including Lulu and Dusty Springfield, as well as the acclaimed actor Donald Sutherland, who needed his hair to be dyed blond for a film role. Nowadays there are loads of products for dyeing hair, but back then it was quite a dodgy thing to do yourself and all your hair could fall out if you got it wrong.

When she hit her mid-20s, Pam decided she wanted something more from life. Between working at the salon and helping her mum run an off-licence, she wasn't meeting anybody special and didn't get much of a life for herself in London. Pam and her cousin Jane had been inspired to move to Majorca after a friend of theirs had married a Spaniard and settled down there. They gave Pam a job in their off-licence and she lived with Jane in a small apartment. I suppose Pam might have expected to meet a nice Spanish guy herself, but instead she met a copper from Shoreditch!

We liked the same music and playing that night in a bar was the song 'Tous les garçons et les filles', the debut single by the legendary French singer-songwriter Françoise Hardy. In English, the song translates to 'All the Boy and Girls', though I doubt I knew that at the time. After one or two Cuba Libras, Pam and I sang that song over and over, as we danced the rest of the night away. Then in the early hours of the morning, we sat on the beach holding hands and watched the sun rise over the tangerine-tinted Bay of Palma.

I had never met anybody like Pam before. She was different to all the other girls I'd known, much more independent and very centred. We shared a very close connection instantly and I felt like we were equals. That evening was magic, and I was truly convinced that I'd met my soulmate. The next morning, when my mates eventually found me, I told them I was passionately in love with the most wonderful girl in the world and that I wasn't going back to England. They thought I was mad, but when they met Pam the next day, they understood.

Pam still had to work at the off-licence during my holiday, but I would meet her for lunch and take her out in the evenings. We were both adventurers and spent her days off on the beach, either hiring a boat or going for a swim. From the start, we just loved being together. As the holiday went on, she introduced me to her friends and we all had a really nice time together. Those two weeks went by far too quickly.

Pam also made some extra money selling tickets for boat trips to tourists at the harbour. She didn't want to be doing both jobs, so I said I would leave the force and take over that job selling the tickets for her. I think she thought I was joking, but I was serious. I was so in love that suddenly nothing else mattered to me, only Pam. At the end of the holiday, Bob and Jock had to work hard to convince me to go back with them.

On the last night, I asked Pam to marry me. I can't remember exactly what I said, but I'm sure I got down on one knee. I felt compelled to ask her. To my great delight, she said yes. I didn't have a ring to offer her, but as she already wore one that she was very fond of, we made that her engagement ring. Before my flight home the next day, Pam gave me a present: a Françoise Hardy record called *Canta*. There are four songs listed on the cover, the first being 'Todos Los Chicos Y Chicas', the Spanish translation for the song we had sang together on our first date.

In a way, as hard as it was to leave Pam behind in Majorca, it was good for us to have a break and for me to get back to reality. Neither of us had a telephone, but we kept in touch by letter. We wrote to each other every other day, exchanging many dozens of letters. I would take mine down to the main post office in the City, in the hope that they would get sent fast, as I didn't want Pam to have to wait too long for my replies.

Below is what Pam wrote in her first letter to me, which I hope gives you some idea of the deep bond we shared right from the start and why I felt I just had to propose to her…

Darling, before I say anything else, I love you. I've never heard that before and it feels wonderful. Yesterday, when I collected your record and I said to the woman at the shop that it was for my fiancé, I had little shivers up and down my spine. You see what you've done to me? I was just a sane ordinary girl until I met you, but its lovely. I was so sorry for our last night when I was thoroughly tight. What a night to choose, I didn't even say goodbye to you properly. Maybe that's just as well, because I would have howled. I hope I didn't show you up too much. I really don't remember very well, please forgive me. Thank you for the message on the photo. You say you were drunk, how about me? I wanted to write on a photo for you and I couldn't even do that. Please Barry, don't change your mind back in England, I couldn't bear it. But if you do, I would rather know. I don't want to stay here now, but I must for a little while. I'll be home as soon as possible. I was so happy last night, I want everybody to know. I'm sure by the time we left the Ali Baba, everyone did. Since this is the first time I've ever written a love letter, I didn't think I'd know what to say, but it came very easily to me. Jane sends her to love to her 'cousin-in-law' as she puts it. I must finish now. I love you very much, take care of yourself. Pamela.

Now the hard part. I had to introduce myself to Pam's mum…

```
DISSOLVE TO:
EXT. TERRACED HOUSES. OFF EDGWARE ROAD. 1965.


BARRY, wearing his best suit and tie, has neatly combed
his hair. He walks down the street, carrying a bottle of
wine and some flowers.


He finds the right door number and hesitates for
a moment. He puts the flowers and wine down on the
pavement, straightens his tie and takes a deep breath.
He tentatively rings the doorbell.
A couple of beats later, ROG, a grey-haired woman in her
mid-50s, opens the door and offers BARRY a curious look.
          ROG
  I can't remember the last time someone brought me
  flowers.

          BARRY
  Mrs. Rogers?
```

                    ROG
Yes?

                    BARRY
Uh, I'm Barry. Barry Appleton. I met Pam on
holiday.

                    ROG
Yes?

                    BARRY
I asked her to marry me.

                    ROG
Oh.

                    BARRY
Sorry to have startled you.

                    ROG
Shocked would be a better word.

                    BARRY
I thought of many ways to tell you.

                    ROG
I'm sure you did!

                    BARRY
In the end, I thought it best to just say it.

                    ROG
Let me get this straight. You asked Pam to marry
you, and she said yes?

                    BARRY
    (chuckling)
I wouldn't have come if she'd said no.

ROG looks anxiously up and down the street before
stepping back inside.

                    ROG
You'd better come in.

BARRY enters and as ROG closes the front door, she
notices a curtain twitch in a window over the road. ROG
rolls her eyes.

Rog made me a cup of tea and after she sat down, I explained everything to her. She laughed at a few things I said and could tell I was hopelessly in love with her daughter. After many a cigarette, and polishing off the bottle of wine I'd brought, she smiled and simply said, 'You'll do.'

Pam's dad, Lewis Rogers, had served as an officer in Germany during the war. He decided to stay out there, only returning once to meet Pam when she was a teenager. He took her to dinner, but there was no affection between them, and he never contacted her again.

Even though they had divorced very early in their marriage, Rhoda Curzon was still affectionately known as 'Rog' by all. She had worked hard to bring up Pam as a single mother, whilst also running the off-licence on the Edgware Road. Rog explained that she used to serve another policeman who was quite fond of Pam. They used to have a drink and a cigarette together, though at some stage he slipped up and blew his chances.

When Pam returned to London, I met her at Heathrow Airport. It was wonderful to see her again. When we got back to my car and I turned the radio on, the song playing was 'Tous les garçons et les filles'. It was meant to be. We would have got married straight away if we'd had the means, but we had to sort out some logistics first. Pam moved back in with Rog while she found herself a new job, which she quickly did by going back into hairdressing, working as a colourist at the famous salon French of London.

The next couple of months went by so quickly as we planned the wedding. When I told the guys at the section house that I was getting married, they were so delighted that they all wanted to buy me a drink. I don't think I was sober for a week, which was unusual for me as I was never a big drinker. I had my stag night at a pub next to Liverpool Street station, though I certainly didn't get drunk. I didn't need to, I was already so happy and just sat there thinking 'I'm marrying Pam tomorrow.'

We got married on 30 October 1965 at St. Peters in Cricklewood, just a few years before the nineteenth-century church was demolished. We couldn't afford a big wedding, but we had great support from friends and family. One of the guys from G Division bought our wedding cake, while others paid for the food and drink. My parents came down from Gloucester, while a few more relatives made the long journey from Monmouth to join us for our big day.

Pam's uncle, Alec Curzon, walked her down the aisle, with her cousin Jane and my sister Susan following as her bridesmaids. I remember turning and seeing my bride for the first time. Pam looked astonishingly beautiful; she literally took my breath away. At the reception, I was introduced to more of Pam's relatives. I learned that Pam's grandfather, Henry Curzon, had been a famous boxer, renowned for having a 'cast-iron head'! I sadly never met the great man, who in later life worked as a stunt man in Hollywood.

We couldn't afford a honeymoon, as we'd already started ordering furniture. Next to Olive House were two blocks of married quarters, containing ten spacious and modern apartments, one of which was to be our first home. This was thanks to another good word from DI Fred Gerrard, who always went out of his way to champion me, along with other young coppers he believed in. I was so happy to be living with my wife. Many people said it would never last, but they were all wrong. It just got better and better.

Pam and I both enjoyed modern jazz and on our first television, we watched the French pianist Jacques Loussier perform with his trio. We loved his arrangements of classical music, mainly Bach and Ravel. In 1966, he made a cigar advertisement famous thanks to his arrangement of 'Air on a G String'. I also greatly admired his lifestyle, as he played concerts for six months of the year and then spent the other half growing grapes in his vineyard back home in the south of France. An idyllic way of life, which seemed a million miles away from chasing villains around the East End.

Our own dream was to save up and buy our own place, which we eventually did in 1966, when we found a very nice semi-detached house in Cheshunt. With three bedrooms, we knew this would be the ideal place for starting a family one day… That magical day came in March 1967, when our son Simon was born. We welcomed him into the world over a bottle of Ruffino Chianti in an Italian restaurant on the Holloway Road. To honour our new arrival, the owner stuck a candle in the top of the empty bottle, which we took home.

In October 1969, our daughter Sacha joined us. Pam gave birth at home, but when the midwife didn't arrive in time, I had to assist a young Portuguese student with the delivery. Pam wasn't very pleased about this, but there was no time to wait. After Sacha's safe arrival, we celebrated with another bottle of Ruffino Chianti. This very proud father now had two lighted candles on the dining room table, for which I said a thankful little prayer.

I loved becoming a father and especially enjoyed reading the kids their bedtime stories. I even changed nappies occasionally, or at least when people were taking photos! Soon we grew the family further with our first pets: Chloe the Siamese cat and Thomas, the King Charles spaniel. My home life was great, which not every copper I knew was able to say. I felt blessed.

As the 1960s drew to a close, the attention of many a police officer was drawn to the conclusion of a major case: a protracted investigation into a family of criminals, and their villainous associates, who had plagued the streets of London for over a decade. Their story has become legend. I was there from the start…

CHAPTER 5

DOUBLE TROUBLE

Ever since I was young, I have been fascinated with boxing. My introduction to the sport came when I joined the St John Ambulance as a kid, where one of the instructors taught me sparring. On a Saturday evening, after collecting our accumulator from the local garage after it had been charged, I would have my ear pressed to the speaker of my grandfather's battery-powered radio, listening to all the big fights of the era. Dick Richardson, Welsh heavyweight at the time, would become a hero of mine.

After landing on G Division, I started looking around for a boxing gym and discovered Fitzroy Lodge, the now famous club in South London. Originally founded in 1908, after the Second World War the gym was re-established under the arches on Lambeth Road, where it remains to this day. Future world champions David Haye and Cornelius Boza-Edwards would train there. This is when I began taking my boxing seriously.

My training would begin with a two and a half mile run from Vauxhall Bridge along the south side of the Embankment, then crossing over Westminster Bridge and running back along the north side. In the early morning sun, that iconic stretch of the Thames really looked spectacular. On my return to the club, with endorphins pumping through my veins, I would hit the gym, working on a punch bag. The two main coaches were Billy Webster and Mick Carney, formidable boxers in their day who had both competed professionally. They gave me a lot of time.

I was never going to be a contender, but I developed fast reflexes, which came in handy when catching villains. After my first motorbike accident, my boxing came to an end. It is a sport that requires you to keep at it all the time and once you stop, and in my case suffer a serious injury, it is very difficult to get back into.

DOUBLE TROUBLE

There is so much more to boxing than simply fighting. While you are trading blows with your opponent, you are not only sharing toil, sweat, tears and the odd drop of blood, you are also learning routine, structure, discipline and respect. It has certainly helped many a young tearaway to get back on the straight and narrow. It is perhaps ironic then that it was through this great sport that I first encountered one of the most heavyweight opponents from my police career.

One early turn shift as a senior cadet, I found myself on my own once again, after the PC I was supposed to be patrolling with had been required at court. Cutting through the back doubles, I came across a small boxing club. The door was open, and I peered inside to see all these kids being coached in the art. I really enjoyed watching them in action, though none of them paid much attention to this young cadet in his very smart uniform observing them from beyond the ropes. However, someone else did, and I soon felt a presence beside me…

```
DISSOLVE TO:
EXT. BOXING GYM DOORWAY. BRICK LANE. 1958.


Standing next to BARRY at the doorway is a BOXER, 20s,
broad-shouldered, greased-back hair, a similar height
to BARRY. He has an intimidating face and wears a sweaty
tracksuit, his hands covered in bandages. Confident and
imposing. A character.
                    BOXER
              (slightly aggressive)
          Can I help you?
                    BARRY
          Just watching the kids working out. One in the
          ring, crew cut. He's fast, definitely got a future.
                    BOXER
          Know anything about boxing?
                    BARRY
          Like those kids, I trained a bit. You?
                    BOXER
          Now and again.
```

                    BARRY
Watch any of the big fights?
                    BOXER
Yeah. I like watching the big guys. Cooper, Erskine,
London.
                    BARRY
I'm a Dick Richardson fan.
                    BOXER
Who the hell's he?
                    BARRY
   (*chuckling)
Wait and see…

The BOXER steps inside and grabs a fresh towel. He turns
to face BARRY.
                    BOXER
If you know so much about boxing, why not come
down and help train these kids?
                    BARRY
I'll think about it.

BARRY starts to walk away.
                    BARRY
See you around.
                    BOXER
Yeah.

CUT TO:
EXT. BRICK LANE. LATER.

BARRY walks away from the club. He is signalled by a
patrol car with two officers inside. BARRY gets in the
back. The DRIVER, 30s, red-faced with a pug nose, turns
around and leans over at BARRY.
                    DRIVER
What d'you think you're doing talking to that
fucking scum?
                    BARRY
Talking about boxing. What's the problem?

                DRIVER
    That fucker you just got so friendly with is
    Reggie Kray!
                BARRY
        (bemused)
    Reggie who?

Exasperated, the DRIVER turns to the RADIO OPERATOR,
late 30s, slightly overweight, balding.
                DRIVER
    "Reggie who" he says! You tell him, Bill. Fucking
    cadets.
                R/O
    Listen Barry, Reggie Kray and his brothers are
    villains. Not big at the moment, but they're
    ambitious. Go back to the nick and check them
    out. Educate yourself.

The DRIVER looks at BARRY in his mirror.
                DRIVER
    And do yourself a favour, greenhorn. Stay away
    from those kinds of people, or you'll be in deep
    shit. You hear me?

BARRY gets out of the patrol car as it races off.
                BARRY
    Loud and clear.

I went back to City Road station and started doing my homework. Looking through the intelligence reports collated on the Kray twins so far, they hadn't yet established themselves as the villains who would go on to rule the East End with an iron fist. The kind of petty crime they were committing early on was to go into a top tailor's and order three made-to-measure suits, which they then wore but never paid for. From little acorns…

The top villain operating in London during the early 1950s was a gangster called Jack Comer, better known as Jack Spot, a nickname he'd apparently acquired for always being 'on the spot' whenever there was trouble. Spot was Jewish and throughout the 1940s he made violent stands against antisemitism, which earned him a reputation as a hardman. When his influence in London began to expand, he began running protection rackets and making serious money from clubs and at the racecourses.

In the 1950s, there were parts of Clerkenwell just like Italy and it was from here that Spot employed Mafia types to help grow his business. Soon he started to search for a wider array of criminals to carry out jobs for him, from burglars and thieves, fences and forgers, to hired thugs and heavies. There was no shortage of young men who had grown up on council estates who were at his beck and call. It was endemic, because they usually wanted to be just like their old man and his father before him. Generations of villains who knew no different. They wanted a flash car outside their council flat or to go into a pub with loads of cash and buy everyone drinks. They felt they couldn't do that by earning an honest living. They wanted more and thought that crime paid.

The Krays were on Jack Spot's payroll for a time, along with many other young men who would become notable villains over the next decade. Ironically, Spot himself was ultimately intimidated out of the underworld he had controlled for so long. The back alleys and side streets of London were now filled with groups of rival gangs, all out to prove themselves and vying for power.

I don't know why Reggie Kray talked to me in the boxing club that morning. Maybe he thought this young copper could come in handy in the future? I never went back to that gym, though it certainly wasn't the last time our paths crossed. I went on lots of raids to pubs, clubs and other 'enterprises' that he and Ronnie owned. On one occasion, we raided 178 Vallance Road, the small two-up, two-down Victorian terrace house in Bethnal Green where the twins allegedly lived with their parents. The house was very grotty inside – the Krays weren't tidy people. The only member of the family at home was their mother, Violet, who unloaded a barrage of foul-mouthed abuse at us.

It felt like we were always turning over the Krays and stopping them in cars to give them a hard time, long before their names ever hit the headlines. By the end of the Fifties, the twins had their own thriving protection racket, built up using a combination of violence and intimidation tactics.

In 1960, Detective Chief Superintendent Tommy Butler of the Flying Squad wrote a report expressing concern that the twins might try to expand their burgeoning activities and target the West End. The potential for an all-out war between rival gangs was becoming a tangible concern. Butler's report described how the twins had cultivated a 'formidable criminal association' with the Nash family, an infamous mob of six brothers.

Jimmy, Roy, Ronnie, George, Johnny and Billy Nash were all born and bred in Islington. I had been warned to watch out for this implacable bunch. I wouldn't be seeing Roy Nash on the Hoxton estate any time soon, as he was serving a five-year stretch for stabbing an unarmed boy to death at a Shoreditch dance hall in 1958. Jimmy Nash was arrested for shooting Selwyn Cooney in the head on 7 February 1960 at the Pen Club, a squalid illegal drinking den on Duval Street. Just four days into his murder trial, Nash was acquitted, after suspicions that the jury had been 'got at'. He was eventually sentenced to five years for GBH.

One evening, I was on night duty when DI John Pritchard from Paddington nick informed me that earlier that evening, two of the Nash brothers had come out of a pub in his area and picked an argument with a guy on the street, who I'll call Peyton. A fight ensued and Peyton made the mistake of producing a knife, which he used to cut one of the brothers. There were roadworks outside this pub and Nash retaliated by picking up a road lamp and hammering Peyton over the head until he was lying in the road, barely conscious. But that wasn't enough for Nash, who got in his car and ran over Peyton. Twice.

DI Pritchard asked me to go to their Hoxton address and, if the Nash in question was there, bring him in. As our suspect had been injured, I thought I would also check the hospitals on G Division, starting with the Royal London Hospital in Whitechapel. I walked into A&E and found Nash being stitched up, with his brothers by his side. I told him I was bringing him in for attempted murder, which he accepted with no fuss. I escorted him to Paddington station, where DI Pritchard thanked me for being so diligent and encouraged me to keep up the good work.

The reason Nash hadn't offered up any resistance when I arrested him was simple: the smarter villains knew that if they didn't come quietly when they were nicked, things would be much harder for them down the line. If they co-operated, they knew they might still have a chance of getting bail, especially if they had the right lawyer. Most of these gangsters had a crooked solicitor in their corner, who were usually more corrupt than their clients.

Criminals didn't have access to Swiss bank accounts back then, so these suits would turn up at court, sometimes unsolicited. They would openly discuss handing over significant sums of cash to represent them and a deal was usually done there and then, right in front of me as if I wasn't there. I couldn't believe some of the excuses these briefs used to spout to the magistrates when trying to get their clients released on bail. Over the years, I got to recognise that it was always the same group of solicitors representing the same calibre of villain.

Even with a dodgy brief on side, if the case was serious enough, or if the prisoner was involved with another crime under investigation, they would be automatically detained. Bail could also be refused if the prisoner didn't have a fixed abode and was considered a flight risk. They often gave a false address, usually owned by a 'friend' or a fellow villain, but we would always visit the property and confirm for ourselves.

Bail was never going to be an option for the Nash brother I arrested. Thankfully his victim survived the attack and was brave enough to take the stand and testify in court. I hadn't thought about the potential dangers of bringing Nash in on my own; I just did what was necessary. That was an easy arrest compared to the time I was checking out a garage under the railway arches near Bethnal Green station, the owners of which were suspected of chopping up stolen cars.

Across the road, I spotted one of the Krays' henchmen, George Kitchener Dixon, coming out of a betting shop. A sadistic piece of work, Dixon had plagued the streets of Limehouse for years and had already done a stretch for causing grievous bodily harm. His weapon of choice was a single-edged razor blade, fixed to a pocketknife. A warrant was out for his arrest, in connection with several serious assaults. I had to bring him in.

DISSOLVE TO:
EXT. SIDE STREET, BETHNAL GREEN. 1961.

BARRY observes GEORGE KITCHENER DIXON, 20s, about six foot tall, wearing stone-washed jeans, a black loose jacket with padded shoulders over a white singlet with a heavy gold chain around his neck. A thug. DIXON leaves a betting shop opposite the railway arches and recognises BARRY. They both walk towards each other, neither with any intention of backing down.

> BARRY
>
> George, you're wanted for a number of serious offences. I'm taking you in.

DIXON pushes BARRY.

> DIXON
>
> You sure you've got the right guy, arsehole?

> BARRY
>
> You want to add assault on a police officer to your list of charges? Be smart.

DIXON shoves BARRY, who resists. Soon, a crowd appears and surrounds BARRY. Nobody in this rabble is going to help. BARRY is on his own in bandit country and in dead trouble.

> DIXON
>
> You ask any of these people, they'll tell you. My name's Harry Jones.

The crowd start to laugh. An old boy with a camera takes a photograph.

> BARRY
>
> You want to stand here arguing? Or are you going to come quietly? Maybe we can get you bail, if you behave yourself.

DIXON knows this is a bluff and he stands closer to BARRY, almost nose to nose.

> DIXON
>
> I'm going nowhere with you. Get. Out. Of my way.

More pushing and shoving ensues. Neither bull is going to back down. Just before things get even more out of hand, the crowd parts, allowing a large black Mercedes to glide forward and pull up by the kerb. On the front wing is a Chilean flag, declaring diplomatic status. The

```
driver winds down his window. It is REGGIE KRAY, who
recognises BARRY.
                    KRAY
   What's the problem, officer?
                    BARRY
   George has been arrested. I've tried to do this
   as reasonably as I can, but all he wants is
   aggravation.


REGGIE KRAY shakes his head with some disapproval.
                    KRAY
       (to DIXON)
   Go with him, George. There's a good boy.


BARRY grabs DIXON's arm, who tries to resist. BARRY
tightens his grip, while KRAY stares at DIXON, who
finally resigns himself to coming in quietly.
```

That confrontation could have gone badly, but being prepared to stand up to villains like Dixon was what I'd signed up for. It took twenty minutes to walk my prisoner to Commercial Road Police Station, during which neither of us uttered another word to each other. I was grateful for the silence. When we got to the nick, Reggie Kray had organised for a solicitor to be there waiting to represent Dixon. Kray wasn't doing me a favour – this was his way of showing that he felt this was his manor and that he was in charge. I checked on his Mercedes and it was an ex-Chilean diplomatic car, recently bought at an auction. As for Dixon, getting nicked didn't stop him in the long-term; this habitual thug was still being found guilty of causing grievous bodily harm in the 1970s.

Detective Chief Superintendent Butler, the first to report on the potential danger of the twins, was an old-school copper and very dedicated. He always worked late into the night, which was unusual for an officer of his rank. Whenever I was on night duty at Scotland Yard, I would walk down the corridor and pass the open door of Tommy's office, where he would always be sat at his desk, diligently working through piles of paperwork.

His position had earned him the right of having a car and driver at his disposal, but he preferred to use the tube or a taxi to travel home. We knew that Tommy lived in a council flat with his mother, but none of us ever knew where exactly their home was. He was a kind of George Smiley character, a lone wolf who gave his life to the job. He was bang on the money when he predicted the twins might end up being glamorised by the media.

The tabloids continued to inflate the twins' egos and, throughout the Swinging Sixties, the Krays would be pictured at showbiz parties mingling with the celebrities of the day. They also began networking with members of parliament. One of the most influential figures in their orbit was Lord Boothby, a former MP who was now a member of the House of Lords. He was also allegedly one of Ronnie Kray's lovers.

I first learned of Boothby's exploits when I was out in a squad car one day and spotted one of the first E-Type Jaguars being driven around the manor. It was a beautiful car and its very distinctive yellow paintwork made it stand out a mile on the streets of Hoxton. I wondered why this brand-new model, which had only just been released, was being driven around by a young lad from one of the local estates.

We followed the Jaguar and, when the teenage driver slowed down to show off to some of his mates, we pulled him over and questioned how he could afford such an expensive motor. He explained that it was a gift from Lord Boothby! We then started to receive reports that Boothby was getting introduced to a steady stream of young men, supplied by Ronnie Kray himself.

Responsible for the Krays' media image was their elder brother Charlie, who fancied himself as a PR man. When the Joan Littlewood film *Sparrows Can't Sing* premiered at the ABC Cinema on Mile End Road in 1963, Charlie had worked his spin and managed to get Ronnie and Reggie front and centre on the red carpet. They were even photographed in a manner that suggested they had accompanied Princess Margaret to the screening.

The press weren't the only ones keeping a watchful eye on the Krays at the premiere. Along with many members of the aide squad mingling in the crowd, I was watching them like a hawk. This was the first time I saw Charlie in the flesh, who I thought looked more business-like than the twins. After the screening, Ronnie and Reggie threw an after party at the Kentucky Club over the road, which the film's star Barbara Windsor attended. Princess Margaret reportedly declined the same invitation.

That premiere was just the beginning. Soon, Charlie was orchestrating for the twins to be seen with as many stars as possible. He also had them supporting charities, donating just enough money to help give the impression that Ronnie and Reggie were upstanding citizens. By 1964, Charlie was even advertising himself in *The Stage* theatrical newspaper, stating his plans to create the Charles Kray Theatrical Agency, representing artistes from an office in Knightsbridge. During the decade where you could be whatever you wanted to be, the Kray brothers were no different to every other young hopeful. Except, Ronnie and Reggie had more dangerous dreams. They wanted to be the Mafia.

The Krays weren't the only villains who had set their sights on making it big in the West End. Gordon Bagier, Labour MP for Sunderland South, had conducted a painstaking investigation which concluded that members of the American Mafia had made secret visits to the north of England, with the intention of buying their way into leading gambling clubs. In March 1967, he raised his concerns at the House of Commons, stating that Britain's gambling laws were too weak and that these notorious gangsters certainly weren't in his constituency for a holiday!

These New York hoodlums had already worked out it was cheaper and safer for their guys to gamble and make easy money in London, rather than Las Vegas. It was even arranged for George Raft, an American movie star of the 1930s, to be placed at the Colony Club in Berkeley Square, Knightsbridge. Raft had been famous for playing gangsters, though by this point his career was over. He had been investigated multiple times for tax evasion and in 1965 was finally convicted, at which point he testified to financial transactions with the Mafia.

Within twelve months, Raft had traded Hell's Kitchen for Hyde Park to run the Colony Club. I wanted to take a look at this fallen movie star for myself and one night an Italian informant of mine managed to get me into the club. I got talking to Raft, who was smaller than his screen persona. He seemed to be a nice enough guy, but maybe that was down to his acting talent.

The Krays didn't take to Raft and his organised crime cohorts stomping on their territory. Perhaps fortunately for George, he made a trip back to the States in 1967, but was banned from re-entering Britain ever again, branded as 'an undesirable'. He never understood this decision and questioned it until his death in 1980. I think you got off lightly, Mr. Raft, because by that point the Krays were no longer playing at being the Mafia. They now had blood on their hands.

The first victim was Tommy Marks, known as 'Ginger'. In January 1965, I was one of the aides assigned to investigate his murder, after he was reportedly gunned down on Cheshire Street, outside the Carpenters Arms, a pub owned by the Krays. When the police attended the scene in the early hours of the morning, bullet holes were discovered, along with blood and Marks' spectacles left abandoned in the street. The only thing missing was a corpse.

The aide squad was always available to work on whatever was required. On a murder case, we would be the officers tasked with knocking on doors, looking for witnesses and taking statements. How many answers we got depended on what kind of murder had been committed. If it was a domestic murder, then everyone in the vicinity had something to tell you. But if it was a gangland killing, forget it. Everybody was too frightened to open their mouths, for fear of having them shut permanently.

We never found Marks' body and legend has it that his remains are buried underneath a motorway. Freddie Foreman, one of the Krays' most notorious heavies on the Firm and known as 'Brown Bread Fred', was arrested for Marks' murder, but later acquitted at the Old Bailey. Over the years, there have been multiple accounts of Ginger Marks' final moments, told by different villains, all claiming that they were there that night on Cheshire Street.

Personally, I think Ginger Marks' big mouth had upset a lot of people, which ultimately got him killed. When my colleague Terry Brown and I went to Marks' flat in Aldgate, we searched through his belongings and I discovered that he had a notebook containing the telephone numbers for a number of Met police officers, as well as the FBI. Was he working as an informant? If anyone else had been snooping around in that flat and found those numbers written down, that would have sealed Marks' fate.

As we left Marks' flat in the early hours of the morning, a member of the public approached us, reporting that they had seen the flash of a torch inside a nearby jeweller's, which was closed. Terry and I proceeded to the front of the shop but couldn't see any light inside the premises. As we walked away, I just happened to look up and I saw someone on the roof, looking down at us, before they quickly disappeared back out of sight. Somehow, we needed to get up onto that roof.

We still didn't have radios in those days, so Terry had to find a phone box and call the fire brigade. During the time it took them to arrive on the scene, there had been no further sign of our mystery man on the roof. When one of the firemen put a ladder against the building, he explained that none of his colleagues would be climbing up it. 'Sorry mate, that's your job.' As Terry was eighteen stone and not very athletic, it fell to me.

I remember the fireman advising me to climb over the top of the ladder, not around it. I followed his advice to the letter, as I didn't fancy falling from three floors up. When I got to the roof, I discovered a large hole. I shone my torch down, but the shop was empty. The intruders must have made their escape across the rooftops not long after we arrived. We later received information that Ginger Marks had been planning to rob the jeweller's that night. Had he been on the way to the jeweller's when he was gunned down? Was it one of his accomplices that I saw, waiting for Marks to arrive, unaware that he was dead? Some cases remain unsolved.

Over the coming months, the levels of violence on the streets continued to grow. The Met had concerns that a full-scale war between rival gangs could erupt at any moment. We might have been serving the City, but south of the river was like another world, a different culture altogether. The most prominent criminals on the other side of the Thames were the Richardsons, who didn't venture into the East End much. But we were aware of their reputation, which was reportedly even more vicious than the Krays. One of their heavies, 'Mad' Frankie Fraser, was a complete nutcase.

One rung down from heavies like Foreman and Fraser were the small-time thugs who willingly got themselves involved in a different league of crime. They did this for the bragging rights that came with working for the likes of the Krays, which they believed would boost their own credibility as a villain. This only added to Ronnie and Reggie believing their own hype. Now fully immersed in their own self-styled mafia world, the protection rackets started getting more violent, with victims getting beaten, cut or worse. Things began to spiral out of control very quickly.

There was one main problem for us detectives investigating the Krays. Even though we'd take statements from people who were involved, or had even been hurt by the Krays or one of their underlings, by the time their case came up months later, they didn't want to know. They had been warned off in between, being forced to change or retract their statements altogether. We found every time we got a step closer to nailing the twins, we were then forced two paces back. The Krays had become untouchable. Something had to change.

On 7 March 1966, Frankie Fraser murdered Richard Hart, one of the small-time villains who aspired to be on the Firm. Hart paid the price when he was shot dead at Mr. Smith's club in Catford. Fraser was charged, but once again he got off after a key witness changed their statement. Hart might have been a bit-part player, but his murder triggered a time bomb. The hatred between the two gangs reached boiling point. It was inevitable that more bloodshed would follow.

I attended many murder scenes in my career. Arguably the most notable was when I was part of the huge investigation team called to the Blind Beggar pub on 9 March 1966. This historic pub is located on Whitechapel Road and was a regular haunt for the Krays. On the night in question, George Cornell, an associate of the Richardson gang, went in the saloon bar for a drink. I believe he had crossed the river to visit a friend. Cornell was originally in with the Krays but had since allied himself with the Richardsons. He wasn't frightened of the twins and was not afraid to say so.

As soon as Ronnie Kray found out Cornell was in the Blind Beggar, he went back to Vallance Road to get tooled up. He arrived with one of his henchmen, Ian Barrie, who fired two shots at the ceiling as a warning. Then, in front of the remaining witnesses, Ronnie went right up to Cornell, pulled out a 9mm Luger and shot him in the head, just above the eyes.

The bullet had gone through Cornell and was still on the floor when we arrived at the scene. Somehow, he was still breathing, and I was one of three officers who accompanied him in an ambulance to Maida Vale hospital. We weren't expecting him to recover, but we had to be there in case somebody from the Firm came back to finish the job. In the end, Cornell never regained consciousness and was pronounced dead a few hours later.

I returned to the Blind Beggar. Back then, crime scenes weren't managed like they are today; we didn't wear special shoes or protective oversuits. What we could do was mark the floor if there was a body, number exhibits and dust the crime scene for fingerprints, while a specialist photographer would document the scene. I never wanted to set foot in that ghastly pub again.

I then joined in with the questioning of witnesses. Many people had seen Ronnie Kray pull the trigger, as he hadn't worn anything to hide his identity. But when we tried taking statements, nobody was prepared to go on the record. Kray was held in custody, but as was proving to be a regular occurrence, we had to let him go. Watching a killer walk away a free man, when you know he is guilty but cannot prove it, is the most sickening feeling for any copper.

But for me, the greatest tragedy of this whole saga was Frances Shea, who married Reggie when she was 21. Just two years later, on 7 June 1967, she took an overdose and died in her brother Frank's flat. Frankie was a Hoxton lad and the only one on the Firm I ever had any time for. We used to meet at least once a month for a drink on the Commercial Road, in a pub that was considered neutral ground for men on both sides of the law.

Frankie Shea was the same age as me and a genuinely nice guy. He wasn't a violent man, and his main function was working as a 'wheelman' for Ronnie and Reggie. He had to wear gloves when he was out on jobs, to cover a large tuft of hair on the top of one of his hands, which kept growing back no matter how many times he shaved it off. This would have made him easily identifiable.

It was fruitless for me to try and persuade Frankie to sever ties with the Krays. He was a product of his upbringing, as with so many families in the East End, who knew no other way. But when Frances died, he vehemently blamed the twins for ruining her life and being the cause of her suicide. Had they not eventually been sent down, I think he would have made his own arrangements. Many years later, Frank also took an overdose and died in 2011. I wonder if his sister was on his mind during his final moments. Rest in peace, Frankie.

The longer the Krays escaped the clutches of the law, the more it deflated me. I told Pam everything. I thought it best that she always knew what I was working on, even though I always spared her the gory details. If she had any reservations about me being a detective, she kept her counsel. She accepted the risks that came with the job, as well as the irregular hours I had to work. But she could see how wading through the grisly cesspit of the underworld without getting a result was affecting me. Pam suggested I was in desperate need of a break from the violence I had witnessed recently and that we should swap the intense baggage that came with the job with some holiday luggage. Yes, ma'am!

I booked a fortnight's leave and we decided to go somewhere new. Bearing in mind that I loved the Mediterranean and hated long flights, Pam suggested Corsica. As this is also a hive of banditry, I initially worried I might be swapping one set of mafiosos for another. But I needn't have worried, as Pam found us a remote log cabin up in the mountains, overlooking a fast-flowing stream. We both enjoyed the invigorating fresh water and the breathtaking scenery. The pizzas were incredible too!

We were a long way from the East End, but even in such a beautiful setting it was hard for me not to wonder what was happening back on those gangland streets. There was a landline in the cabin and on the first day Pam caught me looking at it. She read my mind. 'No! We're on holiday. I'm sure the Met will manage without you for two weeks.' Pam then disconnected and hid the phone to help me forget about the outside world.

I might have returned to London feeling refreshed, but sadly there had been no miraculous clean-up in my absence. The deaths hadn't stopped with Frances. There were new victims and more lives ruined by the Krays. Jack McVitie was a drug trafficker with convictions going back twenty years. Sporting a trilby that earned him the nickname 'Jack the Hat', McVitie was hired by the twins to carry out odd jobs as an enforcer. But he soon became unreliable and by October 1967 was addicted to drugs himself.

Legend has it that McVitie, armed with a sawn-off shotgun, entered the Regency Club in Stoke Newington, a terrible place owned by the Barry brothers, who were in the Krays' pocket. Inside this den of iniquity, Jack bragged that he was going to kill the Krays. As a result, he was lured to a house party at 97 Evering Road on the evening of 29 October. The twins were waiting for him. In front of witnesses, Reggie Kray stabbed McVitie to death. This proved to be the turning point. People were no longer prepared to stand on the sidelines and say nothing. They were ready to talk.

The man ready to listen to them was Nipper Read. Now working as detective chief superintendent of the murder squad, Nipper had been in the force for twenty years. We had quite a lot in common: our careers had started similarly, and he also loved his boxing, which is how he earned his nickname. I first worked with Nipper at City Road, while he was a DI. He just loved being a policeman and was the kind of copper who took his work home with him. The job was everything to him.

Nipper had worked with Tommy Butler and Fred Gerrard, both of whom had already led multiple inquiries to try and nail the Krays. Despite a lot of hard work, these had sadly all failed. It was not due to a lack of resource or effort, but the stumbling block was always the lack of evidence and nobody being willing to testify against them. Armed with all this knowledge, Nipper decided to try a different tactic and set up his operation at Tintagel House.

The building was like a fortress, disconnected from the rest of the Metropolitan Police. I never set foot in there, as Nipper very shrewdly picked officers from outside G Division, who had no prior connection to the Krays, their families or anyone else on the Firm. Operating like MI5, nothing like this had ever been set up before. The squad had their own special phone line installed and all those dedicated people inside Tintagel House were there for one reason only: to build up a solid case against the Krays.

When Nipper got the twins in custody, for what turned out to be the final time, he didn't actually have anything on them. But after the murder of McVitie, he was banking on enough people being willing to come forward while he had them safely tucked away. Thankfully, enough people who had witnessed McVitie's murder, and felt strongly that he hadn't deserved his fate, made statements that helped Nipper put the Krays away for a long time. On 4 March 1969, the twins were both found guilty of murder at the Old Bailey. Ronnie was convicted for Cornell's murder and Reggie for McVitie's. Both were sentenced to life imprisonment.

After the Krays had finally been put behind bars, Nipper was interviewed for a television documentary called *The Name is Kray*. I found watching it again, and revisiting those crime-ridden streets of East London all these years later, a very depressing experience. It especially hit home seeing all those old faces again, people I had known and mixed with, on both sides of the law. Every single person who got involved with the twins had their lives changed. For the worse.

To this day, the Krays continue to be glamourised by the media, even though they were a pair of cold-hearted and utterly ruthless killers, who ruined so many lives. I was one of many coppers who felt a huge sigh of relief when they were finally sent down in 1969. But it was a hollow victory. Despite them being behind bars, there were still plenty of criminals left who fancied taking over the Krays' empire. I was about to take them on, this time from the fast lane.

CHAPTER 6

RIDING SHOTGUN

During my first ten years of law enforcement, I had built up an impressive number of arrests and earned multiple commissioner commendations acknowledging my ability, courage, determination and efficiency. As rewarding as these accolades were, it was more important to me that I had gained a reputation as a diligent officer who could be relied on.

After being impressed with how I had apprehended one of the violent Nash brothers, DI John Pritchard recommended me to the head of the Flying Squad, DCS Tommy Butler, as a promising candidate. Having been his trusted right-hand man on the Great Train Robbery, Butler valued Pritchard's judgement. Thanks to this endorsement, I was offered the chance to join the famous squad in March 1968. I was thrilled.

Formed in 1919, the Flying Squad was an elite unit responsible for tackling serious and organised crime, specialising in investigating and, when possible, preventing robberies. Since the early 1960s, there had been eight squads, each made up of a detective inspector, two sergeants and a few constables. Thanks to their success, it was decided towards the end of the decade to increase the number of squads to ten. As experienced officers were promoted and distributed across the two new squads, an opportunity arose for new blood to join the established teams. I joined Five Squad, also known as 'The Fabulous Five', a formidable team of crimefighters.

Our guv'nor, DI Frank Lovejoy, was a seasoned thief-catcher who meant business. His two deputies, DS Mike McAdam and DS Charlie Snape, both had loads of experience and were guys you could trust with your life. Just before I joined Five Squad, Frank and his team had foiled a robbery at one of London's major airports, catching three villains, all posing as airport personnel in matching overalls, red-handed as they tried to break into a British European Airways strongroom. Five Squad had prevented hundreds of thousands of pounds from being nicked and got the robbers sent down for seven years apiece. If that was the kind of action in store for me, I was all in.

On my first day with Five Squad, we were split into three teams to raid several houses, each containing suspects we believed to have been involved in a bank robbery the day before. As I was the new boy, I was paired with the guv'nor to search a council flat on a big rambling estate in the East End. I was keen to get a result as soon as I could, but initially it looked like this was a fruitless exercise. But as I was going through the bedroom, I checked a drawer and found a brand-new pair of women's gloves in a bag, which still had a price tag and receipt showing they had been purchased at Harrods the previous day, when the robbery had taken place. I showed Frank and pointed out that the famous department store housed safe deposits. It was a long shot, but Frank authorised me to take a car over there.

At Harrods, I discovered our prime suspect had a safe deposit box registered in his own name. Not the sharpest tool. I went to court, got a search warrant and we had the suspect's deposit box forced open. Inside we found heaps of cash and evidence of the robbery. Frank gave me a big pat on the back. 'One day and you've already made a name for yourself!' I was off to a great start.

I had never met such a dedicated band of men until I joined the Flying Squad. I was proud to join the ranks of these highly skilled officers, who saw themselves as knights errant going out to battle on their white chargers, ready to protect workers at banks, building societies, casinos, jewellers, post offices and other commercial premises that were premium targets for robbery.

My first partner on Five Squad was Dave Dixon, a handsome Irishman who I had been a cadet with and worked alongside on the aide squad. We had formed a lasting friendship since spending our afternoons off at the Café de Paris, where one of the singers caught the twinkle in Dave's eye and they fell in love and later got married. Dave and I worked well together; we became known as 'The Jew and the Irishman', thanks to his shock of red hair and because the rest of the squad all thought I looked Jewish.

When Dave and I first went from uniform into CID, we'd had to swap the long baton for a short one. Now, we were trading in our batons for firearms.

The British bobby was just about the only police officer in the world who wasn't armed at that time. It wasn't deemed necessary across most of the country, but that all changed in London after the Shepherd's Bush murders. We needed to be carrying, especially as we were often investigating armed robberies, even though it was initially denied that Flying Squad officers carried weapons.

We were trained at a secret Army facility, where we watched the kind of training films that I had seen in the movies: 'Don't shoot the lady with the pram!' On one course, we had to run around a set of derelict houses and a cardboard cutout of a villain would appear and you had to shoot it before the sound of their gun firing roared out. I was graded as a first class shot.

We practised further at the shooting range in the basement of City Road Police Station. The targets were cutouts of charging US Marines, whilst some also depicted terrorists. The roof was really low in this basement and there were occasions when, if somebody discharged their weapon by accident, you would all have to duck for cover as the bullet hit the ceiling and went ricocheting off the walls. It was dangerous and I felt very lucky to leave that basement alive on more than one occasion.

The Met were trying to model us on the FBI and we were even supplied with the same guns and holsters as our American cousins, with whom we were in regular contact. We each got to choose the weapon we wanted to carry – I preferred the Smith & Wesson snub-nosed .38, along with a shoulder holster, which I found to be more reliable for a quick draw.

Even though we were all very responsible and took these weapons deadly seriously, it was all very casual in comparison with the rules and regulations rightly enforced on officers today. We weren't required to secure the guns in the station and I used to take mine home every night and lock it away there. Not long after joining the squad, I went to court forgetting that I was armed. When the officer on the front desk searched me to check that I was OK to proceed into the building, his hand landed on my firearm and his eyes almost popped out of his head. A look of panic washed over his face until I calmly produced my warrant card.

The Flying Squad was an autonomous organisation, meaning we could have whatever we needed to do the job effectively. As a result, our guns weren't the only things we had in our armoury; we had a choice of vehicles too. We had a selection of nondescript vans, while our cars were mostly Ford Zephyrs and Triumph 2000s. We also had our very own black minicab, which was invaluable for doing observation work around the city. Nobody ever suspected us in that.

We had two teams of drivers: one assigned to the vans and another to handle the cars. Our highly reliable car driver was Bill Parsons, a slightly hunched man in his mid-50s, with thinning grey hair and a little moustache. Very experienced behind the wheel, Bill had driven a tank during the war, when he'd somehow survived being shot in the neck. He had an entrance and exit wound either side of his throat to prove it. Armed with a great sense of humour, Bill was an excellent guy and a father figure to us all.

As he was responsible for the maintenance of the car, Bill would drive it to his home in Southgate every night. As I lived on his way into town, he would kindly pick me up and drop me back every day and wouldn't hear of me relying on public transport. Bill was also very good at spotting faces in a crowd. If we were in traffic and there were twenty people walking along the pavement, he would pick somebody out and say, 'He's not right.' You could always tell the genuine people who were going about their business apart from the odd one with a burglar's head.

One time, Bill was driving me and Dave around when we spotted a car full of villains we recognised. We stopped them and found a load of guns in their trunk. It turned out they were on their way to do a robbery and we arrested them for possession of firearms, which became a stated case.

On another occasion, Bill was driving us through central London when we had to stop due to hordes of people blocking our route. The date was 30 January 1969, the street was Savile Row and, on the rooftop above, the Beatles were giving their final live performance as a band. I also remember Bill driving us through Canning Town to show us what was left of Ronan Point, the tower block that had been partly destroyed by a gas explosion in May 1968, killing four people and seriously injuring many more. After seeing that frightening sight with my own eyes, I vowed never to live in a high-rise building.

If we weren't going straight to a job, Bill would drive us to New Scotland Yard every morning. When I first joined up, Scotland Yard was still based in two very large Victorian Gothic buildings along the Thames near Westminster Bridge, also incorporating Canon Row Police Station and Special Branch. I remember these historic Norman Shaw buildings were very small and cramped inside and walking those corridors felt like I was following in the footsteps of George Smiley in the middle of a John le Carré novel.

In 1967, the Met moved their headquarters to a newly constructed building on Broadway in Victoria, right opposite St James Park underground station. This new HQ was something else and it was quite a nice feeling turning up every morning and passing the famous revolving sign. Knowing we were Flying Squad, security would direct Bill to drive us down to the basement, where he would park his always pristine car.

One of Bill's colleagues, 'Chalky' White, was responsible for a Rover V8, which he kept similarly immaculate. One night, Chalky had to pick up a senior officer who, having had a few drinks, was feeling worse for wear and went to be sick out of the window… only he forgot to wind it down. Chalky went berserk and promptly ejected this senior officer from his prized motor!

The Flying Squad was based on the fourth floor of New Scotland Yard. As you entered, you would first walk down a corridor, where all the high-ranking officers like Tommy Butler had their offices. Then there was a big open-plan space where all our desks were situated. Sometimes we might do a standard eight-hour day there, catching up on all the paperwork that came with the job. At one stage, we were working on so many cases that we were going up to the Old Bailey more or less on a weekly basis!

The powers that be then trialled a system where if we arrested a couple of villains, we could take them to the local police station and hand all the paperwork over to their CID team, who would then appoint someone else to run the case. That didn't work for us, as not only were we giving away big cases, but we were missing out on the potential of getting invaluable information out of villains, which would help us crack more cases. Thankfully after a short time, we went back to running things the tried and tested way.

Information once led us to discover a stolen Transit van, fitted with false plates, hidden under a railway arch. Our source told us that this van was going to be used in a bank robbery. We didn't know which branch was going to be hit, but we believed it would be soon. In the middle of the night, we arranged for a team of specialists to hide a microphone and transmitter in the van for us, which we kept an eye on from an observation post just down the road. Now all we could do was wait and see if anyone turned up.

Two days into the 'obbo' and we were in business. Three guys carrying holdalls got in the Transit and before they'd even started the ignition, they started chatting and we could hear every word, loud and clear. They set off and we followed them in two nondescript vehicles, some way back, but not too far. We would lose the signal at times as we travelled, but we heard enough to get an idea about which bank they were planning to rob. We also learned that they were armed…

```
DISSOLVE TO:
INT. FLYING SQUAD VAN. ON THE MOVE. 1968.


BARRY is riding shotgun in a van with several other Five
Squad officers. Over the surveillance transmitter, they
can hear the conversation of their three suspects in
the Transit van. TOM and HARRY sound irritated by their
nervous colleague, DICK.
          TOM
     (irate)
   How many fuckin' times do I 'ave to tell you?
          DICK
   I'm just saying, what if there's cars parked
   outside?
          HARRY
   I'll double park. Who fucking cares!
          TOM
   Once we're out of the van, we don't stop. Remember my
   psychology. The cash behind the jump is ours. It's
   already ours. If anyone comes between us…
          HARRY
   Two shots in the ceiling. Believe me, there won't
   be any heroes after I give them both barrels.
          DICK
   What if one of the tellers presses a panic alarm?
```

```
        HARRY
For fuck's sake, turn the radio on will you, Tom.
This wanker's even making me nervous!


TOM turns on the radio and all three start singing along
to the Matt Monro song 'Born Free'. BARRY and the rest
of Five Squad are amused by the irony.
        BARRY
Not for long, boys!
```

After a short drive, the Transit pulled up on the kerb alongside a row of shops, where a small bank was located at the centre. We pulled up as close as we could, while our other vehicle parked on the other side of the van. As soon as the robbers got out of the van, we ran at them from all angles. But as I sprinted over with my gun pointed out in front of me, a woman came hurriedly out of one of the shops, pushing a pram right across my path. I went flying head over heels, the woman screamed and the baby cried its heart out. So much for the element of surprise.

I scrambled back on my feet and rushed to assist my colleagues. We arrested all three robbers without a shot being fired.

Once all our suspects were secured, I went to find the woman and her baby, who were being looked after in one of the nearby shops. Thankfully they were both OK, if a little shaken. I bought the woman a bunch of flowers and a present for her baby.

Once a case was closed, hopefully with a good result under our belts, it was onto the next one. If we didn't immediately have a new investigation to work on, we would head out to the streets and find out what was happening on the manor for ourselves. We could go wherever we wanted provided we were 'on the air' via the R/T in the car. If HQ put a call through and, for whatever reason, we weren't able to talk right away, nobody believed that we weren't in the nearest pub!

One pub I found useful for gathering information was the Chelsea Potter, which I had first discovered during lunch breaks from detective training school. I would meet people from different backgrounds in that boozer, from MPs to multi-millionaires. It paid to get to know people from different circles, as you never knew who you might meet who could furnish you with intelligence. From there I started getting invited to parties and it was whilst attending one at a club in the West End that I was introduced to an Italian guy. He was fascinated when he learned that I was a police officer, and I found it strange just how quickly he latched onto me.

The next time we found ourselves at the same party, he invited me to have dinner with him and his wife at their home. I accepted as I was curious about this guy and keen to learn more about him. At his home, whilst dinner was being prepared, I snuck off for a look in his study. He had loads of photographs framed on the wall, featuring all the American sports stars and world-famous entertainers of the day. Standing in the background of every single one of these photographs, clear as day, was my host. That was when I sussed that he had Mafia connections and the reason he was sticking so close to me was to find out information.

He would ask me questions, which I would answer as long as I judged it was appropriate to do so. In return, he would pass on information to me. I remember him once telling me that thousands were being made at Heathrow and Gatwick airports, as well as other terminals all around the world. He was too afraid to tell me how it was done, for fear of ending up under the tarmac. I spent a lot of time cultivating a relationship with this guy, who continued to give me a lot of useful information.

Detectives never reveal the identity of their informants, not even to their colleagues. The only exception is when it is vital to name them as part of an investigation, either to protect them or to ensure they don't get away with a serious crime. When I was on the Flying Squad, the best informants were always the top villains, rather than the ones lower down the food chain. The guys who were running things were always best placed to tell you what was really going on and give you the best intelligence. Some big players from the underworld were informants over the years: names you wouldn't believe were passing on information. They knew how to play the game and keeping the police informed was the main reason these villains were still at the top of the tree. However, it wouldn't stop them getting nicked if they ever committed a serious crime.

A scene that perfectly shows the 'give and take' relationship between a detective and his informant can be seen in *Bullitt*, my favourite film of all time. Not only did Steve McQueen play the part so well, but the dialogue in Trustman and Kleiner's screenplay was spot on. There is a scene where Bullitt wants information and meets his informant, Eddy, on the corner of a busy San Francisco street. After getting everything he needs, Bullitt then asks if there is anything he can do in return? Eddy says a friend of his is in jail and hints he could do with parole. Bullitt can only promise that he'll try.

Thanks to one informant, the Squad received information about some stolen property at a large house in Tottenham. There we searched a horsebox and found what we were looking for: boxes of stolen tobacco and cigarettes. The information was good, now we just had to nail the handlers. The family living in the property pleaded their innocence, claiming they had only been asked to hold onto the horsebox for somebody. They didn't know who would be coming to collect it, or what was inside. We kept this family in their home and waited for the villains to arrive. By the end of the day, there was still no sign of anyone coming to collect the horsebox. Along with a fellow DC, Nicky Birch, I volunteered to stay in the house and keep the family, and their horsebox, under surveillance.

Parked out of sight, around the corner from the house, was Bill Parsons and other members of the team. We had no direct contact with them and couldn't risk going back and forth to the car either, in case somebody saw us. Using the family's landline, we called base at Scotland Yard, who relayed our messages to the rest of the squad over the car radios. We also used the landline to let our families know that we wouldn't be home for supper. Under the cover of darkness, Bill was able to sneak us in some food, while Nicky and I took it in turns to monitor the family and the horsebox all through the night.

On a stakeout, you could never make any solid plans, you just had to commit to the case and wait to see how events unfolded. It helped that I was sharing this obbo with Nicky, a nice guy and a fantastic detective who was very committed to the squad. His ginger hair suited his energetic personality, a real terrier. I didn't know much about his private life, but this wasn't the time to change that. In a movie, two cops on surveillance would most likely while away the hours by sharing their innermost feelings to each other. But in the real world, we had a job to do and needed to maintain our focus.

The next morning, there was still no sign of our villains. We prevented the father from going to work and we stopped their kid going to school. By the end of the second day, unshaven and with heavy bags under our eyes, we were just about to call it a day... when suddenly our villains turned up three-handed! Any tiredness immediately evaporated, we were poised and ready to pounce. As soon as this gang opened the horsebox, boom! We got the lot of them sent down for handling stolen goods.

Other receivers on our manor didn't exactly make their illegal activities a secret. A well-known wheeler-dealer in all things bent was a guy called Kelsey, a shrewd operator who would buy or sell anything as long as he could shift it within a few hours, cutting down his chances of being caught if it happened to be stolen. He'd been arrested a number of times for receiving stolen goods, but never anything of any great value.

On one occasion, we received information from a reliable source that Kelsey was handling stolen Japanese cameras. My old mate DC Terry Brown and I organised a search warrant and we arrived just as Kelsey was locking up his shop, ready to go to the pub for lunch. He was a likeable guy with a great sense of humour and when I showed him the search warrant, he replied, 'You don't need that. You know me, I'm always ready to help the Old Bill anytime any place.' We all had a laugh, until he realised we weren't going anywhere and reluctantly he reopened his premises.

Inside looked like a junk shop, which I think was an intentional design choice. Kelsey watched us for about an hour as we searched, but we couldn't find any cameras. Then just as we were about to call it a day, Terry noticed something that caught his eye. This time he hadn't found the lost chord, but a large, folded carpet that was tucked away behind an old chest freezer...


```
DISSOLVE TO:
INT. KELSEY'S SHOP. SOUTH LONDON. 13:09.


TERRY and BARRY lift out the carpet and try unfolding
it, while KELSEY, early 40s, wearing a second-hand,
slightly stained suit, paces back and forth, smoking
another cigarette.
          KELSEY
     I gave a guy, who was down on his luck, thirty
     pounds for that piece of crap. From the goodness
     of my heart. Honest, guv.
```

                    BARRY
Yeah. You're all heart, Kelsey.

                    KELSEY
Gave me some story that his kids were starving
and his wife badly needed medicine. I must have
been mad!

                    BARRY
Why the carpet?

                    KELSEY
Maybe it was too big for his place? He said he
bought it in Syria years ago. Or was it Afghanistan?
One of those places anyway.

                    BARRY
As you were hiding this, we are going to take it
away with us and check it out.

                    KELSEY
Hiding it? C'mon! It's a load of crap! That's why
its tucked out of the way, I don't want any of my
punters to see it. I told you, it's bloody crap!

                    TERRY
You won't mind if we borrow it then, will you!

The carpet looks tatty and worn, but it is difficult to
judge properly without being in daylight and there is
not enough room to unfold it completely. TERRY begins
folding it back up.

                    BARRY
I promise you'll get it back within a week, Kelsey…
If its straight.

                    KELSEY
I've got a better idea. You keep it! I don't want
it back!

On the way back to the 'factory' we passed a carpet shop. I asked Bill to
pull over and Terry and I took the carpet inside. I introduced myself to the
manager and asked him to value the carpet for us. He checked it over and
said, 'Twenty-five quid. Maybe.'

After Bill got us back to New Scotland Yard, he helped us spread out the fragile carpet so we could look at it for the first time. None of us had ever seen anything like it. I looked up at the guys and said, 'I think this may be worth more than old Kelsey imagined.' I went up to the office and telephoned Sotheby's auction house to ask if one of their experts could give us their take on the carpet. We were invited for an appointment the next day.

The following morning, Terry and I took the carpet down to Sotheby's, where one of their experts was waiting for us, along with two dealers they had invited. While they were talking shop, we spread the carpet out on a big floor as instructed. After a few minutes, the expert came over and asked me how the carpet came into our possession. After I explained, he invited the two dealers over and asked them to give us a valuation.

While the dealers were examining the carpet, the sun suddenly broke through the clouds and cast its glare through the windows. Suddenly the carpet took on a whole other character, gleaming with a beautiful sheen we had not witnessed before. One of the dealers broke cover with the first bid. 'Forty-five thousand.' Terry and I were gobsmacked. The other dealer returned fire, 'At an auction, on a good day, I think it would make fifty.' The expert then informed us that the carpet was in fact a tapestry, which should be professionally hung in properly ventilated conditions.

We never found the guy who sold the tapestry to Kelsey, nor could we confirm if the tapestry had been stolen. If you can't find a loser for the property, then you have no case. After a thorough investigation, we had to admit defeat and reluctantly return the tapestry back to its 'owner'. 'I told you it was a load of crap,' Kelsey moaned. We didn't tell him the value of it but informed him that it was a tapestry and needed to be hung on a wall. By the time we left the shop, it was back behind the freezer.

Everyone on the Flying Squad would take it in turns to do a week of night duty, usually once every ten weeks. This would usually involve sitting in the office filling out paperwork, or occasionally, catching up on some much-needed sleep. One week, I was on night duty with Bill Laver, who I had first worked with on G Division. Bill was tall, good-looking and always impeccably dressed. After doing his national service, he had worked as a door-to-door insurance salesman before joining the Met to carry out different kinds of doorstep inquiries.

Every now and then on night duty, we would get a phone call, usually from an overseas police force, asking us to go out and arrest someone for them. One night, at about 2am, the phone in our office rang. Bill answered the phone in his smooth melodious voice and was told by an anonymous caller that a big drugs deal was going down in an apartment behind Park Lane. We always treated this kind of information with caution, as quite often it would prove false, but we always had to investigate just in case.

We went to the address and rang the bell. A young woman opened the door. She was barely dressed and wearing a man's shirt. Before she could say anything, Bill put his hand across her mouth, while I showed her my warrant card. We went inside and found the apartment to be completely silent. The door to the bedroom was partly open and, thanks to the bedside light being on, I could see a man in bed who appeared to be fast asleep.

I entered the bedroom and saw an opened bottle of vodka on the bedside table, but there was no obvious sign of any drugs and no evidence of dealing. I sat on the side of the bed and woke the guy up. He slowly sat up, shook his head, grabbed the bottle of vodka and started swigging it back. He looked familiar. I introduced myself and asked him who he was. 'Stan Getz,' he replied.

The penny dropped, along with my jaw. I couldn't believe it. 'I'm one of your biggest fans!' I proclaimed. It was true, I am a huge admirer of Stan's work as a jazz saxophonist and loved his West Coast arrangements with Chet Baker, the vocalist who sang so smoothly that it sounded like he was playing the trumpet. Getz had just been playing a gig at Ronnie Scotts earlier that evening and had obviously been set up. He offered me some vodka, which I refused, but we sat talking jazz while Bill checked the rest of the apartment, but we found no drugs. I apologised for waking this jazz legend up and thanked him for his time. We shook hands and I left him to get back to sleep.

Information wasn't always false but sometimes it took time to come to fruition. This is what Five Squad discovered in the summer of 1969, when we were informed that a security van collecting the takings of a department store on Wood Green High Road was going to be hit by armed robbers. The collections were staggered throughout the week, and whilst we didn't know which day the robbery would take place, we had the false registration number for the Ford Transit that the robbers were going to use.

We monitored the store for three weeks, watching the security van make one successful collection after the other without being hit. Eventually our information dried up and we moved onto the next one. This is where fate comes in. Almost a month later, I was on my way back from an operation in North London, travelling in our Fresh Farm Eggs observation van with four officers from different squads. As we approached Wood Green High Road, we got a call from DI Martin Miller in the lead squad car ahead of us. Aware of Five Squad's recent surveillance of the department store, DI Miller announced on the air that he thought we should check the delivery yard while we were in the area. Everyone in the van let out a collective groan, feeling it was another waste of time.

But as we turned into the side street behind the store, I couldn't believe my eyes. There was the Ford Transit with the false plates, motor running, driver ready for action at the wheel. We parked further up the road and DI Miller instructed us over the radio transmitter to use the periscope. A former submariner, he certainly approved of our ingenious device. Five Squad had already planned how we were going to take these guys out, but this time I was in a van with officers from different units. It was too late to make any changes; all I could do was quickly brief them.

DISSOLVE TO:
INT. FRESH FARM EGGS VAN. WOOD GREEN. 1969.

BARRY grabs the radio transmitter.
            BARRY
     (Into R/T)
     All units from Central One-Nine. Suspect vehicle
     is here on the plot! Stay back. Repeat! Stay
     back, out of sight!
            DI MILLER (V.O.)
     (Over R/T).
     One-Nine. Where exactly is the Transit,
     Barry? Over.

            BARRY
      (into R/T).
It's more or less parked right opposite the rear entrance. There's a driver at the wheel. The others must already be in the back.
            DI MILLER (V.O.)
      (Over R/T).
Shit! How the fuck did they get that parking space?
            BARRY
      (into R/T).
Bastards must have had another vehicle parked there overnight.

BARRY turns the periscope a fraction.
            BARRY
      (into R/T).
Guv! The security van has just turned into the street and heading towards us. Highbury end.
            DI MILLER (V.O.)
      (Over R/T).
As soon as the Transit follows the security van into the backyard, we hit it. Wait for my shout!

BARRY keeps lookout through the periscope. He takes a deep breath.
            BARRY
      (into R/T).
Transit up close and reversing in behind the security van.
            DI MILLER (V.O.)
      (Over R/T).
All units. Go!

Within moments, I was stood staring at the back of an empty van and turned to find the barrel of a shotgun being raised towards me. I fired, and the armed robber collapsed to the floor. In a split-second, there seemed to be people and bullets flying all around me. The other two robbers were now on the ground, hands behind their backs, while the shaken security men were both safe from harm. I moved cautiously towards my robber and kicked the shotgun away out of his reach. I then heard him breathing heavily. Thank God he was alive.

As I handcuffed him, I expected blood. But there was none. I asked him if he was wounded. He never said a word. I looked for a bullet hole in his baggy overalls. Nothing. Had I missed him? One of the other officers then pointed to the door of the security van, now dented with the bullet from my gun. The gunman had been so shocked at that fateful moment that he fainted when I fired, the bullet missing him. God moves in a mysterious way.

At the Old Bailey, we were commended for our bravery. The man in the balaclava and his accomplices all pleaded guilty to attempted armed robbery and were each sent down for fifteen years. That operation could have gone horribly wrong, but in the end, we got a good result without bloodshed. The only sour note came when one of the officers from a different squad gave his evidence. When asked by the defence counsel what he thought when I fired at the robber, he replied, 'I hoped he bloody killed him!' That didn't go down well and there was understandable uproar in the court from the prisoners' friends and relations.

After the trial, I had my picture taken for a press release by a Met Police photographer, who joked that my face would look at home in a rogues' gallery. In September 1969, I was named in the subsequent newspaper reports about the incident, where it was written that I had 'fired to miss'. The truth is that was not how I had been trained.

When that armed robber faced me with a shotgun, I had to decide in that split second whether it was going to be him or me who had to fall. Make no mistake, if I hadn't fired first, he would have. I was always determined that my family would never suffer because of my job and having a wife and kids waiting for me to get home safely was the greatest incentive imaginable. But I remain incredibly thankful to God that I hadn't been forced to take a man's life that day.

Life in the Sweeney was like being in a movie – every day was different and you never knew what was around the corner. I loved it. What I didn't know then was the life as a copper in the 1970s would push me and my family to the limit.

CHAPTER 7

LIGHT DUTIES

Away from the action and danger of life on Five Squad, there were many lighter moments that made the occasional tension and jeopardy all worthwhile. We were a sociable bunch on Five Squad and Pam and I would regularly meet up with Bill Laver and his wife Doreen for dinner and drinks. The Met used to hold a lot of black-tie dinners and dances, to which spouses were invited. The Flying Squad dos were particularly grand affairs, usually taking place in the West End with many well-known faces in attendance.

The Met also threw a special family day once a year, where not only could we bring our kids, but also the children from the local orphanages were invited to attend. At one of these family days, where there was always live music, Pam and I were having a drink at the bar when suddenly a familiar voice filled the room, echoing out of all the speakers surrounding us. Our daughter Sacha had jumped onto the stage and started singing!

Another memorable day was when we took Simon and Sacha to the grand unveiling of the Peel Centre, the Met's new Police Training College in Hendon. Performing the opening ceremony was HRH Queen Elizabeth II, and we all felt hugely honoured to stand in line and welcome our very special monarch. We shall never see her like again.

Up until that point, Pam and I hadn't strategically planned anything in our lives, we had just let things happen organically. But as our children started growing up, we wanted the best for them. We were aware that a school in Cuffley, a village just up the road from where we lived in Cheshunt, had an excellent reputation. One weekend we decided to go for a drive and investigate the area.

The great thing about not planning things too carefully is being open to change and possibilities. On a road called King James Avenue, not far from Cuffley train station, we came across a big overgrown plot of land with a dilapidated bungalow at the centre. A sign in front read, 'Up for Auction'. I said to Pam, 'Why don't we put a bid in? You never know.' We did and we got accepted... but what we hadn't realised was that we had to complete the purchase within three weeks. Not only hadn't we sold our place yet, we didn't even have it on the market!

It all worked out though and eventually we got the keys to the bungalow, which had been in a sorry state for a long time. There had been an old couple living there in terrible conditions. We got to know our new neighbour, a schoolmistress who had previously offered fresh flowers in an attempt to befriend this elderly couple. When she knocked on the door, it only opened slightly enough for a frail hand to come out, take the flowers and shut the door again, without saying a word.

Inside, the bungalow was in a sorry state. When the old residents had previously decorated, they had painted around all their furniture in situ, leaving perfect outlines of untouched wallpaper showing where all their chairs and dressers had stood. But it had serious potential and my parents kindly came down to help us get settled in. Dad and I cut down all the trees and shrubs in the overgrown garden, eventually discovering an air raid shelter at the back, with mushrooms growing in there. They turned out to be safe to eat, meaning we had an endless food supply. We did live in relative squalor for a long time, but it was a great adventure and a perfect way for me to unwind on my days off.

Pam and I thought the best way to meet the locals was to go to Sunday service. When we arrived at the very modern and stylish St. Andrew's church, there was an extraordinary mass of people waiting to enter. We went over to introduce ourselves and enquire why there were so many people there. Someone explained that the vicar was retiring after many years and this was to be his last service. He had served in the First World War and later offered comfort as a chaplain during the second conflict. I'll never forget the closing words of his sermon: 'You won't find God in here. You'll find God out there. In the fields, in the hedgerows and along the riverbanks.' Those powerful words inspired us both and were a very positive way to begin our new chapter in Cuffley.

The 1970s also got off to a great start when I passed my sergeant's exams and was promoted to detective sergeant. This did however come with a caveat: I would have to leave the Flying Squad. The idea of promoting Squad officers and moving them back onto Division for a while was to cut down the potential for corruption, which was possibly a risk for anyone who stayed in one department for too long. Even though it didn't apply to me, I understood why the rule was there. My two years serving on Five Squad had been the happiest of my police career to date and I hoped to be able to rejoin their ranks again in the future.

In May 1970, I was tasked with running the CID offices in two stations. My new routine began by first calling in each morning at Potters Bar station, where I would review and sign the crime book and liaise with the two detective constables posted there. From there, I would report to Barnet nick, where I had my desk. These two stations were at the far end of S Division, a vast area north of London. At that time, Barnet was on the up, with lots of commercial premises and restaurants opening. But this sprawling terrain was much more challenging to police than the relatively compact East End.

One of the biggest cases I worked on in the area was a terrorist attack on 12 January 1971, when two bombs were detonated at the home of employment minister Robert Carr. He and his family lived just around the corner from Barnet train station and were inside when the first bomb blew out their front door and windows, before a second device destroyed their kitchen. The house was a mess and the Carr family were left understandably shaken by the incident. The devices hadn't been set with a timer, meaning the attackers had been present just seconds earlier.

While forensics, explosives experts and Special Branch were investigating the crime scene, me and my CID team were tasked with conducting house-to-house inquiries and taking witness statements. We didn't have long to wait before the culprits, the so-called 'Angry Brigade', claimed the attack. This British terrorist group were responsible for twenty-five similar bombings during this period, though thankfully nobody was ever killed.

Potters Bar was only a ten-minute drive from Cuffley, meaning I could have breakfast with my family every morning before work. Pam was pleased that I was working more sociable hours and especially happy for me to be away from the more dangerous side of life on the Flying Squad. Having now served as a copper for thirteen years, I felt I had enjoyed a pretty good run of fortune. I always expected that, sooner or later, something bad might happen to me, but I thought I'd had my near miss with the shotgun incident in 1969. I was wrong.

I was at home one night when a friend of mine called Carlos rang. He managed a pub in Barnet and we'd first got chatting about our mutual love of motorbikes. I used to pop in quite often for a drink on my way home from work. Unlike some other coppers I worked with throughout my career, my wife and children were the most important part of my life. Following my promotion, I vowed that once I came home safely at night, I wouldn't go out again until the next morning. Except for this one night.

Carlos ran a nice pub with a restaurant and outside he had converted a big barn into a function room, complete with a sound system, dance floor and private bar. That night there was a disco in the barn, and some youngsters were getting out of hand, helping themselves to drinks and refusing to pay. I said I'd get a car over from Barnet Police Station and that I would also come down personally to help my friend sort this little problem out.

Somehow, I managed to get there before the patrol car and I went inside, where Carlos met me and thanked me for coming. We walked through to this barn at the rear, where everybody was dancing to loud music and flashing lights. It was packed out, though I quickly worked out who the main troublemakers were. I started to walk towards them when suddenly the barn went pitch black.

One of the kids had pulled the mains, plunging the place into darkness and the air filled with lots of panic and screaming. Someone then tried to knock me to the ground, but I managed to grab my mystery assailant. I wrestled them down onto the floor, while Carlos tried to make his way over to the mains switch. Whilst I was restraining one of these teenagers, somebody hit me with something heavy from behind. It felt like a stool. I went down and before I knew it, I was being kicked from all angles.

Thankfully, Carlos got the lights back on just as two uniformed constables from Barnet nick arrived on the scene. My attackers all made a run for it, though three of them were apprehended. Carlos felt awful about what had happened, but I assured him that I was fine. After I got my breath back, I made a few suggestions on how he could prevent something like this from happening again and left him to mop up the mess.

When I got home, I noticed that the fingers on my right hand were numb and I couldn't hold anything. Soon, I couldn't bend my arm and suddenly my shoulder hurt badly. The pain was getting worse and the only way I could get any relief was to lie on the floor with my arm pressed against the radiator. Something was wrong. Pam called a doctor, who came and examined me at home. He said I needed to go to hospital immediately.

After an initial examination at Barnet A&E, I was told I would need to be kept in overnight for more tests. By this point, the pain had extended to my neck, and I couldn't turn my head. I was laid out on a bed, while a medical team started attaching a selection of weights to my body. Nobody explained what these were for and the only instruction I got was 'try not to move please Mr Appleton'. 'Chance would be a fine thing,' I replied.

Standing at the end of my bed was a hospital doctor and a neurologist. I couldn't look down to see them, but I could faintly hear them discussing what might be wrong with me. Their discussion then turned into a disagreement, which then escalated into a heated argument. Distracted by this war of words, the nurse somehow managed to knock one of the weights off the side of my bed, which dragged my head with it. The pain was indescribable.

In a typical Barry Appleton move, I used my good arm to rip off all these contraptions and I stormed out of the hospital, wearing only my pyjamas. I hadn't made it very far when a patrol car spotted this strange man walking around Barnet in the dead of night in his pyjamas. The PC at the wheel couldn't help himself: 'You must really miss walking the beat, Sarge!' I explained what had happened and got a lift home, back to a very concerned wife.

The next morning, Pam called our doctor again and I was taken to Southgate Hospital, where I was admitted into the care of an Egyptian neurosurgeon. Once again, I was stretched out with wires and weights, which this time I learned was to try and ease the strain on my neck. A metal plate was fixed around my head, over which was a frame containing my now completely numb right arm. Except for my left arm, I was completely immobilised and unable to move. The television was behind me, so they fixed up a mirror so that I could at least watch some entertainment.

People came to visit me, including one of my informants, who brought me a book on the Mafia to read with my good arm. He even gave me some intelligence, hoping it might come in handy when I returned to work. Pam came in every day, but I wouldn't let her bring Simon and Sacha as I feared it would have been too upsetting for me to see me all bolted up like the Tin Man.

A deflated Carlos also came to see me, still feeling awful about my attack. Despite me reassuring him that it wasn't his fault, the incident had shaken him to the extent that he had put his business on the market and was planning to leave London altogether, hoping to start a new venture on the coast. I said we'd come and visit him once I got better. The only problem was I wasn't getting any better. I was getting worse.

The main reason for my decline was my neurosurgeon had gone back to Egypt, without warning, to attend a conference. The hospital didn't have anyone else suitably qualified to attend to me and their regulations meant that as I had been assigned to this specific neurosurgeon, I couldn't be released into anyone else's care without his express permission. Pam went berserk.

As a steady stream of new patients came and went, I continued to lie there immobile, day after day, week after week. I ended up being stuck in that bed for months, literally wasting away. Some patients felt so sorry for me that they would come over in their wheelchairs and keep me company.

Then, on 11 April 1971, something changed inside me. It was a beautiful Sunday afternoon, and all the windows on the ward were open. I could feel a slight breeze and I watched the shadow of a sun-kissed tree dancing on the ceiling above me. It was Easter and there had been a mass exodus of patients at midday, who one by one had waved goodbye and wished me a Happy Easter. Now the ward around me was empty and a quiet hush had descended. At that moment, I felt at one with God and I was convinced he was about to take me… And I wasn't going to fight it.

Then suddenly, I heard footsteps in the corridor outside. They paused at the door. I looked in my mirror and saw the reflection of the Ward Sister. She approached me...

```
DISSOLVE TO:
INT. HOSPITAL WARD. 1971.


BARRY is lying immobile in his hospital bed. The WARD
SISTER, mid-40s, voluptuous, long brown hair tied into a
bun. Verbally abrupt, she never stands for any nonsense.
She sits by BARRY at his bedside.
```

                SISTER
    How are you feeling, Barry?
                BARRY
    A little sorry for myself.

Unusually, the SISTER offers a warm smile and gently
brushes back the hair from BARRY'S face.
                SISTER
    You'll be okay.
                BARRY
    Are you an angel?
                SISTER
    I'm flattered.
                BARRY
    Or am I dreaming? You don't have wings or a halo.
                SISTER
    This morning you told me I was a witch. Yesterday
    I was a witch. The day before I was a witch.
                BARRY
    Did I really say that?
                SISTER
    And all the weeks before.

BARRY thinks for a moment, considering his next words.
As always, he feels honesty is the best policy.
                BARRY
    Pam thinks you're a bitch.
                SISTER
       (chuckling)

I've been promoted! Your wife and I had a heart-to-heart
talk yesterday and we came to an understanding. She's your
angel.
                BARRY
    I've always known that.
                SISTER
    I'm not going to let you die on my watch, Barry.

                    BARRY
That's good to hear. But can't you get me out of
this hell hole?
                    SISTER
And where would you go? Wait till your doctor is
back from his conference.
                    BARRY
It's been some conference!
                    SISTER
Like I explained to your wife, it's complicated.
                    BARRY
And in the meantime, I'm supposed to just waste away?
                    SISTER
Barry, listen to me. By four o'clock, this place
will be heaving again. All those DIY people will
be falling off their ladders or having accidents
with their lawnmowers. And they'll all be turning
to you for advice. You'll be the star attraction.

The SISTER leans in and kisses BARRY on the forehead.
                    SISTER
I'm counting on you, Barry.

The SISTER leaves to continue with her duties. A tear
runs down BARRY's cheek.

I'll never forget that beautiful moment, where it felt like the sister seemed
to know exactly what was happening in my mind. She was also spot on
when she described Pam as my angel and that moment proved to be the
turning point in my fortunes. Just as I had been considering letting go, Pam
was fighting tooth and nail to get me help and was now desperately close to
finally cutting through the hospital's red tape.

    After going through all the usual healthcare channels and then seeking
advice from the Police Federation, Pam had managed to get a meeting with
our local MP in Broxbourne, who was appalled to hear about my situation.
Suddenly, I was transferred by ambulance to the Royal London Hospital

and within hours, I was greeted by the eminent neurosurgeon Professor Sid Watkins, who would later make a huge impact in the world of Formula 1 racing and became best known for trying to save the life of Ayrton Senna on the fateful day of his final race.

Exuding a charming and sensitive manner, Professor Watkins explained my condition to five of his medical students, who were also encouraged to ask me questions. There was no front to Sid, he was a really down-to-earth person. He then braced me for a potentially chilling prognosis which, had I been able to feel my spine, would have sent shivers down it. 'I'm going to operate on you tomorrow morning, Barry. It's best that you know now… you may end up being partly paralysed.' Despite this possibility, my overall feelings were relief and gratitude that something was finally going to be done. I thanked Sid, who promised to do his best to help me. I believed him.

I remember being taken to be showered. Because of the apparatus I had been permanently rigged up in, I hadn't been able to have a proper bath or wash for months. When the nurse took me to the shower unit, she removed this rig and for the first time in months, I saw myself naked in the mirror. It was a considerable shock; my whole body was skeletally thin and I couldn't believe it was me. I was unrecognisable.

The next day, I went for the operation. I didn't really want to know all the gory details, but during the procedure I believe they took out a couple of discs and put something else in their place. When I awoke, I saw a bar above my head that I was encouraged to reach out and use to pull myself up when I felt ready to do so. As soon as I could, I was doing that exercise all the time, day and night. All I was interested in was getting discharged and being back home with my family.

At one stage, the patient in the bed next to me was Jack Dash, the top union official for London's docks. He told me that he could have had a private room, but he didn't want to be antisocial. We got quite friendly, and I think it was quite good for the union man to be seen chatting with an injured policeman in the next bed. We even swapped books to read, though only after my tome had been carefully checked by one of his bodyguards, two of whom were with him at all times.

I remember the hit record at the time was Tony Christie's 'Is This The Way To Amarillo' and one day, the hospital held a concert outside in the grounds. I was wheeled to the window so I could watch and there down below was the great man himself, singing his heart out. That upbeat song was in my head for weeks as I continued my exercises. I was getting better and the feeling of returning home was hugely exciting.

By the time I was discharged, the only trace of my injury was a scar on the back of my head down to between my shoulder blades, as well as a numbness in one of my fingers, which remains to this day. Thankfully it wasn't my trigger finger and, considering how much worse the outcome of my procedure could have been, it felt like a small price to pay. Thank you, Sid Watkins!

It was brilliant to get back home to Pam and the kids. The first thing I wanted to do was eat a great big steak meal, which Pam kindly prepared. Every day I did my exercises, turning my neck and building up my strength. I had to go for regular physio sessions, which Pam was able to take me to, having passed her driving test while I was in hospital. She had been determined to succeed in time for my return home and I felt so proud when she showed me her driver's licence for the first time.

In the evenings, while Pam cooked us a meal, I spent time playing games with the kids before reading them a bedtime story. I would then carefully lay the table with serviettes and candles, with a nice bit of jazz in the background. These moments with Pam were more important to me than anything else, especially after my injury.

The Met were very supportive while I recovered and looked after me, paying me my full salary throughout. I never considered leaving the police and Pam would never have suggested that either, as she knew how much I enjoyed my job. She just focused on helping me get better and started encouraging me to do some gardening and little DIY jobs around the house.

Another really good source of exercise was taking our new addition to the family for a walk. Anatole, named after the Eve Titus books I read to the kids, was an Afghan Hound with luxuriously long, flowing blond locks. On his first night with us, Simon and Sacha were laying on their stomachs watching the TV when he went and laid between them, best friends from day one. Anatole did however make a bit of a name for himself out on the streets of Cuffley, where he had a terrible habit of sticking his snout up women's dresses. Upon realising Anatole was the culprit, one lady once quipped, 'Shame, I thought it was my lucky day…'

As much as I was enjoying spending some precious time with my family, I was very keen to return to the job. To ease me back into work, I was put on light duties and assigned to Wood Green CID. It was a little unsettling to be transferred to a new division. Just like a village, every police station has its own unique environment and customs, occasionally inhabited by some quite weird coppers. You usually found a Reg Hollis working in most stations. Thankfully there were a few friendly faces at Wood Green, who all helped me settle in on my new manor.

One of my first cases was to investigate a leading manufacturer of sanitary products, who had recently installed some new Swedish machines into their factory, which produced thousands of disposable products an hour. On average, one in every thousand products wouldn't be quite up to standard, meaning there would usually be a box containing about 40 rejects at the end of the week. I was called in after it was noticed that the machine was suddenly producing 50 rejects in every 1,000. Whoever was responsible at the factory was now selling all this dodgy stock at all the markets across the division. Quite an enterprise.

During my investigation, I discovered that the factory employed occasional labourers, who allegedly only worked weekends. I asked to see all the timesheets for these part-time workers and as I started going through them, I couldn't believe my eyes. Every single one was signed by a famous composer: Beethoven had worked a shift, followed by Handel, Mozart, even Mendelssohn had been on the factory floor! What was going on?

I asked a member of their accounts team, 'Do you know anybody working here who likes classical music?' He said, 'Funny you should say that. There's a cleaner who is always whistling symphonies!' I found this cleaner and called him into the office. 'Have you been signing these timesheets?' He nodded, so I asked him why. 'The manager asked me to sign these things for him, but to use different names. I wrote the composers because they were the only names I could think of…'

With my star witness on board and the manager in the frame for defrauding the company, I was then able to uncover all the main players down at the market. I had exposed the whole network, which I hoped would be my ticket to get off light duties… But when we got the case to the Crown court, halfway through giving my evidence, I discovered that all my witnesses from the company were claiming taxi fares, even though the company had laid on a bus for them. It turned out that they were *all* committing fraud and, as a result, the case was thrown out. Some comeback.

One of my responsibilities on light duties was to write monthly performance reports assessing the four CID aides working in the office. I never saw myself as their guv'nor and certainly never pulled rank or courted publicity like other officers I had worked with. As far as I was concerned, I was still one of the lads.

One of the aides was called Peter Nelson, a friendly, well-educated guy. He was very self-assured and perhaps an unlikely detective. One day, he turned up in a brand-new Ford Corsair, which I went out to admire along with a couple of the lads. Soon standing beside us was a grumpy detective sergeant from another station, who had come over for some files. I knew him of old. He was one of the CID officers who had shared a whisky with my first major arrest back at City Road. Now well-known for desperately waiting to be eligible for early retirement, he could only afford to drive a second-hand Hillman Imp, which kept breaking down. When he saw Nelson's brand-new Corsair, he wasn't impressed and I had to restrain him as he aggressively demanded to know how an aide could afford such a nice new car.

The next day, Peter didn't turn up for work. When I questioned his absence, I was told he had been transferred. Many years later, I was watching an evening news report covering the House of Lords when I spotted a familiar face above a caption that read 'Lord Peter Nelson'. It turned out that Peter was a direct descendent of Horatio, 1st Viscount Nelson. Perhaps I had prevented a smaller version of Trafalgar in the car that day…

All the aides at Wood Green were good lads, who each did their job with little fanfare and never let me down. Except on one occasion. One of the younger members of the team, whom I shall name Jones, was having bad trouble with his girlfriend. Only she wasn't technically *his* girlfriend; he'd fallen in love with the mistress of a high-profile businessman, who I knew had underworld connections. I did my best to make him see sense… 'Jonesy, there are plenty more beautiful girls out there who will break your heart just as easily.' But he insisted, very emotionally, that this girl was the love of his life and nobody else could possibly take her place.

I asked the other lads in the office to keep an eye on him and let me know if things became a problem. A few days later, I arrived at the office to check the duty book and noticed that Jones hadn't booked on. I asked the other lads in the office if they knew where he was, but they shook their heads in suspicious unison. I decided not to do anything immediately and, as I didn't want to get him into trouble if he really did have a reasonable excuse, I booked him as being on duty before a senior officer noticed his absence. Big mistake.

The next morning, I found the duty book was missing and I was informed that the chief super wanted to see me urgently…

```
DISSOLVE TO:
INT. CHIEF SUPT. GROUT'S OFFICE. 1971

BARRY is standing in front of CHIEF SUPERINTENDENT GROUT,
mid-50's, very tall and slim. None of the officers have
ever seen him in civilian clothes, he wears his uniform
with fierce pride. GROUT has the duty book on his desk,
which he turns to face BARRY and taps at the bottom of
the page.
                    GROUT
        Your signature?


BARRY leans forward for a closer look.
                    BARRY
        Yeah?


GROUT removes his black-rimmed glasses and taps the
badge on his shoulder with a finger, before shooting a
look of sheer disapproval at BARRY, who promptly stands
up straight.
                    BARRY
        Yes, sir.

                    GROUT
        Why did you book him on duty when he wasn't here?

                    BARRY
        He was in an emotional state, sir. Problems with
        his girlfriend.

                    GROUT
        You bloody fool, you could get the sack for this!
```

             BARRY
He was one of my lads. Thought I'd give him
time to sort himself out. It's just twenty-four
hours, guv. He's probably down in the office
right now.

GROUT sits back in his chair in disbelief.

             GROUT
Oh you think so, do you Sergeant?

             BARRY
      (suspicious)
Do you know something I don't, sir?

             GROUT
Yesterday evening, young Jones was arrested for
causing a disturbance in a nightclub!

             BARRY
Oh shit!

             GROUT
The nightclub is in Vancouver.

             BARRY
Canada?!

             GROUT
So it's time to tell me what this is all about.
The truth, Barry.

             BARRY
Jones fell in love with a girl who is the mistress
of a high-profile businessman with underworld
connections.

GROUT stands up, looking like he is chewing a wasp.

             GROUT
You should have come to me. It's called trust!

             BARRY
I'm sorry, sir. I did what I thought was best.
I told him in no uncertain terms to leave her
alone.

             GROUT
Well he doesn't appear to have taken your advice!

                    BARRY
          No, sir.
               (suddenly)
          Why Vancouver?

                    GROUT
          Your friendly mafioso sent his mistress there to
          be out of Jones' way. The young fool decided to
          follow her.

                    BARRY
          Wow! Determined lad is Jones, sir.

                    GROUT
          This isn't funny Barry! I've got lunch with the
          Chief Constable this afternoon. If he catches
          wind of this you'll be for the high jump!

GROUT takes a deep breath and sits back down.

                    GROUT
          This is what I want you to do. The Vancouver police
          have put Jones on a flight to Gatwick, arriving
          tonight. I want you there to bring him back here
          immediately. Do you think you can handle that,
          Sergeant?

                    BARRY
          Yes, sir. I'll be there.

BARRY leaves the office. in the corridor, he looks
heavenward.

                    BARRY
               (to himself)
          Thank you, Jonesey…

When Jones' flight arrived back in Gatwick that night, he did a runner when he saw the reception committee waiting for him. We caught him before he got very far and I'm sad to say that he was forced to resign that evening. I was sorry to see him go.

One of my final tasks on light duties was to go back to the detective training school in Chelsea, this time as an instructor. I was responsible for an overseas class, where some of my students were the sons of some notable dictators. They were considered so important that they each had a bodyguard assigned to them for their protection. I'll never forget the sight of a line of four heavily armed bodyguards stood at the back of my classroom, all reading *Beano* comics! If those students passed the end of term exam I set for them, they already had high-ranking jobs lined up back in their home countries. One of them was in line to become Chief of Police!

Before I could start tackling serious crime again, there was just one outstanding matter to deal with. The Met's Solicitors Branch had appealed to the Criminal Compensation Board on my behalf, as I had only received a small amount which didn't take any long-term injury prognosis into account. Eventually, I was called to appear before the Board in central London with my solicitor, who said I had no chance as they very rarely increased their original offer. I had done some research on the Board's previous appeal awards but found nothing that could really help my case.

Soon the day of judgement arrived. I remember sitting in a huge queue of claimants who, one by one, would go in and then come back out looking disappointed and dejected. Eventually my name was called, and I entered the room, which reminded me of a juvenile courtroom. I stood before a board of two women and a chairman in the middle, who were seated at a long desk on a raised platform, with an antechamber behind them.

After I was invited to take my seat, my solicitor started to address the Board on my behalf. He was suddenly stopped mid-sentence, when the chairman addressed me directly. He asked me how my injuries were affecting me on light duties. I stood up and said, 'I feel fine. I'm getting stronger every day and I'm not in any substantial pain. To be truthful, I'm just glad to be alive and happy to be back on duty.' There was a hushed silence around the room as the panel glanced at each other poker-faced. My solicitor looked like he wanted to bang his head against the desk.

The chairman asked me about my prognosis, and I explained I was concerned how my injury might affect me later in life. The members of the board exchanged some looks, before announcing they would adjourn for ten minutes. Everyone stood as they got up and went into the antechamber behind them and closed the door. Maybe it was their tea break?

After ten minutes, they returned. The chairman said, 'Detective Sergeant Appleton, we cannot base a grant on something that *may* happen in the future. However, your total honesty has been a breath of fresh air in this room today. For that alone, you will be awarded an extra £100. Thank you and good luck for the future.' A small amount of compensation considering what I had been through, but I probably walked the tallest out of all those assembled to appeal that day.

I was now off light duties and couldn't wait to get back out on the streets again. Despite what I had been through, I had missed the danger that went with the job, which could perhaps be most easily experienced whilst working undercover…

CHAPTER 8

THE MAN WHO MURDERED KING

Undercover work is usually reserved for specialist officers who are trained to be dropped into a long-term investigation, be it for a few days, several weeks, or even many months. During that time posing as someone else, the copper in question must cut themselves off from their own life completely, having only minimal contact with a designated handler from the job. They are now living out a fantasy, playing a character in somebody else's storyline.

In my opinion, this type of dedicated and often dangerous work is best reserved for an officer who isn't married and doesn't have a family back home to worry about. But my marital status didn't stop me from doing my fair share of roleplaying when the job required.

One of my first cases after coming off light duties was to investigate a suspect in the Barnet area, believed to be selling arms. I'd heard him down the local pub at lunchtime, boasting to another face that he could 'get any firearm you want'. Posing as another interested party, I got this guy's telephone number and, later in the week, I called to arrange a meeting.

He set the meeting point: in the car park of a busy supermarket in High Barnet. Aware he might have other guys watching us, I made sure that my team were a discreet distance away, poised to move in at the first sign of trouble. S Division didn't have access to the hidden transmitters or vans with periscopes that I'd played with on the Flying Squad. We just had to rely on our eyes and ears. It was my job to convince this self-styled arms dealer that he was meeting another villain and not get a whiff of Old Bill.

He had given me a time and told me he would be parked in a grey Cortina. I drove along the high street and, sure enough, there he was. I parked alongside and joined him in his car, sitting in the passenger seat. I got straight down to business.

DISSOLVE TO:
INT. ARMS DEALER'S CAR. HIGH BARNET. 1971.

BARRY sits next to the ARMS DEALER. Late 20s, sporting a long black ponytail and trying hard to grow a beard. He is dressed smart casual in an open-necked shirt, wearing a thin gold necklace.

    BARRY
 Do you have what I am looking for?

    DEALER
 I think so.

The DEALER looks around the car park.

    BARRY
 What have you got?

    DEALER
 All in good time. Have you got what we agreed?

    BARRY
 I'm not handing over any cash until I've seen the goods.

The DEALER leans forward and picks up a small lunchbox from under his car seat.

    DEALER
 Cop a load of this...

The DEALER opens the lunchbox. Inside is a small 2.2 Beretta. He gives it to BARRY, who takes out the magazine and makes sure the weapon is unloaded before he says another word.

    BARRY
 This piddly little thing's not going to do much damage, is it?

    DEALER
 You don't want to be on the wrong end of that when it's loaded, trust me.

                    BARRY
This is a peashooter. I want some real firepower.
I can pay, what else have you got?
                    DEALER
Oh I can get you whatever you want, just say the
word.
                    BARRY
That's what you promised in the pub and you've
turned up with this water pistol. Don't waste my
time.

BARRY puts the Beretta back in the lunchbox.
                    DEALER
I can get big weapons, don't worry about that.
                    BARRY
Can you get me sawn-offs? Then we can do business.
                    DEALER
Whatever you want. Listen, all I need is a £1,000
deposit and I'll call you later in the week when
they're ready to collect.
                    BARRY
Do me a favour, I don't do business like that.
I want to see the merchandise before I'm buying…

Round and round in circles we went, but he still couldn't tell me what kind
of guns he had. Realising the only thing this guy was dealing was bullshit, I
got out of the car and made a signal to my guys, which in copper language
roughly translated to, 'Get the bastard.' They swooped in and we nicked
him, ultimately just for possession of that tiny little firearm. I'd been hoping
to get him for something bigger, which would have done me no harm in
trying to get back on the Flying Squad.

My earliest undercover work was on aide squad, thanks to DI Fred
Gerrard's admiration of my supposedly villainous visage. One of my first
assignments was investigating a string of illegal gambling clubs frequented
by many a villain. Fred made it clear that as soon as I entered one of these
places, I would become 'a face'. His main advice was: 'Whatever you do
when you walk into a club, don't start looking around, that will make you

stand out like a sore thumb!' I followed his advice to the letter. I would walk straight over to the nearest card game and just watch the play unfold. Then, in between games, I'd try to make conversation with someone.

I knew that as soon as I opened my mouth I would need a cover story, so I adopted the persona of a car dealer. If anyone I got talking to in the club was looking for a motor, I could offer to get it for them outside of the big dealers. Similarly, if they had a car they were looking to get rid of, I could offer to find someone who would buy it. The fact that I sourced vehicles as a middleman meant that I had no overheads, which all helped sell my story. It was acting really, taking on the role of somebody else and maintaining that character for long enough to be able to gather information.

Whenever I went to one of these clubs, I had to look the part. I had my first mohair suit made to measure, which even a dapper dresser like Fred had to concede I looked the business in. I also had a fake business card designed, complete with a 'business' number, which if dialled would have called a public phone box. I didn't use my real name and never carried my warrant card or anything else that could identify me.

I would be given £100 in notes, as it was important for me to gamble to help maintain my cover. I tried not to as a rule, but if the situation required, I would play three-card brag, which is my personal game of choice. If the club had a roulette wheel I would have a go on that too and just let things play out naturally.

When each club was raided, the team knew exactly where to find the money or drugs hidden within, thanks to the intelligence I had gathered. I would never go on the raids, as I would already be working undercover at another club, where I would often see the same line-up of punters. The raids would also be done on a night when I wasn't in a club, which helped maintain my cover and prevented any of my fellow gamblers from putting two and two together. I helped shut three of these illegal dens down in total.

Another time I needed to blend into a crowd was during the 1966 General Election, when fascist politician Oswald Mosley stood as a candidate for Shoreditch and Finsbury. During his previous attempt, Mosley had pushed an anti-immigration agenda in the wake of the 1958 Notting Hill race riots, calling for regulations to oppose mixed marriages and demanding forced repatriation of Caribbean immigrants. The understandable backlash to his extreme views had prompted him to leave Britain altogether.

When he made his unwelcome return to politics, protest marches were scheduled to take place all over London, meaning the Met needed to be out in force. Dressed as a protestor, I joined an angry rabble at Dalston Market, where Mosley was due to make a speech. For some reason, amongst the hundreds of people airing their grievances, the one protestor that a young bobby decided to arrest… was me!

I decided not to tell this greenhorn who I was, but after being escorted to Dalston Police Station, I tipped off the custody sergeant about my identity. The next thing I knew, the Assistant Commissioner came down to see this angry protestor with his own eyes. He couldn't believe it when I announced I was an undercover aide from G Division! I never got to hear Mosley's speech, but the genuine protestors did a good enough job to persuade him to leave politics, and Britain, once and for all.

My undercover work changed when I joined the Flying Squad. We were department C8 and next-door to us at Scotland Yard was C11, the intelligence unit. Members of their team were working undercover permanently, whereas part of our brief was to be seen out on the streets, getting our faces known and for the local villains to know we'd be watching them. This occasionally meant enlisting a new face when an operation required.

We once selected a uniformed constable who was new to the manor to infiltrate a drug gang for us, posing as a buyer. He was dressed in plain clothes and given £2,000, with strict instructions to only flash the cash and not hand it over under any circumstances… After we'd raided the place and got him out of harm's way, the young constable explained that when he flashed his cash, the villains simply grabbed the money and made a very quick getaway. They were now at large with a useful cash injection, courtesy of the Metropolitan Police. Not everyone is suited to undercover work.

Sometimes we also got the villains to take care of business for us. Once, Bill Parsons was driving me back to the 'factory' after I had set up a sensitive undercover job in Hertfordshire when we got a message on the R/T that an informant, who I shall call 'John', wanted to meet urgently. Bill drove me into town and, from a phone box, I arranged to meet John at a bar in Smithfield Market.

John was a very fleshy Jewish man, with greying hair parted to the side. He never stopped talking, except to take breath. He was a small-time receiver, and I didn't trust him one bit, but he had in the past provided some valuable information. He told us he knew a guy who wanted to sell an ivory chess board, which was 'priceless'. He'd seen one of the chess figures and was impressed. I told John to get back in touch with the seller and say he wanted to see the whole set before making an offer.

The trap was set. John would meet the seller in a hotel foyer at Heathrow airport in the evening. We would be in the car park. I briefed John that if the seller had the chess set with him, he would say he would think about it. Keeping it friendly enough that they could walk out of the hotel together, John was then to blow his nose as a signal as they left, only if the seller had the complete chess set with him.

After an hour, nothing had happened and we thought something must have gone wrong. It was now getting dark and heavy rain was making it difficult for us to see. Just when we were thinking one of us might have to go in, John came out of the hotel with a guy carrying a large carrier bag. They stood on the steps a while and talked. Subtlety wasn't in John's vocabulary and he produced a very large, theatrical nose blow. Thankfully the seller obviously wasn't much of a critic, and he drove off in a Datsun 240Z sports car without a care in the world. We followed him.

We had no danger of this guy realising he was being pursued with Bill Parsons at the wheel, but we couldn't act too quickly. I might not have liked John, but I didn't want him identified as a grass. I got on the radio and called up a local traffic car, asking them to pull over this Datsun on a technicality. A few minutes later, we watched from a distance as a traffic car pulled the seller over. The officers got the driver to step out and open the boot for them. We waited and sure enough, they called us up over the air and informed us that a chess set had been discovered. Boom!

We arranged for the officers to take the suspect to their local station in Feltham, where we later arrived to interview him. The driver turned out to be football star Ian Hutchinson, then centre-forward for Chelsea. He said he had bought the chess set in a pub and wasn't aware it had been stolen. We arranged for another squad to search his address, where the detectives found other stolen property, including several stamp albums. I remember one of the team labelled Hutchinson a 'magpie'. We couldn't prove that he had stolen any of the items in his possession, but he was clearly acting as a receiver. I deduced that he had been suckered into trying to sell items like the chess set by shrewder criminals, who knew they would be too hot to handle on the open market.

Like the case with Kelsey and his tapestry, we needed a 'loser' who could prove that they owned the property that had been stolen. We hadn't found a loser for the chess set, but we were able to find the rightful owners of the stamp albums, meaning we were able to charge Hutchinson. I had been happy for the traffic guys to get the credit, but as I had signed the charge sheet and set up the job, I was required in court.

I accompanied Hutchinson to Feltham magistrates court on 27 October and asked for remand. When I left the court with this famous footballer, I was hit by a barrage of flash photography and television cameras, which caused my planned undercover work in Hertfordshire to be abandoned. Hutchinson never appeared to be worried about the scandal and he continued to play for Chelsea, despite reports of his arrest making front-page headlines.

But what about the chess set? Two weeks had gone by and we still hadn't traced an owner. We'd had the set valued and it was indeed priceless. Our last chance was to launch an appeal on the television programme *Police 5*, where the public were asked for information to help locate missing people or stolen property. Viewers were given a telephone number to ring if they could offer information that might assist the police with their enquiries. A film about the chess set went out and we manned the phones, expecting many a crank call, but hoping that one might help us.

Eventually, I took a call from an excited woman, who claimed to know precisely where the set came from. 'In fact, I'm looking at it right now.' I paused. 'Could you explain yourself please, madam?' I asked politely. 'I'm looking at a glossy magazine of Knebworth House and one of the pages shows that chess set on display amongst antique furniture.' It turned out she was spot on! The chess set had been stolen from the famous stately home and had unbelievably not been missed. Not even the security guards who patrolled the home had clocked its absence… They obviously didn't watch *Police 5*, where presenter Shaw Taylor used to sign off with the catchphrase, 'Keep 'em peeled.'

Despite occasionally making the press, there were still plenty of times on Five Squad when our well-established mugs could blend into the background, especially if a new face appeared on our patch. Once, on night duty, we received a call in the early hours from the Playboy Club in Park Lane. They reported that an American guy was playing poker and kept losing a great deal of money. But every time he came down to his last dollar, he would angrily leave, only to miraculously return within half an hour, armed with more cash and ready to play again. Suspicious, one of the club's security guards checked one of the waste bins and discovered Swiss bank wrappers inside…

Bill Laver and I headed down to the club, posing as customers, to watch the last of the big spenders in action. Tall and lean, he was dressed as only an American can, with cowboy boots, light blue Oxford button-down collar and a large plaid jacket. His constant cigar smoke, as well as the allure of the 'Bunny' Girls dotted around the club, helped obscure Bill and me from his gaze.

We observed from a nearby dining table, where we were issued with fillet steaks, compliments of the management. To look the part of a seasoned diner, I tucked a napkin into my shirt. After about an hour, our steaks duly consumed, it was almost daylight and the American lost big time once again. He got up, swore at the croupier, and stormed out. Bill and I followed him.

Park Lane was now heaving with commuters making their way to work. I couldn't understand why so many people were staring at me… I then realised I still had my Playboy Club napkin tucked in my shirt. We pursued our mystery gambler, who turned sharply into the Hilton Hotel and got a lift to the third floor. With some assistance from security, we followed him up there and knocked on the door to his suite. There he was, just about to leave armed with yet more cash. It turned out that he was wanted in the States for a million-dollar insurance fraud and had stashed the money in a Swiss bank. Another result for Five Squad.

My most prominent piece of undercover work actually came shortly after I had joined the Sweeney. In July 1968, Tommy Butler tasked me with posing as a prisoner at Canon Row Police Station to investigate a fugitive awaiting extradition. My fellow inmate was James Earl Ray, who just a few months earlier on 4 April had committed one of the greatest crimes of the twentieth century: the assassination of Dr. Martin Luther King.

Ray had been intercepted at Heathrow trying to board a plane under the name Ramon George Sneyd. Thankfully, the resourceful ticket inspector spotted that Ray was carrying two passports with different names and he was arrested. While preparations were being made for him to stand trial back in America, Ray was transferred to Canon Row for further questioning. I was placed in the adjoining cell, posing as a prisoner being detained in connection with an armed robbery. My brief was to try to befriend Ray and discover if anyone else had been involved in the assassination of Martin Luther King.

Canon Row had already been open for business for over sixty years and the cells in this old-fashioned station were very basic, just a concrete slab for a bed, with a very thin mattress on top. Each prisoner had a toilet, but no sink, meaning you had to ask for permission to be allowed out to wash your hands, which as you can imagine was rarely allowed.

To help maintain my cover, the officers would routinely drag me out of my cell, making it loud enough for Ray to hear that they were taking me for another interview. I'd then be brought back again, usually making rude remarks as they took my cuffs off and slammed the cell door in my face. They used to bring food to our cells at the same time and he would have been able to hear me shouting, 'What's this crap? I wouldn't feed my dog this shit!'

Then, after the loud clank of the huge door slamming in the corridor, Ray would have known it was just me and him left, a couple of fellow cons. I couldn't see him, and he couldn't see me, but he just had to be able to hear me through the wall. Similarly, I could also hear when his lawyer visited him in his cell.

Unlike Ray, I didn't have to spend the night locked away in my cell. On our first night, the officers made a return visit and I protested loudly as they put the cuffs back on me. 'You're being taken back to the scene of your crime, let's see if that refreshes your memory!' I'd then be smuggled back in the following morning, just before it was time for us to come face to face in the exercise yard…

DISSOLVE TO:
EXT. EXERCISE YARD. CANON ROW POLICE STATION. 1968.

BARRY is escorted into a small yard, surrounded by tall, grey stone buildings that tower into an open sky. BARRY lights up a cigarette as a UNIFORMED OFFICER enters the yard with JAMES EARL RAY, 40, short, slim, steel blue eyes, a man who has lived a life of crime.

RAY approaches BARRY and takes out a pack of Lucky Strike cigarettes. RAY flicks his thumb, wanting a light. The UNIFORMED OFFICER stands at the door and watches BARRY light RAY's cigarette.

            BARRY
On your way back to the States then?

RAY shoots an inquisitive glance at BARRY.

            BARRY
My cell's next to yours, couldn't help overhearing you talking to your brief.

RAY takes a long drag on a cigarette before responding.

            RAY
Maybe.

The pair start slowly walking around the yard.

            BARRY
They say you killed a black guy?

            RAY
Bullshit.

            BARRY
Not one of those Ku Klux Klan geezers are you?

RAY stares at BARRY with a look that could kill. BARRY knows he needs to be careful.

            BARRY
I'm interested, that's all. I'm from a long family of villains. My dad was a fucking psycho. His

```
dad before him. My kids will probably grow up
to be right wrong'uns. It's the natural order of
things.
```

```
RAY takes another long drag of his cigarette. He is now
curious, but remains suspicious.
```
```
                    RAY
Why are you here?
                    BARRY
Fucking robbery. Remand for a week in this
shithole, see if I'll put my hands up to other
blaggings. They'll send me to prison whatever
happens when I go back to court. That's the way
it is. That's life.
                    RAY
Yeah. That's life.
```

```
It starts to rain and BARRY watches RAY lift his head
up to the sky, his face impassive as the raindrops run
down his cheeks. They make their way back to the door.
                    BARRY
Send me a postcard from Alcatraz.
```

Standing face to face with Ray, the thing that struck me most were his eyes. When he looked at me, his eyes were completely still, cold and devoid of life. I remember going home that night and telling Pam, 'If ever there was a killer, this guy is it.' When the job introduced me to darkness, I was so glad to have Pam as my light.

Over the following days, I continued to gain Ray's trust in the exercise yard. We kept talking, a little more each time. On the second day, he said he wanted a skipping rope. 'I want to exercise with it.' I replied, 'They're not going to give you a rope, they'll think you'll want to top yourself.' Then the officer would pipe up and say, 'No more talking you two!' helping keep up the act.

On the third day, Ray told me he wanted to be a mercenary. Even though he had the eyes of a killer, he was the last guy you'd ever want to hire to commit a murder. In fact, he bungled every crime he committed. When he robbed a bank in 1959, he was arrested after falling out of the getaway car and landing in the middle of the road, still holding a sawn-off shotgun and covered in all the stolen bank notes. Similarly, when he assassinated Martin Luther King, Ray left the rifle in the apartment opposite the Lorraine Motel, covered in his fingerprints.

After a few days, they swapped me out for another officer to have a go. Ray never spoke about Martin Luther King. A few weeks later, after his extradition was granted, he was transferred to the US Air Force base at RAF Mildenhall. Five Squad followed behind his vehicle as backup. Until then, he hadn't seen me outside of the exercise yard. At the airbase, he saw me in a corridor and suddenly put it all together. 'You didn't fool me,' he lied. 'I knew you were a cop all the time.' I just smiled and nodded.

After he was extradited back to the USA, Ray finally confessed to the crime on 10 March 1969. I'll never forget having to look into those cold steel eyes of his. It still seems unthinkable that he was responsible for killing one of the most influential figures in modern history. Despite Martin Luther King's tragic demise, he continues to inspire generations. I often think of his words:

> Power properly understood is the ability to achieve purpose. Power without love is reckless and abusive, and love without power is sentimental and anaemic.

Despite Ray's claim, I never got sussed as an undercover police officer and I always felt like I could talk my way out of any situation. Except once, when I felt I had no choice but to take my undercover work to new 'heights'.

On some Flying Squad cases, I needed an informant to make an introduction that would hopefully gain me access into a suspect's circle. Whoever handled the set up tended to make up a backstory, not always thinking to consult me about it beforehand. This meant I often had to think on my feet and improvise. The usual approach was, 'I was in prison with him', but this could be a very dodgy move. In the criminal fraternity, every villain seemed to know where everyone had done their porridge. It was risky business to say too much in case it gave the game away.

To avoid the usual traps, the informants would sometimes spin a yarn that wouldn't look out of place in a movie. I discovered this for myself when, one very cold February night, I met a Luton detective in a pub just outside a football ground. There he introduced me to his snout, who had boasted he had some very good information regarding a team of upmarket housebreakers. The plan was for me to infiltrate this den of thieves and help catch them in the act…

```
DISSOLVE TO:
INT. PUB. LUTON. 1972.
```

BARRY sits at a table in the corner of a loud bar, with a jukebox blasting out and lots of young men and women playing on gaming machines. Sat next to him is WYATT, a snout, late 30s, burly with a crew cut, very impressionable and credible. Sitting opposite is DETECTIVE CONSTABLE DAVID BROCK, 20s, tall, athletic, clean-cut, a friendly face that BARRY feels he can trust.

> BARRY
>
> What did you tell them about me?

> WYATT
>
> I told them you did some work for me occasionally.

> BARRY
>
> Doing what?

> WYATT
>
> Driving. Whatever.

BROCK leans in.

> BROCK
>
> Just tell him what you told me.

> WYATT
>
> They're a team of housebreakers, though they have grand ambitions. They are going to do a museum and they want someone to fly them and the gear to France.
>
> They've got a contact out there who can flog the stuff for them.

> BARRY
>
> So where do I come into this?

                    WYATT
They're still looking for someone to fly the plane.
I told them you're a pilot.

BARRY almost drops his pint glass in shock.

                    BARRY
You did what?

BARRY shoots a look of disbelief at BROCK.

                    BROCK
Sorry, this is news to me.

                    BARRY
     (to WYATT)
What the hell made you tell them I was a pilot?

                    WYATT
Listen these guys aren't your usual slag, you
know. They are intelligent. I wanted to impress
them.
BARRY downs his beer.

                    BARRY
I'm out of this.

                    BROCK
I don't blame you.

                    WYATT
Hang about. Just come and meet them. You don't
have to commit to anything.

                    BARRY
I don't believe this.

The jukebox begins playing 'Fly Me To The Moon' by Frank
Sinatra.

WYATT and BROCK share a smile and look at me with eager
anticipation. BARRY has always held Sinatra in high
regard. He takes a deep breath.

                    BARRY
OK. Set up a meet with these guys for a week
today. But don't come out with anymore bullshit,
or you'll be the one that gets nicked!

```
                WYATT
      One for the road?
                BARRY
      I think I need it!
```

I was more than ready to walk away from this case, but I knew that if these guys really were planning to rob a museum, gaining the intelligence to catch them in the act would be a massive result. However, maintaining my cover on this job wouldn't be as easy as just turning up with a fancy business card, with 'Pilot for Hire' on it. I needed to do my homework and give myself the best chance of being able to answer any questions and convince this gang that I was the real deal.

Ahead of the meet, I urgently got in touch with Chief Superintendent Martin Grieves of the Fraud Squad, one of my oldest and closest friends. He had met his wife around the same time as I'd met Pam and we'd lived near each other in Cheshunt and Cuffley. A very good sportsman, Martin could ride horses, swim, fence and had even competed in the Olympic pentathlon. He was also the only person I knew who had a pilot's licence.

When I told Martin about my predicament, he laughed out loud. 'I'll say something for you, Barry, you're dedicated to the job!' Martin took me to a private airfield in Blackbushe, near Heathrow, where he was a member of a club. He took me up in a single-engine Cessna, showing me how all the controls worked and taught me the basics and filled my head with enough technical jargon to help me bullshit my way through any awkward questions. He even let me take over the controls for a while. I cherish those memories with Martin, who was tragically killed in 2005 whilst on board Bellview Airlines Flight 210, which mysteriously crashed moments after take-off in Nigeria. I still miss him terribly.

I never got the chance to put my dear old friend's invaluable teachings to the test. My targeted housebreakers got caught on another job, shifting a van-load of stolen property in Bedford. No museum pieces, only everyday household belongings. Perhaps the whole thing had been nonsense from the start? I wouldn't have long to ponder this, as I was soon assigned to a new station, where once again fate played its hand…

CHAPTER 9

RELOAD

Fate could be a copper's best friend or their worst enemy. It varied from case to case, but it was always a silent partner on every investigation. In March 1972, not long after I had been transferred to Golders Green Police Station, I got to find out whether luck was on my side around my new manor…

```
DISSOLVE TO:
INT. GOLDERS GREEN STATION. FRONT OFFICE. 1972.

BARRY enters and checks the crime book. Standing at the
desk on the phone is Station Sergeant MATT JONES, 40,
tall, a Welshman turned committed cockney. Hair combed
forward to hide his bald spot. An efficient officer with
a great sense of humour. An ODD COUPLE, both in their
late 40s, stand impatiently waiting to be seen. The
man is tall and gaunt, the lady short and plump. After
signing the crime book, BARRY closes it, only for JONES
to place a ladies' handbag on top of it. BARRY gives
JONES a quizzical look.
               JONES
        (into mouthpiece)
     And the same to you, sir.


JONES puts the receiver down. BARRY leans on the desk
and points at the bag.
               BARRY
     It suits you. Not sure green is your colour
        though, Matt.
JONES thrusts the bag at BARRY.
```

Right: War child, growing up in Monmouth.

Below left: With my parents, Jack and Millie. I didn't get to know them until after the war.

Below right: Proud cadet no. 9093 reporting for duty.

Playing football at Hackney Marshes during my Hendon days.

Top of the Cops – Me towering over the rest of City Road's formidable Aide Squad, posing with some notable figures in the front row, including Neil McElligott QC (bottom left) and DI Bert Wickstead (centre).

Diplomatic immunity – Undercover for a station wind-up.

Right: Soulmates – with Pam during our first magical fortnight in Majorca, 1965.

Below: Popping a cork after popping the question.

Our wedding day, 30 October 1965. My parents Jack and Millie, the happy couple, Pam's mum Rog and her uncle Alec Curzon, who gave her away.

And they said it would never last.

Right: Serious Business – Reggie Kray with associates in 1968. (Public Domain)

Below left: The eyes of a killer. James Earl Ray, who I went undercover to investigate in 1968. (Public Domain)

Below right: Photographed after receiving a commendation for courage in 1969.

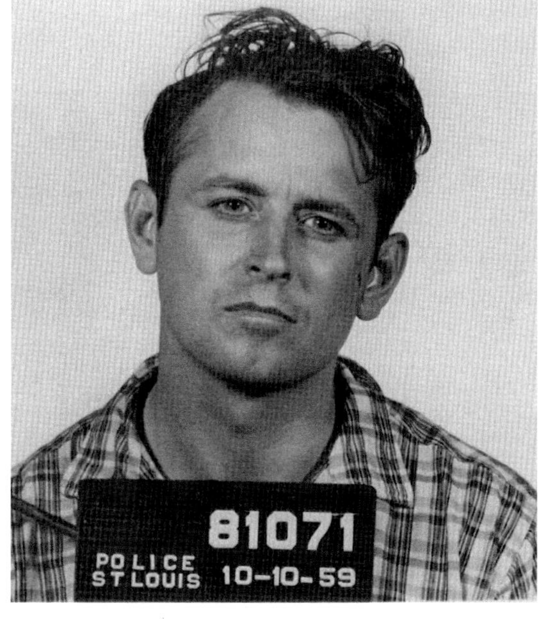

Fabulous Five Squad. (L–R) DC Dave Dixon, DS Charlie Snape, DI Frank Lovejoy, me, DS Mike MacAdam, DC Nicky Birch and driver Bill Parsons. All guys you could trust with your life.

A Royal Occasion – The Appletons standing in line to welcome Queen Elizabeth II at the opening of The Peel Centre in 1974.

Simon and Sacha with my parents. Seeing them with my own children reminded me of what we had all missed during the war.

A New Chapter – I became proud landlord of The Lion in 1978, where I poured many a pint of Old Casanova. (Courtesy of Potters Bar Museum)

Back on the beat – I watch on (bottom right) as 'Ringer', my episode of *The Bill* based on my first major arrest, is brought to life by Thames Television in 1985. (© Ralph Brown)

Above left: Nick Reding as PC Pete Ramsey, my creation loosely based on myself.

Above right: Michael Chapman, the producer of *The Bill* who launched my television career. (© Nigel J. Wilson)

Sun Hill's finest. Some of my favourite actors to write for included Nula Conwell (WPC Viv Martella), Eric Richard (Sgt. Bob Cryer) and Jon Iles (DC Mike Dashwood). (© Ralph Brown and Nigel J. Wilson)

Above left and above right: Zero to hero. Speaking at a Writers Circle in 1985 with Teresa Howard, my first agent who got me started and opened so many doors for me. (© Teresa Howard Archive)

First book brings author overnight success

WORKING undercover, cracking international crime rings and getting involved in gun battles may sound like glamourised crime fiction to most people, but for one former Flying Squad officer such adventures were all in a day's work.

By combining that experience with a love and talent for writing, 46-year-old Barry Appleton is now enjoying overnight success with his first book, "A Walking Shadow", and as a scriptwriter for Thames Television's new police series "The Bill".

By Anna Averkiou

As Barry discussed the book and the series at his home in Holmwood Avenue, Cuffley, he said: "There are not many success stories in writing. For me it's all happened at once and now I have so much work coming in."

Barry was born in Monmouth and spent 20 years in the police force, beginning his career attached to stations in the East End and continuing on to serve eight years in the Flying Squad at Scotland Yard.

"The Flying Squad was marvellous," recalled Barry. "I would probably still have been in it if it hadn't been for a spinal injury I received in a fight while on duty.

"The Sweeney" is very true to life. I travelled throughout the country and was involved in some big jobs."

Having had to give up his duties he took over The Lion public house, in just about getting there when something would happen. I didn't want to change anything I wrote and I suppose I was naive about publishing and agents."

Two years ago Barry decided to concentrate purely on fiction and the result was "A Walking Shadow" which was published in September. It is a gripping crime story based on the world of international terrorism.

Detective Christos Mackenzie is working on what is supposed to be a simple Home Office assignment. He has been told of a secret training camp somewhere in England where stolen Greek gold is being used to finance a terrorist plan to overthrow the Turkish Government in Cyprus.

Former Sweeney detective steps out of the literary shadows

● Barry Appleton

He explained that he has many Greek Cypriot friends which sparked the idea of using the problems in Cyprus as the basis of the plot.

"A Greek Cypriot friend has a clothing fac- killings, cover-ups and danger, Barry replied: "It's difficult to tell what's truth and what's fiction but in my writing I draw on true-life experiences."

The training camp in "A Walking Shadow" is that they might need a technical advisor on any police series.

He was in luck as Thames were doing a pilot show which they liked and they asked Barry to try his hand at writing scripts.

entirely on location on video tape and Barry is already working on another series which is set to equal "The Sweeney" and "Z Cars" in popularity.

Deadline

with his success. He describes his wife, Pam, a "my memory! And sh[e] does my typing for me. She knows the book better than I do."

Barry is also able to see more of his two children

Making the headlines. (© Teresa Howard Archive)

Above: Is that you, Stephen? Dreaming of Spielberg levels of success.

Right: Renewing our wedding vows in 1995 at St Mary's Sturmer, the church which also inspired two of my *Taggart* storylines.

Above left: Celebrating our silver anniversary in style.

Above right: Licence to Thrill.

Below: Of all the gin joints…

Above left: Proud grandparents – with Simon's daughters Phoebe and Zoe.

Above right: Pam with Merlin, our gentle giant. (Author's Collection)

Below: We're back, my son. The great John Salthouse visiting us in Paphos. John has a fantastic energy and was so committed to *The Bill*.

All Shook Up. With Willie Clarke on the set of my first play, No Room at the Pub in 1997. (© Stage One Theatre Group)

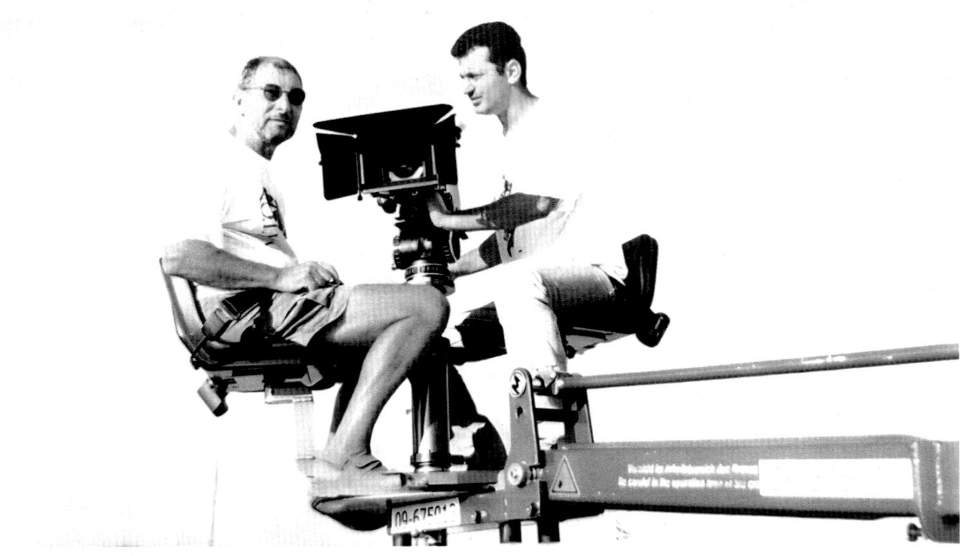

The sky's the limit! Filmmaker Andros Achilleos made me an offer I couldn't refuse and brought me out of retirement to write *East of Wild Goat Rocks* in 2000.

Making it up as we go along...

Above left: A long way from Potters Bar. Reunited with Teresa Howard at Viklari in 2024.

Above right: Where it all began. With my original shooting script for 'A Dangerous Breed' the first ever episode of *The Bill* to go into production.

Does a writer ever truly retire?

Keeping the faith. Without God I could easily have turned out to be one of the bad guys.

          JONES

Got a mystery for you. This was handed in about an hour ago, by a woman who found it in her front garden. Looks like someone threw it over her fence.

          BARRY

I assume you think it's connected to a crime and you're not trying to lumber me with a uniform job?

          JONES

Would I do that?

          MAN

Excuse me?

          JONES

I'll be with you in a moment, sir.

The phone rings.

          JONES

There's a name inside. Do me a favour, Barry?

          BARRY

Okay. Leave it with me.

JONES answers the phone, much to the ODD COUPLE's annoyance. BARRY walks up to CID, intrigued by the handbag.

CUT TO:
INT. GOLDERS GREEN STATION. CID OFFICE. LATER.

BARRY tips the contents of the bag onto his desk and notices a Co-op loyalty card, addressed to a Martha Atkinson from Leicester. BARRY calls out to one of his aides.

          BARRY

Skinner, get me the number for Leicestershire and Rutland Constabulary please.

CUT TO:
INT. GOLDERS GREEN STATION. CID OFFICE. LATER.

BARRY is on the phone to Leicester police. He has been transferred to DETECTIVE INSPECTOR TESSA FRANCIS from the murder squad.

>   FRANCIS
> I'm glad you called. This is a fucking horrible crime! The victim was battered to death in her house, we think yesterday evening. We will know for sure later after the autopsy. We think the killers were a couple of housebreakers. The poor dear lived alone, salt of the earth by all accounts. I don't know what this fucking world is coming to.

>   BARRY
> Is there anything we can do to assist down here?

>   FRANCIS
> There was a Ford Cortina seen close by with two guys inside. It was dark and the witness didn't get the registration or colour. But she thought it had some damage on the left rear. The back light was broken, like it had been in a collision. It may be nothing, but that's all we've got.

>   BARRY
> This could be two London guys?

>   FRANCIS
> Looks that way. Finding that bag is a Godsend! I will send a couple of our boys down to you straight away. Thank you for your cooperation, Barry. I'll let you know if anything else comes up.

>   BARRY
> Thank you, Ma'am.

BARRY puts the phone down.

>   BARRY
> Skinner, is the D.I. in yet?

>   SKINNER
> Canteen, sarge.

CUT TO:

RELOAD

EXT. GOLDERS GREEN STATION. YARD. LATER.

BARRY makes his way across the yard, heading towards
the canteen. He passes six cars, all of which have been
involved in a crime. A 'Preserve for Fingerprints' sign
has been placed against the rear of a Ford Cortina. The
car has a damaged left rear end and broken light! BARRY
immediately heads back to the front office.

CUT TO:

INT. GOLDERS GREEN STATION. FRONT OFFICE. LATER.

JONES is writing a report when BARRY rushes in.

> BARRY
>
> Matt! The Cortina in the yard?

> JONES
>
> Stolen. The area car nicked two youths racing
> around Hampstead Heath in it at 4am.

> BARRY
>
> (with urgency)
>
> Where are they now?

> JONES
>
> At court. One in custody, one on bail. Or should
> be…

JONES glances up at the clock.

> JONES
>
> They're probably waiting to go in.

> BARRY
>
> Ring the court. Don't let them go!

> JONES
>
> What's the matter? It's only a nicked motor.

> BARRY
>
> By tonight they'll probably be charged with
> murder. I'm on my way to the court now.

> JONES
>
> Bloody hell! I'll call them. Leave it to me.

BARRY heads to the doorway.

I arrived at the court to find both youths in custody and had them transferred back to Golders Green, while we awaited the arrival of two detectives from Leicester. It turned out that one of these two London lads had a girlfriend up in Leicester, where they had nicked the Cortina before robbing and killing the elderly victim. They had driven back down to London to get rid of the car when one of our patrol cars spotted it racing through Hampstead and, on discovering over the radio it was reported stolen, took chase. The youths tried to evade capture and sped off around a corner, chucking the victim's handbag out of the window and into a front garden. Transferred to Leicester CID, they were both charged with murder and eventually given heavy sentences.

That's how fate helped me solve a murder in a day. I was glad it was on my side.

A little later during my posting at Golders Green, Matt Jones handed me another item of lost property: a very old and incredibly ornate urn, depicting scenes from ancient Greece. It was a work of art. In this case, the owner of the urn was no mystery, as their name was engraved on it: Sigmund Freud. The world-famous neurologist spent his final years living in Hampstead until his death in 1939. Freud had requested that his ashes be placed in this urn, a sealed Greek bell krater, which had been a birthday present from Princess Marie Bonaparte, granddaughter of Napoleon. He reportedly loved the piece so much that he wished to literally take it to the grave…

The urn had been stolen from Golders Green Crematorium, where it sat on top of a large black marble plinth in front of a window. Possibly, the thieves realised they could never sell such an item and it somehow found its way to the police station. I returned the urn to the Freud family home in Maresfield Gardens, where they thanked me for its safe return, despite not having been aware of its theft. They explained that the ancient artefact was 2,000 years old and depicted Dionysus, the god of wine, vegetation, fertility, festivity, ritual madness, religious ecstasy and theatre. 'You learn something new every day on this job!' I replied.

Another face I got to know in Golders Green was a guy who 'sponsored' John Conteh, a promising young boxer who was on the up. This so-called sponsor, who I'll call David, was an entrepreneur who had supposedly made his fortune by selling Swedish electric storage heaters. In reality, he'd made a decent crust from doping greyhounds, which he'd done a short stretch for.

Eager to present himself as a respectable citizen in the boxing world, David felt that being seen as a friend of the police was the best way to cultivate his image. As I was the new detective in town, he turned up at the front office one day, dressed in very expensive clobber, and invited me for a spin around the block in his brand-new Rolls-Royce. I thought he might make a potential informant, so I humoured him. I got in the front with the chauffeur, while he sat in the back with a young girl who proceeded to give him a manicure. It was all very bizarre.

He then started to invite me out to parties and dos, but I only accepted on one occasion, when he invited me to attend a gala boxing dinner in the West End. I was late arriving at the ringside, where food was already being served to the guests at the tables. The lights were down low and, as I took my seat, I made my apologies. But when I looked up and saw the other guests at the table, my blood ran cold. My dinner companions were none other than the notorious Nash brothers and sat directly opposite me was the one I'd arrested in the Sixties for attempted murder. He had only just been released after his lengthy stretch and when our eyes met, I was positive he remembered me. Without saying a word, I got up and left the table.

As I walked out, I kept an eye over my shoulder to make sure the Nash brothers weren't in the mood for vengeance. I got into the foyer, but just before I reached the exit a hand gripped my shoulder. I thought 'Here we go…' I turned around ready to defend myself, but thankfully it was David, who wanted to know why I was leaving. I made my excuses, and he said I should come to Conteh's next big fight. I was non-committal, I just wanted to make a quick getaway, but he wouldn't take no for an answer. Before I could utter another word, he waved over a very tall, well-built black man.

'Give him a couple of ringside tickets for the next fight.' A bitter argument broke out, then the big man reached inside his jacket pocket. Our eyes met and, after a moment, he reluctantly took two tickets out and gave them to me before walking away in disgust. David revealed that the man was Conteh's father, Frank. Perhaps encouraged by his dad to keep better company, Conteh soon signed up with George Francis and went on to become light heavyweight boxing champion of the world. I don't know what happened to David – I chucked the tickets in the nearest bin and never saw him again. I didn't like the company he kept.

As I drove home, I made sure I wasn't being followed as I didn't want the Nash brothers knowing where my family lived. Seeing those vicious men again certainly made me think back to my early days on the job. Then in December 1972, I was contacted by another blast from the past, this time from the right side of the law. Bob Robinson, who had started out with me as a cadet, had continued to make shrewd moves in his career. Having now risen to the rank of DCI, Bob was made head of the Flying Squad and offered me the chance to return to Five Squad, this time as a detective sergeant. Christmas had come early.

After two and a half years on S Division, I was thrilled to be rejoining the 'Fabulous Five'. When Bill Parsons picked me up from Cuffley on a crisp Monday morning, it was like I'd never been away, especially as I would be partnered once again with Bill Laver, who was also returning after a secondment to the Regional Crime Squad. It felt great to be back in the saddle and I couldn't wait to get stuck into some action. I didn't have long to wait.

One bitterly cold evening the week before Christmas, four villains wearing winter clothing robbed a large house in Hampstead. They knew that the businessman owner of the property usually came home around 7pm, so earlier in the evening they knocked on the front door and captured the maid who answered. They then grabbed the businessman's wife from the kitchen and forced her and the maid into the lounge, holding them hostage.

The robbers had somehow learned that there was a safe in the bedroom, hidden behind an oil painting. The wife pleaded that she didn't know the code to the safe, nor what time her husband was due home. They'd planned a quick getaway, but after a couple of hours there was still no sign of the businessman's return. Two of the gang searched the house and found some cash, along with a pair of Purdey shotguns. The youngest robber was left guarding the wife and maid. He took off his old army coat, as the heating in the house was on full blast, and threw it over the back of the sofa.

When the businessman eventually arrived home, much later than planned, he walked in and was surprised by two of the villains, who dragged him upstairs. Under threat of violence to his wife, he was forced to open the safe and the intruders took all the contents, along with the two shotguns, and made a swift exit. A witness saw the gang driving away in a white Ford Zephyr.

Five Squad happened to be in the area when the robbery call went out and we were at the house in minutes. I discovered the old army coat, which had fallen behind the sofa and obviously been forgotten about in the heat of the moment. I checked the coat, which had a surname and Army personnel number stitched on a label inside. Schoolboy error. I made a few phone calls, and the Military Police put me in touch with their records office in Gloucester. They confirmed the full name of the soldier, who had a home address in the East End.

In the early hours of the morning, we drove over to the address and parked outside was a white Ford Zephyr. Bingo! We hit the place and caught them all red-handed, sharing out the cash whilst getting drunk. We also recovered the two shotguns, which these crooks had been just about to saw in half and turn into sawn-offs. I did some digging and discovered that these masterminds had been planning on taking a hacksaw to a pair of shotguns that were worth £125,000 – more valuable than the contents of the safe!

With all the stolen property recovered and returned within 24 hours, the businessman was so over the moon that he requested all our names. A couple of days later, a small parcel from Harrods was delivered to Five Squad. Inside were personalised gold pens for us all, each with our names engraved. This marvellous result was a great way to return to the action.

Later that week, I received information about a lorry loaded with stolen tobacco and booze, apparently parked on a farmyard near Cheshunt. Under the cover of darkness, Bill Parsons and I went out to check this farmyard and found the lorry. The next day, with warrant in hand, we hit the lorry, which was packed to the rafters with nicked cigarettes and whiskey. The guy who owned the farm claimed that the driver had broken down and abandoned the lorry. Whether this story was true or not, we were able to recover and return thousands of pounds worth of goods.

During the season of goodwill, criminals were often nicking lorryloads of gear, unaware of Scotland Yard's little helpers... The information gathered by Intelligence Department C11, located next door to the Flying Squad, could sometimes prove crucial in our work. This team of sleuths helped me identify a pair of crooks who had done over a bonded warehouse, using a JCB to take down a wall in the middle the night and make it away with hundreds of parcels. We raided their hideout and recovered thousands of pounds worth of Avon make-up and perfume products. Whilst this might have been a great result for us, it was still a disaster for Avon. Even though the boxes were still sealed and wrapped up with Christmas labels, the company's policy meant that they wouldn't allow them to be delivered and they ordered their destruction.

Just after Christmas, one of my informants tipped me off about a house loaded with stolen Scholl driving shoes, all pinched from a factory. We already had one job lined up for the first Saturday of the new year, but I knew that if we were quick, and had our old friend Fate on side, we would be able to handle both jobs. Sure enough, we found a basement full of these stolen shoes. We got the receivers and, eventually, the guys who had nicked them. Another solid result.

Being successful on the Squad relied on knowing when to be patient and let things unfold. Over the years, people have got the impression that the Flying Squad is all about kicking down doors, punch-ups and car chases, mainly thanks to our action-packed portrayal in the hit television series *The Sweeney*. Whilst there are more differences than similarities, fact and fiction did collide for Five Squad in the summer of 1974...

DISSOLVE TO:
INT. FLYING SQUAD MAIN OFFICE. 1974.

Twenty officers, including BARRY and BILL LAVER, are catching up on their paperwork, surrounded by copious cups of coffee and cigarette smoke. BARRY nudges BILL as he notices DET. CHIEF SUPT. RON PAGE enter the room. PAGE is in his late 40s, sporting a lovely smile and good at hiding his slight corpulence, a real gentleman who treats his officers with genuine respect. PAGE is accompanied by two familiar faces either side of him, standing like two boxers at a weigh-in.

          PAGE
Listen up everyone!

There are a few double-takes around the room.

          PAGE
This is Dennis Waterman and
John Thaw, who I can see
you've already recognised.
They are going to be playing
the leads in a new police
series called, believe it
or not… 'The Sweeney'.
There is a cheer from the squad.

          PAGE
They are going to be shadowing the squad
for a while.

The officers trade looks and a few smiles.

          BILL
Which one's playing you then, guv?

DENNIS and JOHN both giggle at the question.

          PAGE
A very distinguished actor called Garfield Morgan
will be playing their supervising officer, thank
you Bill. He however doesn't need to pick up any
of your bad habits.

Good-natured laughter fills the office.

          PAGE
To make John and Dennis welcome, I'm taking them
down to the Tank for a little light refreshment.

Those of you who don't have pressing police
business are welcome to join us.

BARRY and BILL share a nod and a wink.

CUT TO:
INT. NEW SCOTLAND YARD. THE TANK. LATER.

Based in the bowels of the building, the Tank is where
the squad entertained visitors. The large grey room had
a bar, tables, pictures on the wall and a piano in the
corner. The Tank is almost empty so early in the day,
frequented only by members of the Flying Squad and their
special guests. BARRY sits with DENNIS WATERMAN.

          DENNIS
Why do they call this gaff the Tank then?

          BARRY
That's a mystery that remains unsolved. Cheers.

          DENNIS
Cheers, pal.

          BARRY
How long is your series going to be on for?

          DENNIS
Thirteen episodes. We made a pilot called 'Regan',
that's John's character. We want to make it as
real as possible. I can't wait to see you guys in
action.

          BARRY
From a distance. If there's any trouble you'll
have to step back. Sorry. We can't afford to let
you get involved.

          DENNIS
That's fine by me, I just want to get to know you lot.

          BARRY
You've come to the right place.

CUT TO:
INT. NEW SCOTLAND YARD. THE TANK. LATER.

The bar is now busy with lunchtime customers. JOHN, DENNIS and the Squad gather around the piano as one of the officers plays a tune. Everyone is starting to get merry, there is a great atmosphere.

           DENNIS
So, you're a detective sergeant then?

           BARRY
Right. Four years now.

           DENNIS
Carter's a detective sergeant. John's only playing a DI because he can do the *Times* crossword and he's a brown-nose crawler, the shit!

           JOHN
    (smiling)
You taking my name in vain again, Waterman?

           DENNIS
You see, Barry, he thinks he's going to be the star attraction. Some fucking chance.

JOHN puts his arm around DENNIS

           JOHN
I'm going to have to pull rank on Carter, get him transferred to traffic!

The three men laugh.

The good humour and singing continued for many hours and we all lost track of time. When the barmaid wanted to close down, John and Dennis each bought a bottle of Scotch and the merriment carried on until they eventually drank us all under the table. That first day gave the two stars a great taste of the camaraderie on the Squad. The following day, with a couple of fragile heads in tow, it was time for us to show them what the job was all about.

There was a limit to how many shouts we could take John and Dennis out on. Aside from the obvious need to protect them from harm, if either of them witnessed a case that went to court, their involvement could have threatened the programme's tight film schedule. They both shadowed us in the office and we took them out in the car with us. John Thaw spent a lot of time talking to Bill Parsons and I like to think he requested that Regan's faithful driver in *The Sweeney* be named Bill in his honour.

I had enjoyed showing John and Dennis the ropes and we subsequently saw them out and about filming on the streets of London. *The Sweeney* and many other dramas would film outside New Scotland Yard, using it as a backdrop to add an air of authenticity to their programmes. If there was ever a film crew outside when Bill drove us up from the underground car park, he would screech around the corner, beep the horn and we would cheer as we drove past, completely ruining their take!

The Sweeney became an instant hit when it began airing in January 1975, storming the television charts with 17 million viewers tuning in. John and Dennis were great in their roles and the series was easily the most realistic police drama on television at the time. The writers had done their research and the programme makers got the tone exactly right. *The Sweeney* was occasionally dark and shocking, just like the job itself. We all got reminded of this on 26 February 1975, when we heard another of those calls over the radio that all coppers dread: 'Shots fired. Officer down.'

Stephen Tibble was a 21-year-old police constable with a wife, who was tragically in the wrong place at the wrong time. He was off-duty riding his motorcycle when he saw plain-clothed officers pursuing a suspect in West Kensington. After being flagged down and quickly briefed by training Detective Constable Derek Wilson, PC Tibble bravely volunteered to pursue the suspect on his motorbike and block his exit. Pulling to a stop at the junction of Gledstanes Road and Charleville Road, Tibble dismounted from his motorbike, crouched and spread out his arms to block the path of the suspect. As he tried to catch hold of him, the suspect pulled out a .38 Long Colt revolver and shot Tibble twice in the chest at point-blank range. He died three hours later in hospital.

The fleeing suspect was Liam Quinn, an American member of the IRA. He had been observed entering a house on the adjoining Fairholme Road by Wilson and his fellow plain-clothes officers, who were investigating burglaries in the area. When Quinn returned to the premises, the officers approached him and asked him to empty his pockets. It was then that he made his escape and, within moments, had committed a cold-blooded murder. None of those officers could have known that Quinn was armed, nor that the house was in fact an IRA bomb factory.

Five Squad was drafted in after we got a possible lead on Quinn's whereabouts. Throughout my career, the kind of criminals I was dealing with evolved; from arresting small-time thieves and pickpockets, I was now chasing bomb suspects and terrorists. Quinn was believed to be having a relationship with a high-profile barrister, who was possibly hiding him. We raided her chambers in Lincoln's Inn, but she had not come to work. We got her home address and hit the road.

We arrived at a quiet residential street in a village way outside of London, ready to hit this barrister's home. While some officers took the front, Bill Laver and I jumped over the back walls and ran through neighbouring gardens. One lady hanging out her washing got quite a shock when two armed detectives jumped over her fence! When we raided the house, there was no sign of Quinn or the barrister.

Quinn managed to evade capture and fled back to the States. After years of extradition wrangling, he was eventually sentenced to life imprisonment for PC Tibble's murder at the Old Bailey in 1988. Appallingly, due to his IRA allegiance, he only served eleven years before being released under the Good Friday Agreement. I can't imagine how Tibble's widow Kathryn must have felt about that crazy decision. Her late husband was awarded a posthumous Queen's Police Medal for gallantry and a memorial stone was placed on Charleville Road, marking the spot where he fell. Stephen Tibble only served in the Met for six months, but his name will never be forgotten.

That same year, we got word that three armed robbers, who had managed to evade arrest and had become a serious problem, had threatened to gun down any Flying Squad officer who came after them. We had a department meeting, where Bob Robinson announced that he wanted these guys put away once and for all. We started asking around and were told that one of the trio had gone missing. It was rumoured that an argument had broken out within the gang, which resulted in two of them killing the other.

This was all speculation, until one of my informants was in a pub in North London when one of these guys sat down at the bar beside him and ordered a drink. He was carrying a holdall. My informant asked, 'How's Sean? We haven't seen him in here lately.' In front of the whole pub, the man with the holdall calmly replied, 'Sean? I've got him here.' He then unzipped the bag and looking back at my informant was the severed head of the third robber. A gruesome trophy. We had to find this maniac and fast.

We soon learned where their hideout was and Five Squad launched a full-scale raid. The holdall villain wasn't home, but his accomplice was: a slim, long-haired man with vicious eyes. He fled up to the top floor of this terraced building and escaped out onto the rooftops. We followed him up there, but before I knew what was happening, a bullet whizzed over my head. One of the officers behind me saw that the suspect was armed and, remembering their threat to kill any of us they encountered, fired a warning shot over his head and ordered him to stop. He gave himself up, but not the whereabouts of the holdall man, who disappeared without trace. That one still haunts me.

During my time on the Flying Squad, our biggest result arguably came in 1976, when we got eight suspects sent down for carrying out a multi-million-pound robbery from the deposit boxes at the Mayfair branch of the Bank of America. Among those being sentenced was a familiar face. Remember my first major arrest, when I nicked the driver of that Ford Consul ringer? This is where his life of crime had led him. Peter Colson was now a 32-year-old car dealer, sentenced to a twenty-one-year stretch. Judge Alan King-Hamilton described Colson as "a dangerous professional criminal", armed with 'a mind and body as fast and slippery as quicksilver'.

I had to hand it to Colson and his mob, they had been very creative with their bank robbery. They found an electrician who used to work for British Telecom. Knowing how to hack into the bank's wiring, they put up a maintenance tent outside the bank and, from inside, opened a manhole cover and went underground. They then operated the phonelines between the bank manager and, allegedly, another bank. Using a script, they arranged the transfer of millions of pounds. It must have been the easiest money they'd ever made.

Despite this massive haul, Colson still lived in the same council flat that he and his brother had first fled to when I pursued them two decades earlier. Like many criminals, they just didn't want to leave the estate they had grown up on, but they also couldn't just blend into the background either. For a while, Colson parked a Lamborghini Esplanade outside, just to show off his earnings. Older, but no wiser.

Bob Robinson was in charge of this case and I was one of the men he picked to accompany him down to Eastbourne, where we suspected one of the bank robbers was hiding. Waiting for our suspect to leave a house, hopefully carrying a load of cash, we all hid in different places down a very dark street, filled with parked cars. Time was ticking by without any sign of movement.

From our van parked at the top end, we spotted a different guy making his way down the street. He had a burglar's head if ever I saw one. Sure enough, he started trying door after door on these parked cars. I knew we had to get him out of the way before he blew our operation. Just as he was checking out the next car, we drove up in the van and boom! Executed like a kidnapping, we swiftly grabbed this old lag and pulled him into the back of the van before he even knew what had hit him.

While the rest of the squad continued with the operation, we got this chancer back to Eastbourne Police Station. It turned out they'd had a warrant out for his arrest for the last forty years, in connection with all manner of crimes. After decades of getting away with it, he'd thought that night was no different... not realising he'd walked straight into a Flying Squad operation. Fate played its hand once again and he literally landed in our laps!

Another high stakes case came our way later that year, when the government informed us that a great deal of money had been lost through stolen benefit cheques. They had no idea how it was being done. I went to meet with an old informant, who suggested that the whole scam was down to just one man...

DISSOLVE TO:
INT. PUBLIC HOUSE. 1976.

BARRY drinks in a saloon bar, waiting for his informant to turn up. Further down the bar there are a few noisy City types, all getting over another bad day on the

Stock Exchange. Through the window, BARRY observes his snout, TONY, late 20s, short dark curly hair, turning up in a brand-new Rover V8. He parks it and makes his grand entrance. He is dressed smart casual, wearing pointed shoes. BARRY is overpowered by the smell of TONY's aftershave as he sits down to join him.

>   BARRY
> Nice motor.

>   TONY
> Picked it up yesterday.

>   BARRY
> Villainy must be good.

BARRY waves over to the barman.

>   BARRY
> Same again please, and whatever he's having.

>   TONY
> Gin and tonic. A little ice.

>   BARRY
> The motor must have cost you a few bob?

>   TONY
> Just the deposit. They'll never see it again.

>   BARRY
> That's fraud.

>   TONY
> They never asked me if I could make the repayments. All they wanted to do was sell me the car. What you guys call an "unsatisfactory business transaction."

>   BARRY
> You know all the angles.

>   TONY
> That's why I'm still here talking to you.

>   BARRY
> Not for long if you don't give me something.

The BARMAN brings over the drinks. TONY waits until he has gone.

            TONY
How would you like to save the government thousands
of pounds?

            BARRY
I'm listening.

            TONY
There's a guy who has duplicate keys to the back
door of a Post Office sorting office. He knows
exactly what time everyone goes to lunch. He
goes in with a carrier bag, knowing where all
the brown envelopes are stacked. Payments to
deserving cases.

            BARRY
The poor and needy? I don't like the sound of
this.

TONY takes a sip from his drink.

            TONY
He has a team of trusty housewives who cash the
cheques for him and get paid a percentage. Local
shops, garages, grocers accept the cheques. No
one loses out, except the government.

            BARRY
It can't be that easy?

            TONY
Every Friday, regular as clockwork. You interested?

Come Friday lunchtime, three of us were in the back of an observation van, hidden amongst other vehicles, with a good view of the sorting office back door. Occasionally some staff came outside to have a smoke, but no sign of our man. I really hoped my snout hadn't given me the runaround. Then almost at 1pm precisely, our suspect approached the back door, wearing a hooded tracksuit, jeans and trainers. He looked up and down the street before taking out a set of keys, opening the door and closing it behind him. We got out of the van and waited for him to return with his illicit takings. Within minutes, we caught him red-handed.

This happened on Detective Chief Superintendent Jack Slipper's manor. 'Slipper of the Yard' had just earned the headline 'Slip-Up of the Yard', having finally tracked down train robber Ronnie Biggs in Brazil, only to return empty-handed when he was refused permission to extradite Biggs back to the UK. Now desperate to salvage his reputation and career, Slipper wanted to meet my informant after hearing about my sorting office result. I was reluctant to deal with Slipper, but as I was keen to sever ties with Tony, who was getting too clever for my liking, I arranged for them to meet. They were welcome to each other.

I loved being on Five Squad. Every day was different and I felt truly excited to be going to work. It was a wonderful experience, beyond my wildest imagination. Perhaps that's why I started to lose some of my grip on reality…

CHAPTER 10

EXIT WOUNDS

Early one damp morning, after a long night wasted on a fruitless observation, Bill Parsons was driving Bill Laver and me through the back streets of Islington when we got a call about a couple of guys who had rented a one-bedroom flat in the area. They weren't locals and had been spending a lot of money on a couple of girls in a pub while making a bit of a nuisance. It was between shifts at the local nick and as they had no CID available to investigate, we were asked if we could take a look while we were passing. After an all-night obbo, it was the last thing we felt like doing, but experience taught us that it was worth investigating. These two high-spending strangers in town could have been a couple of terrorists waiting in the wings, or maybe no-one of any importance at all. There was only one way to find out…

We parked up in a side street next to a large three-storey Edwardian house, which was badly in need of repair. The flat these two guys had rented was on the top floor. Inside, Bill Laver knocked on their door several times, but there was no answer. We could have kicked the door in, but we didn't have a search warrant and as the information was so sketchy, it wasn't worth taking the chance. Either through exhaustion or blind faith, for some reason I volunteered to try looking for signs of life through their bedroom window. There was only one way to do that.

From the third-floor landing, I climbed through a window and out onto a narrow ledge. I started to shuffle across, with my back and arms tightly pressed against the wall. I got a fright when I came to a piece of the ledge that was missing. I managed to step across the gap, but mistakenly looked down at the drop below. I froze for a moment and suddenly came to my senses. 'What the hell am I doing up here?! This is stupid!' But, having committed to my reckless mission, I took a deep breath and managed to make it to the edge of the window.

There was no way I could make the return journey, and I couldn't risk the occupants opening the window and forcing me off the ledge. There was only one thing for it: pressing my arms firmly against the brickwork for purchase, I kicked the window with the heel of my shoe and the glass shattered with one blow. I tumbled straight into the bedroom and quickly scrambled to my feet, miraculously without a scratch on me.

At the same time, the two Bills crashed through the door after hearing the glass shattering. These two young lads and the girls they had picked up all screamed in terror as we burst into their room, pointing guns at them. With adrenaline and relief pumping through my veins, I angrily shouted, 'If you guys had answered the fucking door in the first place this wouldn't have happened!'

The teenagers turned out to be housebreakers from Harlow, who we handed over to the local police once they eventually turned up for their Early shift. I later discovered they confessed to several burglaries in the area, as well as a stolen car. But what had I been thinking? It was clearly not worth risking my life over. When I got home and confessed what I'd done to Pam, she told me I was mad! 'What if you had fallen? What about your family? Didn't you think about us!' My brain was so tired that I couldn't form a logical answer. I simply put up my hands in surrender, kissed her and went to bed.

Pam was delighted and relieved when, a few months later, I was promoted to detective inspector on 6 July 1976 and reassigned to N Division. Once again, this meant leaving the Flying Squad. I didn't want to leave the Fabulous Five, but my promotion came with a substantial pay rise, meaning I could make life more comfortable for my family. Five Squad took me out for a few drinks to celebrate, where I secretly vowed to rejoin my comrades in arms as soon as possible…

As DI, I would be based at 76 King's Cross Road, in an impressive, yellow-stoned Victorian building that had previously served as Clerkenwell Police Station. My new routine was very similar to my time at Golders Green, beginning every morning by checking the crime book in the front office. Once, the desk sergeant pointed out that I had something in my beard. At that time, Sacha had started getting up early in the morning to join me for breakfast. She used to have Ready Brek, which she liked so thick she could stand her spoon upright in it. That morning, she had given me a kiss on the cheek, and I had walked into the station with a lump of the stuff glued to my beard! After signing the books, I would go up to CID and receive updates on the cases my team were working on.

Not long after I had been assigned to King's Cross, we worked on a case that required us to stake out an old warehouse overnight. I arranged for my team to have access to a pair of state-of-the-art night vision binoculars. I thought my son Simon would be interested in this equipment and I drove him down to the observation in my red VW Beetle. After checking in with the troops, I let Simon have a look through the goggles, which turned everything green. As a young kid, he found it all very exciting.

I had expected to feel a similar level of excitement about setting up my own little squad at King's Cross. But to be honest, I felt that these young coppers weren't as engaged or committed as officers I had served with on other divisions. These lads only seemed interested in getting plenty of overtime and claiming expenses, but not in the art of thief taking. It just wasn't the same.

I soon found my new role as DI to be quite boring and mundane. I was now working traditional nine-to-five hours, spending most of my time writing reports. My new rank meant I was no longer required to be out on the jobs as an operator anymore; I had become an administrator, mainly sat at my desk smoking too many cigarettes and thinking, 'What am I doing here?' I wanted to be going back into battle with my fellow knights errant again, chasing down the bad guys. I missed the danger.

After stepping away from the action and taking on a largely deskbound job, I started suffering increased muscular problems, hailing from my spinal injury six years earlier. Maybe the adrenaline that came from life on Five Squad meant that I hadn't felt the pain in recent years. I started going for physiotherapy sessions again, but found that the treatment only offered a little relief. A friend of mine suggested that I might try acupuncture and recommended a male nurse from a local hospital who did home visits. I thought anything was worth a try, even though the recommendation came with a warning that the male nurse was 'a little weird…'

I vividly recall this nurse turning up at the bungalow late at night on an old motorcycle. He wore a shabby billowing raincoat and carried a schoolkid's canvas briefcase, which had comic transfers on the sides. He removed his raincoat to reveal his nurse's uniform… 'Just come off duty?' I asked. He put the briefcase on the dining room table and smiled. 'Acupuncture is a hobby of mine.' I was hit by the overpowering smell of stale tobacco, emanating from beyond his badly stained teeth.

Out of his briefcase, he produced a crumpled medical chart, which he unwrapped and spread out across the dining room table. 'This is what I am going to do…' he announced, as Pam and I exchanged glances. After a reasonably detailed explanation, he produced an Old Holborn tobacco tin. I thought he was about to light one up, but inside were a selection of long needles, each wrapped in cotton wool. At this point, Pam looked to the heavens and left the room. I kept reminding myself that this guy had been highly recommended, so what could possibly go wrong…

I was instructed to take my shirt off and lie face down on the floor. I then felt some strange liquid being rubbed around my neck and shoulders, followed by the odd sensation of the needles being stuck into my body. I just closed my eyes and pretended it wasn't happening. After it was all over, I couldn't wait to get rid of him and pour myself a large drink. But to my complete surprise, I woke up the next morning and felt no pain. Hallelujah! However, after a few weeks the pain came back. Rather than call 'Old Holborn' back in, I decided to just try to live with the pain.

I couldn't wait to finish my posting at King's Cross and made my feelings clear to the powers that be, who organised for me to attend a four-week pre-promotion course at the Police Staff College in Bramshill, Hampshire. For over fifty years, the college was based in a Jacobean mansion and, to fit in with this grandeur, I was required to go to the Lambeth clothing store and get measured for a special uniform to wear on the course. Complete with white gloves and a baton, I looked like a glorified bus conductor. This felt like the wrong move for me.

Sensing my disgruntlement about the course, I was made an offer I couldn't refuse: a vacancy for DCI on the Flying Squad would be coming up next year. If I did the course, I would be assigned my own squad. The chance to return to the Sweeney, this time as guv'nor to my own merry band of crimefighters, was what I wanted more than anything. I couldn't wait to get home and share my exciting news…

When I told Pam, she broke down and pleaded with me not to go back to the Flying Squad.

In our twelve years of marriage, she had never once complained about the unsociable hours I worked, which she understood came with the job. But things had been different since I'd been posted to King's Cross; working regular office hours had meant I had been able to spend more time with her and the kids. The thought of that changing, especially to put myself back in the firing line again, was her limit. 'You've got a son and a daughter. We should be spending time together as a family. What happens if you get injured again? Or worse, you don't come back at all…'

I realised that Pam had hidden her frustrations for a long time, putting my feelings before her own. I loved my family above all, but my desire to return to the action of the Flying Squad had clouded my judgement. I thought I could have it all. But Pam pointed out that if things had been going wrong for Simon and Sacha, I wouldn't have noticed because I wasn't fully present. It never occurred to me the pain and misery I had been causing Pam and the thought of being a neglectful husband and father upset me greatly. It was the reality check that I badly needed.

Once again, I thought back to the film *Bullitt*. The titular detective is confronted by his girlfriend Cathy, played by Jacqueline Bisset, who has stumbled in on a murder scene and noticed how calmly Bullitt examines the corpse of a young woman. 'I thought I knew you. But I'm not so sure anymore.' She tells him he is 'living in a sewer' and he calmly points out, 'That's where the crime is.' But she is having none of it, and continues, 'Your world is so far from the one I know. What will happen to us in time?' Realising he has a choice to make, Bullitt replies, 'Time starts now.'

I knew that if I couldn't get back to the kind of hands-on policing that I knew and loved, that anything else the job had to offer me would only make me unhappy in the long run. Having realised how selfish I had been to my family, I knew it was time for me to leave the force behind me. I put my papers in the next day. My resignation did not go down well…

DISSOLVE TO:
INT. DET. SUPT. ANDREWS' OFFICE. 1977.

BARRY stands at an open door. A SECRETARY places files into DET. SUPT. BOB ANDREWS' in-tray. BARRY's former Best Man is tall, with short dark hair greying at the temples. ANDREWS paces uneasily behind his desk, holding BARRY'S resignation letter. The SECRETARY winks at BARRY as she leaves the office and closes the door.

> BARRY

You wanted to see me, sir?

BOB waves the resignation letter at BARRY.

> ANDREWS

What's this shit?

> BARRY

Looks like my resignation letter.

> ANDREWS

You can't be serious?

> BARRY
>   (lying)

It's something I've been thinking about for some time, sir.

BOB slams the letter down on his desk in disgust.

> ANDREWS

Don't "sir" me, mate! You must be fucking mad?! Throwing your career away like this! You'll make DCI by Christmas!

BARRY shrugs his shoulders.

> ANDREWS

I'm not accepting this, and that's final!

ANDREWS crumples up BARRY's letter and chucks it at the bin in the corner of his office. He misses.

> BARRY

I'd like to do this in a nice, pleasant way, Bob. Stay friends. Have a drink together sometime.

> ANDREWS

Just tell me straight. What the hell's brought on all this crap?

> BARRY

I need to spend more time with my family. My kids are growing up...

                    ANDREWS
              (interrupting)
        Don't bullshit me, Barry! I know you. You're
        hiding something!

BARRY silently waits for ANDREWS to calm down.

                    ANDREWS
        You're not having a fucking midlife crisis are
        you? Wishing you and Pam were back on Majorca
        beach, running around like a couple of lovesick
        teenagers again?

                    BARRY
        With respect, Pam and I are fine. And no, I'm
        not having a midlife crisis. It's just time to
        leave.

                    ANDREWS
        Listen, Barry. I wouldn't do this for anyone
        else. Do me a favour. Just for old times' sake.
        Go and see the shrink at the medical centre.

                    BARRY
        I'd be wasting his time...

ANDREWS flicks through his filofax.

                    ANDREWS
        What's his fucking name again, that shrink?

                    BARRY
        McPatterson...
ANDREWS starts dialling the number.

                    ANDREWS
        I'm telling him you're on your way over and that
        he's to see you immediately. A month's leave,
        that'll straighten you out. Then we'll get you
        back on the road to promotion again.

BARRY shakes his head and smiles to himself as he leaves
the office.

CUT TO:
INT. POLICE MEDICAL CENTRE. LATER.

DR. MCPATTERSON, 50s, spectacles, long greying hair with a bushy beard, wearing an open white smock over a smart tartan shirt. MCPATTERSON leans against the side of his desk and studies BARRY, who is sitting casually on a couch, doing up his tie after a medical examination.

> MCPATTERSON
>
> Many officers, particularly detectives, who come through that door, have turned fighting crime into a personal crusade, like seeking out the holy grail. Much to the detriment of their loved ones, I might add. Your exclusive mission, it seems to me, is chasing down the bad guys. Am I right?

> BARRY
>
> Maybe once. Not anymore.

> MCPATTERSON
>
> Justice for the ordinary Joe, or Jane, so they can safely walk the streets in peace?

BARRY looks around the room and smiles.

> BARRY
>
> I must have left my cape at home.

The phone on the desk rings. MCPATTERSON gestures for BARRY to take a seat opposite him. BARRY removes his jacket from the back of the chair and takes a seat while the doctor speaks.

> MCPATTERSON
>
> (on phone)
>
> Yes. He's here right now. I certainly will.

MCPATTERSON puts the phone down.

> MCPATTERSON
>
> Many people are concerned about you, inspector.

> BARRY
>
> I just want to walk off into the sunset. No fanfare.

> MCPATTERSON
>
> I've been asked to consider giving you a month's leave on medical grounds.

                    BARRY
I wouldn't take it.

                    MCPATTERSON
Why?

                    BARRY
I've neglected my family for long enough. You
said it yourself, the signs were there, I just
missed them or didn't want to see them. I don't
know. I just want to do the right thing now.
Before it's too late.

MCPATTERSON flicks through BARRY's personnel file.

                    MCPATTERSON
You've had several serious injuries in the line
of duty. One almost fatal. I don't think your
body can take anymore. I have enough evidence to
discharge you from the force right now on medical
grounds. Is that what you want, inspector?

                    BARRY
Are you calling my bluff?

                    MCPATTERSON
You've had an exemplary career. There's no shame
in bowing out now, before the job takes an even
heavier toll on your health. Do you want me to
discharge you?

                    BARRY
Yes.

                    MCPATTERSON
You're sure?

                    BARRY
Absolutely.

MCPATTERSON nods. He removes some forms from the top
drawer of his desk and continues talking to BARRY whilst
filling in the paperwork.

                    MCPATTERSON
"What is this life, if full of care. We have no
time to stand and stare."

                    BARRY
        William Henry Davies.

MCPATTERSON looks up with some surprise.
                    MCPATTERSON
        Indeed. A very gifted poet.
                    BARRY
        He was born in Newport, just down the road from
        me.

MCPATTERSON signs his paperwork with a flourish and holds
out the paper to BARRY.
                    MCPATTERSON
        This is your chance to stand and stare, Barry.
        You are now unemployed. Go home to your family.
        Do not go back to the station. Leave them to me.
        You can say your farewells another time.

They stand up and shake hands.
                    BARRY
        Thank you, doctor.

I was discharged from the force on 24 October 1977, after 19 years and 222 days service. My conduct was described as 'Exemplary', which I remain very proud of. None of my mates on Five Squad could believe that I wouldn't be returning to join them. I never discussed my decision with them either. When I had my leaving drinks at a pub in King's Cross, I didn't even stay to the end. While everyone was still drinking away and talking shop, I quietly walked out and left. No fanfare.

When I look back on my two decades in the police, I feel most proud about the fact that I actually enjoyed my job. I loved being a copper and I was lucky to do things that most people only read about or see on television. I got to do it all for real, in vivid black and white. Many retired cops join security firms and instantly regret leaving the job. That wasn't going to be me. Apart from the few ex-cops I have stayed in touch with because they are genuine friends, rather than the only thing we had in common being that we once wore blue serge, I chose to completely cut myself off from the force. I never attended reunions or retirement parties and thought it best to keep moving forward. No going back.

I had no idea what I was going to do for work, or what my future held, but I had faith that somehow, I would make a living. I wasn't going to worry about that yet though – for now I was going to dedicate my life to being a better husband and father. I decided to take twelve months off to purely focus on spending time with my family and enjoy living my new life as a civilian.

It was nice being able to drop the kids off at school and meet some of their friends for the first time. We started taking the dogs out for regular walks together and going to the cinema as a family. I also got to learn more about what my kids were into; Simon was a war gamer and enjoyed painting his own little figures, while Sacha was very sporty and was so passionate about tennis that we helped her join the Northaw & Cuffley Lawn Tennis Club.

As for Pam, we started living like a couple of kids again, forgetting about the future and just enjoying the moment. It was sheer freedom. In the winter, we thought we'd escape the cold and took the kids on a holiday in the Algarve, where we had a wonderful time. One day, we decided to go to Sagres Point, the furthest west you can venture in Portugal. From this incredible landscape, we would be able to look out across the Atlantic and take in the same view that Columbus must have at some point in history.

Standing along this coastal peninsula is a lighthouse, called the Farol do Cabo de São Vicente. But even here, in this vast open space with nobody to be seen for miles around, I couldn't escape the shadow of my career as a law enforcer. When we got to the base of the lighthouse, we found a middle-aged woman standing alone, looking out across the waves. Hearing our footsteps in the gravel, she turned around and, to my utter amazement, she said, 'Hello Barry.' I was speechless and it took me a moment to remember who she was. This lady had worked in the canteen at City Road Police Station back in the Sixties. It already felt like another life.

Back home in Cuffley, I was really enjoying being a nobody, quietly living my life away from the fast lane and blending into the background. I started to feel like an 'ordinary' person again and embraced having time on my hands. I really got into DIY and decided to try and build a stone fireplace. I pictured a large wooden oak beam on top of it, with bookcases standing either side. After sketching out my vision, I knew that I could do some of the labouring but would need some help with the stone bricklaying.

I was introduced to a designer, whose most famous client was Elton John, who said he would be happy to give me a quote for the fireplace. Arriving in a Jaguar, his engaging smile was surrounded by a Mexican moustache and a tuft of hair under his lower lip. His long hair almost masked a looped gold earring. Speaking with a slight Scottish accent, he agreed to take the job on. He told me what stones to order, and we fixed a date.

I duly ordered all the stones and associated materials but come the day this guy never turned up and I couldn't get hold of him. After a few weeks with no follow up, I decided to have a go myself. Having solved murders and foiled million-pound-robberies, how hard could this be? I got all the stones and planned how they could fit together, like a big jigsaw puzzle. I then joined them with cement and by the end of it I had myself a fireplace.

Within moments of taking in my masterpiece, I heard the sound of a car horn on the driveway… It was Elton John's mate! He strolled inside, took one look at the fireplace and asked, 'Have you got a sledgehammer?' After knocking my creation down right in front of me, he said, 'I'm going to need some more gear, I'll be here tomorrow.' This time, he kept his appointment and I have to confess that he did a much better job than I did.

I had started to think about what I might like to do for work. Pam suggested that it might be nice for us to do something together and we decided to try running a pub. I did some digging and found a lease for The Lion, a pub on Barnet Way in Potters Bar, was up for grabs. I applied and to our amazement we got it! We were now proud landlords of our very own boozer and, while the paperwork was being finalised, we both got some experience doing shifts behind the bar at the Two Brewers in Northaw.

The Lion was almost derelict when we got the keys and it needed a good clean. All the other pubs in the area had been modernised and turned into restaurants. Years later, this fate would fall upon The Lion, but not on my watch. We were the last public bar standing in Potters Bar, which proved to be very popular with the locals, who would be knocking on the door at 6:00pm ready for their first sup after work.

I wanted The Lion to have a bit of an ambience, so I played some music on cassette. On the night after opening, a guy came and sat at the bar. He said, 'Nice music.' I thought he was a fellow jazz lover, but he promptly held up his ID and informed me that he was from Performing Rights. 'Can I see your music licence please sir…' Being new to the game, I hadn't even thought about it! I apologised and paid for the licence then and there. That was the first time I'd experienced what it must have been like every time I waved my warrant card in the face of an unsuspecting villain.

The Lion was on the corner of a big junction in Potters Bar, with two housing estates nearby – one containing the overspill from Tottenham, the other catering for Highbury. The fans from both of their football clubs, Tottenham Hotspur and Arsenal, hated each other with a vengeance and every time they played a match, our windows would get smashed by the fans brawling outside.

Aside from these hooligans, we had some very nice customers. One of our greatest regulars was 'Jim the Bin', a remarkably slim man considering how many pints he consumed. I became a good listener to Jim, who was in his 40s and had been a dustman ever since leaving school. In the summer, Jim would take his pint outside and sit on a wall in the car park, where he was prone to falling asleep. People would often watch him through the window, strangely hypnotised as he gently rocked back and forth, still somehow staying upright and never spilling a drop of his pint. But one night, Jim had obviously drunk more than usual. He nodded off and rolled backwards over the other side of the wall, breaking his arm in the fall. We kept a closer eye on him after that!

We were really enjoying running the pub, but disaster struck when we were plagued by regular strikes at the brewery. Our customers didn't stay happy for long when we couldn't serve them any beer. Being a creative thinker, I thought I would get around this by having a go at making my own beverage. After lots of experiments, I created my very own ale, which I christened 'Old Casanova'. All my customers loved it, though arguably people who frequent a public bar during a beer strike will drink anything!

During another strike, we were 'untied' by the brewery, meaning we were allowed to buy beer from other suppliers. I remember going out with Simon to collect a barrel of beer, but because my car was out of action, we had to squeeze this massive steel barrel into the back of Pam's tiny Citroen 2CV. The drive back to the pub was very wobbly. To get barrels into the cellar, I had to lower them down by rope, which was a great workout. But despite all the effort we made, all my real ale regulars asked me if I could get Old Casanova back in instead.

Eventually, after a ropey start, it felt like The Lion was a roaring success. Pam and I couldn't have done it without my parents, who had volunteered to come and help us get the pub all set up before we opened for business. I still didn't feel like I really knew Mum and Dad that well on a personal level, as they were of a generation who didn't really discuss their feelings. But setting up the pub with them did a lot for our relationship and they even stayed on to work a few shifts after we opened, which was lovely.

Dad also showed off his engineering prowess by building my kids a very impressive sledge, which he handmade with incredibly varnished wood and shiny metal runners. Jack and Millie really enjoyed being grandparents and it was interesting for me to see my dad letting Simon and Sacha ride around on his back as he crawled along on his hands and knees. It reminded me of what my parents and I had missed out on during wartime, and I realised how much they had sacrificed. My kids called my dad 'Daddy Jack', which was a spin-off from me asking them to call me 'Barry', as I thought them calling me 'Daddy' would make me feel old.

Whilst working in the pub had brought me closer to my parents, they had their own lives to lead in Gloucester and returned home once they saw we could manage the pub by ourselves. When I went up to visit them later in the year, I discovered that my dad was not well. He had recently had an operation, apparently for ulcers, but he was clearly in a bad way. I urged my mum to get him back into hospital immediately. She did, but sadly he never came back out. Jack Appleton died on 11 June 1979; he was only 59.

I stayed and looked after my mum for a while. I felt sorry for her being left alone and feared that I hadn't done enough to support them, even though I had no idea that dad had been ill. It had all happened so quickly and I'd never imagined that he would die so young. I wish we'd had more time, as there was still so much left unsaid between us. Now it was too late.

If I could relive one moment with my dad, it would be one Saturday morning back in Monmouth during the late 1940s…

DISSOLVE TO:
EXT. BOROUGH ARMS. BACK YARD. SATURDAY MORNING.

BARRY is cleaning JACK's motorbike. JACK leaves the house and calls out to his young son.

          JACK
I'm going down the railway station to load up. I could do with a hand, if you fancy earning some pocket money?

          BARRY
Okay.
CUT TO:
INT. JACK'S VAN. LATER.

JACK drives a large van, which in the week he uses to deliver tins of Kemp's biscuits to shops over a huge area. Every Saturday, the cargo containing next week's goods arrives at the railway station. BARRY enjoys riding in the van, sitting high up with his elbow on the open window, taking in the panoramic view and waving to people. The journey takes about fifteen minutes.

          JACK
What are you going to do with all the pocket money you're earning?

          BARRY
Don't know.

          JACK
Thought you were saving for a racing bike?

          BARRY
I wish. Richard Wills has got a new Raleigh, with dropped handlebars and four speeds. It's the business!

          JACK
Oh yeah? Well, you can forget about that.

          BARRY
It's got lights as well, so he can ride it around at night.

                    JACK
    Can he ride about in a big van like this?
                    BARRY
    I don't think so.
                    JACK
    See, you've got something he hasn't got. Makes
    you even.
                    BARRY
    I suppose so.

BARRY stares out of the window, daydreaming. JACK glances
over at his son and smiles.

CUT TO:
EXT. RAILWAY STATION. PLATFORM. LATER.

BARRY has been helping JACK load up the van in the goods
yard, which has taken about an hour. JACK is now signing
papers at the ticket office. While he waits for his
dad, BARRY stands on the platform. A blue racing bike,
leaning against a bench, partly covered in wrapping,
catches his eye. JACK leaves the office and notices BARRY
looking at the bike.
                    JACK
      That's a nice bike.
                    BARRY
    It's a Runwell. They're really fast.

JACK turns around and calls out to STAN the station
master.
                    JACK
      Stan!

STAN, 50s, almost bald, short, barrel-chested in a
uniform he has outgrown, leaves the ticket office. He has
a jovial manner, keen to please.
                    STAN
      Yes, Jack?

                    JACK
          Who's that bike for? It'll get stolen if you leave
          it leaning there. Want me to deliver it for you?
STAN walks over and examines the bike.
                    STAN
          There should be a label on it somewhere. Oh,
          I haven't got my glasses on. Young Barry, can you
          read the label on it please?

BARRY joins STAN and finds the label.
                    STAN
          What does it say?

BARRY stares at the label in disbelief.
                    BARRY
          It says…
                    STAN
          Yes?
                    BARRY
              (tears in his eyes)
          "To Barry. Thanks for your help. Dad"

BARRY looks over at JACK, who offers him a warm smile.
BARRY runs over and hugs his dad, something he has never
done before.

CHAPTER 11

LAST CHANCE SALOON

Running a pub was much harder work than we had imagined. Once we knew we had a popular boozer that was making money, we invested in a manager to take over the day-to-day duties. We invited a husband-and-wife team to become our live-in managers, including the flat above the pub in our offer. We would work in the day and they would take over in the evenings, which we hoped would allow us to spend a bit more time at home.

Sadly, it didn't work out. Every time we got home for our evening off, the phone would ring. 'We've got trouble.' Whenever I went back, it would be something trivial that they could have easily dealt with themselves. We soon went back to running The Lion full-time ourselves and I hired bar staff from the local estates to come in and help us during the daytime.

Every morning, it was Pam's job to go out and get fresh produce for the lunchtime trade, where we served sandwiches and traditional bar snacks. One day, I was at the bar when I heard a squeal of brakes and a big bang. There were always accidents at the junction outside the pub, so I didn't think much of this latest one and I just carried on pulling pints. A few of the customers went outside to see how bad the accident was and, after a few minutes, one of them came back in, carrying a bag of groceries. 'I don't know how to tell you this Barry. It's Pam. She's been hit by a car.'

A police car pulled up as I rushed outside, where I found Pam lying in the road with a blanket over her. I was told that an ambulance was on its way. Pam said she was okay and told me not to worry. I thanked God she was alive, but I could see she was in discomfort and was putting on a typically stoic face. One of our bar staff kindly offered to hold the fort so I could go with Pam in the ambulance to hospital, where an x-ray revealed that she had broken her pelvis.

During the following weeks, while Pam rested up and recovered, I took over the cooking. Simon and Sacha didn't eat many vegetables in their youth and I thought it was time they started. I began by making something quick and easy – a bubble and squeak stew, full of fresh veg, inspired by my canteen days at City Road. 'Awful and terrible' was Sacha's review and, to this day, she maintains that I put her off stew for life. The next morning, I somehow managed to serve grey eggs for breakfast…

To try and restore my family's confidence in my cooking abilities, I decided to cheat. Opposite The Lion was an upmarket Greek restaurant ran by a sophisticated Cypriot guy called Costas, who we affectionately nicknamed 'Costas a lot!' I confessed that I needed to amaze my family with my cooking skills and Costas kindly provided me with a piping hot duck a l'orange to serve up at home… I wasn't fooling anyone, but I think Pam and the kids were just grateful not to be eating my bubble and squeak.

As Pam got better, she started to teach me how to cook properly, much to the kids' relief. As with many things, Pam was ahead of her time, with one of her specialities being Chinese food. Later, she enrolled in a cordon bleu course, which blew our taste buds away even more. After lots of negotiation with the bar staff, Wednesday became our night off from the pub. As a family, we would alternate into different teams of two, having fun working together in the kitchen cooking different dishes.

We might have been spending more time together than when I'd been in the force, but we were undeniably a lot more tired. Deciding it might be time to change tack, I started applying for different jobs I saw advertised in *The Times*. Rather than assume that nobody would be interested in hiring a 40-year-old ex-copper, I was ambitious with my applications, even though I often had no suitable experience.

One job I applied for on a whim was to be a political agent for the Conservative Party, which would involve working with a Member of Parliament. To my great surprise, we were invited for an interview at their Cambridge office. I say 'we', because they specifically wanted to meet the wives of all the candidates as well…

Come the day of the interview, Pam and I sat down at a large oak desk, behind which sat a frustrated-looking bespectacled man, wearing a flamboyant bow tie. As he looked through my application, he sighed with some relief and explained that we were his last interviewees of the day. A smile then cracked his stern face. 'How nice to see a mature couple for a change.' He then began a twenty-minute rant, telling us about the young men he had interviewed throughout the day, fresh out of university with partners who he deemed 'completely unsuitable…'

'This job involves a lot of entertaining," he continued, "and having the right personality is paramount. I know from my considerable experience that the candidates I have interviewed so far today wouldn't be able to hold their drink on such occasions. They would be an embarrassment to the party and that's before they have shagged their way across the political landscape!' Pam and I offered a polite, if slightly bemused, smile.

The 'interview' ended without us being asked a single question and our host said that we would be informed of the decision the following week... Incredibly, I received a letter telling me that I had got the job. Pam and I couldn't stop laughing. I was to be sent on a political course at Leicester for a few months, before being let loose on the public. But before that could happen, a general election was called, which Margaret Thatcher won on 3 May 1979. Now the Conversative Party was in power, my course was cancelled, along with my new job.

Things might have changed in the political landscape, but not for me on the job front. We were now running the bar six days a week, with the kids upstairs in the flat keeping themselves amused in the evenings. We used to close the pub after the lunchtime rush and then re-open at 6pm. One evening, a group of young people came rushing in as soon as I opened the doors. After I poured each of them half a lager, they sat down and started harmonising, obviously for an act of some kind. It turned out that they were Performance Arts students from the nearby Middlesex Polytechnic.

I took a shine to this bunch of performers and offered that if any of them wanted a part-time job in the evenings, I'd be happy to take them on. I soon had four new recruits, including Peter Walsingham, who told me he was a pianist. With his blessing, I got a piano for the pub and on Sunday evenings Peter would play all the classics, which the customers loved as much as I did. The Lion finally had that great ambience I had dreamt of at the start, which completely revitalised the experience for us.

Peter shared a flat around the corner with another of the students, Alan Riley. One evening, they invited Pam and me back to their apartment for a drink after we closed. We ventured down to the small flat they were renting above a butcher's shop and walked up this narrow staircase, along the balcony and stepped inside. I couldn't believe what I saw… In the middle of this tiny flat was a white baby grand piano, which was almost as big as the room it was standing in. How they got it up there I will never know.

We had a lovely evening as Peter played the piano and Alan performed his brilliant mime act. He then passionately explained his dream of touring the country with a box of handmade masks and a pop-up trestle stage. I loved hanging out with these young creatives, who made quite an impression on me. Their world was so different to mine; they were very relaxed people, living their lives in a romantic way. I found their company very inspiring.

As we walked back to the pub, I found myself saying to Pam, 'I would love to live that kind of life…' She smiled, pleasantly surprised to hear the former detective she loved professing such thoughts. 'What do you mean?' she asked. 'What those guys are doing. Drama and storytelling. I like it.' I barely slept a wink that night, as I pondered whether their creative world had a place for me…

As I got to know the students more, I started opening up about my police career, sharing some of the stories you have read about in this book, as well as others you have yet to discover. I was surprised how my tales of old could captivate a young audience, the age gap between us suddenly evaporating. Alan suggested that I might like to meet his girlfriend, who worked in publishing.

Enter Teresa Howard, also known as Tracy, an impressive young Performing Arts graduate and emerging playwright. Teresa was then working for Gordon & Breach Science Publishers and helping Alan get the Trestle Theatre Company up and running. She came to see me at The Lion on 9 September 1981. We met in the saloon bar, where her positive energy and powerful presence filled the room. Once I'd got Jim and the other regulars fixed up with a pint of Old Casanova, I poured Teresa a glass of wine and started telling her about some of my old Flying Squad adventures, cracking international crime rings and taking on the underworld.

She encouraged me to turn these escapades into a book, enthusing that it could be a best-seller. I joked that I could barely write a postcard, let alone a book, but I promised to get around to it when I had time. She leaned forward and looked me in the eye. 'Make time, Barry. You're a natural storyteller.' Teresa revealed that she had a good friend who was a literary agent and that she would be more than happy to put a word in. She recommended that I write a short treatment for an action-packed book and, as my stories were so visual, that I consider writing a screenplay as well…

At that moment, something changed inside me. This young creative professional wasn't looking at me as an ex-copper working behind a bar, harping on about his glory days. She was talking to me as a fellow writer, one of her own. I was so empowered, I felt like I could walk through a wall. For the rest of that shift, I did my best to calmly pull pints and clean glasses, but behind my eyes, my brain was in overdrive as my imagination started to run wild. A seed had been sown.

The following night was our Wednesday evening off from the pub. Armed with Teresa's encouraging words, I sat down with Pam and spoke to her from the heart. 'I'd like to write a book. I think I can learn how to do it. What do you think?' My soulmate couldn't have been more encouraging and with Pam's support I knew anything was possible. But where to begin? Having long admired the work of John le Carré and Frederick Forsyth, I thought I would try my hand at writing a crime thriller.

My first big idea was for a novel based on my experiences in and around the Colony Club back in the 1960s. I dreamed up a scenario where George Raft hadn't been extradited back to the States, forcing the rival gangs of the Krays and the Richardsons to put their own feuds on temporary hold to try and rid London of the growing presence of the American Mafia.

After writing the idea down on paper, I bought myself an old-fashioned second-hand typewriter, which Pam then used to type up my treatment, along with some information about my background and police career. True to her word, Teresa kindly passed this treatment on to her friend, Lizzie Jackson at Film Rights Ltd. I couldn't believe how quickly I got a response. Just two days later, I received a letter from Lizzie, informing me that my treatment had potential and that they would be willing to represent me as my literary agent. Lizzie suggested we meet once I had a few sample chapters in hand. I couldn't believe I was being taken so seriously and knew this was an opportunity I needed to grasp with both hands. But what about the pub?

I knew we weren't able to just walk away from our only source of income, based on the hope that I might write a bestseller. I'm impulsive, but not crazy. Pam suggested that, as I had made so many DIY improvements to the bungalow during my sabbatical, that we might be able to sell it and make a decent profit. We wanted to stay in Cuffley, as the kids were happy in their schools and we loved being part of the community. We saw a recently built detached house on Homewood Avenue in Cuffley up for sale. It was a decent price and the house would suit us down to the ground. We got it and were able to reduce our mortgage payments so that we could afford to give up the pub and I could dedicate some time to try and make it as a writer.

We both felt a mixture of sadness and relief to be leaving The Lion. It had been very hard work, but we had made a lot of new friends. The customers hired out a hall in Potters Bar to throw a leaving do for us, where Teresa booked a singing telegram to entertain us all. Everyone also clubbed together to buy us a leaving present: a 'hostess trolley' for keeping food warm, which we still treasure and use to this day. After we got home, having closed the saloon doors for the final time, we were so exhausted that we slept until the following lunchtime.

With enough money in the bank to survive for a year, I was now free to try my hand at writing. My new routine was to get up at 5am and write for six hours solid. I placed the typewriter on top of a big Victorian chest of drawers and decided I would write standing up, as I was so used to being on my feet all day and didn't want to start putting on weight. Then at lunchtime, I would go for a long jog, employing an old trick of wrapping a bin liner around me to help sweat and burn off fat.

Getting a decent rhythm going on my new means of expression was initially hard for a one-finger typist, so sometimes I would write down my ideas on pen and paper, which Pam would kindly type up for me and format into proper pages. I still had no knowledge of writing from a technical aspect, but I didn't let that worry me. Once I began writing, the ideas started to pour out, I felt like I'd found my calling and just wanted to write and write. It was a very exhilarating feeling.

Pam and Sacha used to read my writing and point out any mistakes I'd made. I wanted my work to look professional and when I made a mistake, even if I was really tired, I would take out the paper, carefully apply a dab of Tippex, then do my best to carefully type over the mistake once the magic ink had dried. I made so many typos that I quickly went through boxes of the stuff!

I had made a scrapbook of newspaper cuttings during my police career, including many reports about the growing Mafia presence in London during the 1960s, which I used to ground my story in reality. After a couple of months typing full-time, I had my first completed manuscript. The following text is from the prologue of my writing debut, which I called *Let's Kill George Raft*…

The 'Flamingo' in Vegas was the chosen venue for this little gathering of businessmen, who had arranged to hold their 'convention' in a private room on the second floor. When all the delegates were present, the door was locked, security checked and the business in hand put into motion. The big, silver-haired man standing at the end of the table began by outlining their present interest in London and the problems encountered. Then, like a skilful salesman, he gradually paved the way for his own ideas. With open arms, knuckles pressed to the polished tabletop, he leaned forward.

"Our man in London has on good authority the British Government's next move. That, Gentlemen, is why I called this meeting."

The room fell silent, no pencil tapping, no scribbling. The only visual movements were the occasional twitch in their otherwise impassive features and the odd 'Havana' that crossed from one side of an expressionless mouth to the other.

"Their intention is to keep out gambling syndicates by excluding foreign nationals from having one hundred percent stakes in casinos, clubs and all those other joints that bring in a quick buck. So, this is what I'm proposing…"

Because I had enjoyed writing my first novel so much, rather than submit a few sample chapters, I sent the full manuscript to Lizzie in December 1981. I awaited their feedback with huge anticipation. However, the book did not progress any further. Film Rights were concerned about the risk of libel, as the Kray brothers were still alive at this time and, whilst Ronnie and Reggie were serving life sentences, Charlie Kray had been released in 1975 and was looking after the twins' business interests. The potential of a lawsuit meant that no publishers would take a risk on *Lets Kill George Raft*. After such a promising start, I had experienced my first rejection. It would be the first of many.

Any thoughts about a new book had to be put on hold in January 1982, when Pam's mum was rushed to hospital. Rog had been found unconscious on her living room floor by a neighbour and, by the time we got to her, she was in a coma. Three days later, she was taken from us. Rog was one of the good people, with a heart of gold and possessing a great feeling for humanity. A faithful Christian, I am sure there was a place in heaven waiting for her. Pam and I went to church and prayed for her mum many times during this period. We missed her terribly. God bless you, Rog.

It was a while before I returned to the typewriter. When I did, I decided to create a novel that, whilst still drawing on my experiences as a detective, this time only used fictional characters to avoid another risk of libel. *A Walking Shadow* followed the story of Detective Inspector Christos Mackenzie, who had received information about a secret training camp in England, where stolen Turkish gold is being used to finance a terrorist plan to overthrow the Turkish government in Cyprus.

Mackenzie must locate the secret camp before its political significance upsets the balance of the Mediterranean NATO alliance. But he soon encountered a problem: a man holding the plans of the secret base is impersonating the detective. As the political tension rises, so too does the body count. Mackenzie must catch his doppelgänger before time runs out.

The novel begins in a big, rambling old house, tucked away along the tree-lined borders of Hampstead and Swiss Cottage. Mary, a teenager who is ready to leave at the end of her cleaning shift, is surprised to hear the melodious sound of the front door chiming. After adjusting her hair in the hallway mirror, she opens the large mahogany door…

…The large gasp had little chance of developing into a terrified scream as the strong, outstretched gloved hand of one of the hooded men quickly muffled all sound. With thumb and fingers acting in unison, he clamped a vice-like grip to the underside of Mary's cheekbones. The hand lifting her on tiptoe caused a furious back pedal, her delicate frame coming to an abrupt halt against the far wall. He held her rigid body flat against the golden flock, silently allowing her to recover. Cool and unhurried, he waited until her breathing became steadier, the dilated eyes although stricken with fear contracted. Then he leaned and gently whispered in her ear. "Listen carefully Mary. We've got your boyfriend outside. He's safe, nobody's going to hurt him as long as you do as you're told…"

Not exactly le Carré, but I was pleased to have created my first work of complete fiction. But when I submitted *A Walking Shadow* to Film Rights, I realised I had still been very naïve about the world of publishing. Without the real-life true-crime angle, my agent didn't feel confident that they would be able to find a publisher for my novel. It was a rude awakening. I was frustrated; nothing was happening, time was marching on, and my money was running out.

Aware that I hadn't yet found any employment as a writer, our vicar, the Reverend Jim Sykes, offered to try and help me financially through the church. I thanked him for his kind gesture, but politely declined, explaining that there were others much more in need than me. I could survive for another six months, but realistically I knew I needed to get myself another job. For now, the dream was over.

My experience as a pub landlord made me eligible for a role with the Hotel and Catering Industry Training Board. Thanks to the government introducing a scheme where they would pay restaurants to employ kids who wanted to go into catering or hospitality, despite leaving school with little qualifications. I became a coordinator for this scheme, going around schools to recruit kids who wanted work placements in professional kitchens. I would then take them to be fitted up in all their chef whites and find work for them. I started off in Essex and, after I proved successful at the job, I was assigned Cambridge and Bedford.

As rewarding as it was helping these young people, I was still feeling very frustrated that nothing had happened with my writing. Having left the pub with a literary agent in my corner and such high hopes, I still hadn't earned a single penny as a writer. Seeking inspiration, I joined the Cuffley Writers' Circle, a creative workshop run by local librarian Audrey Curzon, a lovely person who became a dear friend. Audrey kindly read *A Walking Shadow* and was very encouraging. She enjoyed reading a crime novel for a change, as most of the other writers in the circle were older women who penned romantic fiction. Some of Audrey's blue-rinse brigade had quite wild imaginations, often making her blush…

Once a year, the Cuffley group joined up with many other writers' circles from across the country for a big convention at St Albans town hall. These annual meetings would always be packed with hundreds of keen hopefuls, all listening intently to the experiences of a guest speaker. At the 1983 event, a book was passed around, in which everyone was invited to write down how much they had earned from writing. Like most of the names on the list, I had to write sweet Foxtrot Alpha. I saw that somebody had earned £80, which at the time seemed like a mind-blowing amount. I remember thinking to myself, 'If only I could earn £80 from my writing, at least I'd feel like I'd made a start.'

I went home that night feeling utterly deflated. I thought I had some good ideas, but now I was back working full-time and felt like my writing 'career' was over before it had even started. I was still at the bottom of the mountain and, lacking inspiration to start climbing again, I confessed to Pam, 'I'm not going to make it. I'm going to have to think of another dream.' But Pam's faith in me never diminished, 'You will make it. Keep going.'

In need of some fresh advice, we invited Teresa over for supper. She had now had her own breakthrough as a writer, with her first full-length play *Grock* lined up to be performed at the Liverpool Lunchtime Theatre. A creative thinker, Teresa suggested I think outside the box and write to all the television companies, offering my services as a technical adviser for any of their police dramas. At this stage, it felt like anything was worth a try…

The Sweeney would have been perfect for me, but wanting to shake off the shadow of Jack Regan, John Thaw was now focusing on working in the theatre. Meanwhile, his former partner in crime-busting Dennis Waterman was starring in *Minder*, a comedy drama for Thames Television. I enjoyed that series and paid close attention to the end credits, where the final caption read: 'Produced by Verity Lambert for Euston Films.' In May 1983, I sent a letter to Verity, along with all the other producers I could find contact details for. A few days later, I received a response:

> Dear Mr Appleton
> Thank you for your letter of 21 May addressed to Verity Lambert.
>> I have passed your letter to our Producers for their future reference.
>> Thank you for thinking of us.
>
>> Yours sincerely
>> KARINA BREWIN
>> Secretary to Lloyd Shirley,
>> Controller, Drama
>> Thames Television Limited
>> Teddington Studios
>> Teddington Lock, Teddington
>> Middlesex TW11 9NT

The days went by and, every time the phone rang, I answered with eager anticipation, hoping it would be a producer offering me my big break. But no-one called and I never had a response to any of my other letters. After the days turned into weeks, I felt thoroughly disillusioned, while the typewriter sat gathering dust. I had failed. When the phone rang on 7 June 1983, I was so depressed that I didn't even bother getting up to answer it.

```
DISSOLVE TO:
INT. HOMEWOOD AVENUE. 1983
```

```
BARRY ignores the phone ringing as he sits in front of
the television, looking the picture of gloom and doom.
The phone is eventually answered by PAM, who rushes
```

```
through from the kitchen to answer it.
                PAM
        Hello?
          (pause)
        Yes?
          (longer pause)
        Yes that's right…

PAM clicks her fingers and waves at BARRY. She covers the
mouthpiece and whispers loudly.
                PAM
          (to BARRY)
        Thames Television!

BARRY jumps out of his chair, like a Flying Squad
detective who has been on a stakeout for three weeks and
finally gets the chance for some action. PAM buys her
husband some time while he composes himself.
                PAM
          (on the phone)
        If you could please hold on, Barry has just
        returned from a Writers' Circle meeting. I'll go
        and get him for you.

PAM places the receiver in BARRY's hand and tenderly
kisses him on the cheek.
                PAM
          (softly)
        Good luck, my love.
```

I took a deep breath and answered the phone. On the other end was the well-spoken voice of Michael Chapman, producer of a Thames programme called *Storyboard*, an anthology series of single plays that also served as pilots for potential new series. Michael had commissioned a script telling the story of a new police constable's first day in uniform.

Having learned of my experience via Karina Brewin, Michael felt I would be well suited to look at the script and assess its accuracy in terms of police procedure. He asked if I would be willing to read the script and then meet him in person to discuss my thoughts. I did my best to play it cool and thanked him for the opportunity. After the call, I said a thankful prayer. The next day, the script arrived by courier, enclosed with a letter:

> Dear Barry,
> Herewith, the script WOODENTOP by Geoff McQueen, which I hope you will find interesting – and not too full of holes!
> I look forward to meeting you.
>
> Yours sincerely,
> MICHAEL CHAPMAN
> Producer
> STORYBOARD

Six years after leaving the police force, my old friend fate had finally returned to my side, ready to partner me once more as I began an unbelievable journey back onto the beat of London's East End…

CHAPTER 12

FITTING THE BILL

The script for *Woodentop* told the story of young probationer Jim Carver working his first day as a police constable. My letter to Verity Lambert had landed on Michael Chapman's desk just at the moment he had been unable to get hold of the script's writer. Geoff McQueen had since been commissioned to create a new series for the BBC called *Big Deal,* making him unavailable for further rewrites. My job was to assess the script and check that everything was accurate from a police perspective.

Michael Chapman had already been working in television for twenty-five years. Prior to this he had served in the Royal Navy, before working in the Civil Service Guided Weapons and Electronic Defence Department, where after an extensive vetting process, he was allowed access to highly sensitive information, including the nuclear codes. Since then, he had written many hours of television, including crime dramas *Public Eye*, *Special Branch* and *Van der Valk.*

The *Woodentop* script needed a lot of work; parts of it were handwritten and there was Tippex all over it, meaning Michael was not yet in a position to hand it over to a director. I made copious notes about the story, which had some interesting ideas, but had clearly not been written by a copper. I also found my own imagination firing up with ideas. I was to present my thoughts to Michael at Thames' Euston Road studios the following day, where together we would work out how to finish the script.

I don't know who was more excited, me or Pam, as I left home the next morning. She gave me a kiss and wished me luck. It was a glorious day and the sun was shining. Finally, something was happening. I was dressed very casually, wearing a smart lightweight sports jacket and stonewashed jeans. I arrived bang on time.

DISSOLVE TO:
INT. THAMES TELEVISION STUDIOS. EUSTON ROAD. 1983.

BARRY makes his entrance through a set of blue revolving
doors. Waiting at reception is MICHAEL CHAPMAN, mid-50s,
tall, a distinguished looking gentleman with a twinkle
in his eye. He wears a smart brown suit jacket and black
tie. He greets BARRY with a firm handshake and a warm
smile.

>MICHAEL
Nice to meet you, Barry. Fancy a bite to eat?

CUT TO:
INT. THAMES TELEVISION STUDIOS. CORRIDOR.

MICHAEL and BARRY walk and talk as they make their way
to the canteen.

>BARRY
I don't see any signs for Studios 1-3?

>MICHAEL
I can see you were a detective. Well spotted.
Studios 1-3 are down at Teddington, where our
comedy and drama productions are made. Here at
Euston, Studios 4-6 produce Thames' news, current
affairs, schools and religious programmes. As you
were coming from Cuffley, I thought this would
make a convenient halfway point.

CUT TO:
INT. THAMES TELEVISION STUDIOS. CANTEEN.

BARRY and MICHAEL sit at a table, adorned with a couple
of empty plates and beer glasses. MICHAEL is reading the
last page of BARRY's detailed notes about the *Woodentop*
script.

>MICHAEL
Thank you for your valuable contribution, Barry.
I'm very impressed. You've put my mind at ease
on a number of things that were troubling me in
this script.

> BARRY
> The main problem is that a young single man does not live at home, no matter how convenient. Maybe if this was Dixon of Dock Green it would be nice and cosy and might work. But the Met have spent millions on section houses to house single officers, who are readily available at any time in an emergency. Jim Carver would be living in a shared building like I did as a young bobby.
>
> MICHAEL
> We will get over this somehow. Now that Geoff McQueen is writing a series for the BBC, I will have to rely upon you some more, especially if *Woodentop* becomes a series. We have almost finished casting all the parts and will be having a readthrough later this month. Would you be able to join us? I would pay you for your time of course.
>
> BARRY
> I'd be delighted.

The readthrough for *Woodentop* took place on 29 June 1983 at 11am in the Steadfast Sea Cadet Hall, Kingston-Upon-Thames. I arrived early to have a coffee with other members of the team and was introduced to director Peter Cregeen, who had a wealth of experience directing police dramas like *Z Cars* and *Softly, Softly*. Peter had just finished work on the espionage series *The Sandbaggers* and his extensive theatre background meant that he was an expert with actors, as I was about to witness.

The readthrough began with Peter introducing each of the cast around the table. Playing rookie PC Jim Carver was Mark Wingett, who had already made a name for himself on the big screen, starring in the British film *Quadrophenia*. Sitting next to him was Trudie Goodwin, who had shone in Euston Films' gritty crime series *Fox*. She would be playing WPC June Ackland, who would be 'puppy-walking' Carver on his first day. Completing the main cast around the table were Gary Olsen as PC Litten, Colin Blumenau as PC Morgan, Peter Dean as Sgt. Wilding, Jon Croft as Inspector Deeping and Robert Pugh as Detective Inspector Galloway. They each read their lines out loud, while Peter called out the action and Isobel

Neil the PA wrote down the timings of each scene using a stopwatch. It was fascinating watching all these actors, dressed in their civvies, reading out the dialogue like a play.

After the reading, a number of the actors ran outside and made the most of the hot weather by diving in the Thames for a swim. It was a pleasant atmosphere and I was very happy to have been invited. Peter Cregeen thanked me for my time and asked if I would be able to join them on 5 July, when they would be shooting scenes on location, featuring Carver and Ackland discovering human remains in a flat on their beat. Thankfully that realistic scene was shot after breakfast, so it didn't put me off my bacon butty! Whilst I was 'tucking in' with the rest of the cast and crew at the catering wagon, I remember thinking, 'I could get used to this.'

Peter Cregeen had been impressed by *Police*, Roger Graef's fly-on-the-wall documentary about the Thames Valley Police the previous year, which inspired him to approach *Woodentop* in a similar style. A hand-held camera would be used to follow the actors on location, shooting on videotape rather than film, which at the time was very unusual for a drama production. The aim was to represent that documentary 'look' and I was very blown away watching camera operator Roy Easton following the actors around, especially considering the large and cumbersome television camera on his shoulder, which looked incredibly heavy. I felt a shiver up my occasionally tender spine.

After the location shooting wrapped, Peter invited me to attend a run-through of the interior scenes at Teddington Studios on 11 July. Set mainly in the police station, these scenes would be shot in a more traditional multi-camera studio environment. Until now, the actors had only rehearsed these scenes in the Sea Cadet Hall, with tape on the floor marking out the various sets. Now, they would get the full experience working with props and in costume.

Part of my brief from Michael Chapman was to help the designers understand exactly how the station sets should be laid out in the studio. I also helped the stage manager with all the little details for dressing the set, from what kind of paperwork would be on each officer's desk, to the posters on the walls. During my time teaching at the Detective Training School, I'd had an e-fit photo of my face created to show the process to the students. I'd kept this and gave it to Philip Blowers, the designer, who put it up on the Sun Hill station set. That's my cameo in *Woodentop*.

Recording a television programme is a huge operation and I could not believe how many people were involved, all working hard on the various ingredients that helped make the final product. Once the studio recording began, I was very reluctant to interfere, but I was surprised to spot a continuity error. Jon Croft, playing Inspector Deeping, had started off as a chief inspector with three pips on his lapels. But when shooting a later scene, for some unknown reason, his costume now only had two pips.

I put my hand up and stopped production, which I later learned is a rare and very costly thing to do during a studio recording. All eyes were on me, including Michael Chapman's. 'I'm sorry to do this, but Inspector Deeping has been demoted.' There was a big panic by the wardrobe department, followed by a large sigh by everyone else. I worried that I'd done the wrong thing, but Michael came over, patted me on the back and said, 'Thank you, Barry. That would have been bad if it had gone out unnoticed.'

Personally, I felt these interior scenes lost the edge that the handheld camera offered on location. Michael explained to me the huge cost difference between shooting with an Outside Broadcast camera unit, versus using the studios, where all the lighting and sound can be controlled. I was enjoying learning about the craft of making television, soaking up information like a sponge.

Just over a month after the studio recording, *Woodentop* was broadcast on 16 August 1983. Michael arranged for me to be credited as the programme's Technical Adviser and, after the credits rolled, our phone rang at home. It was my mum, who couldn't believe that her son's name had been on television. Millie was among the 15 million viewers who watched the pilot, which also went down well with the critics.

A short while later, Michael Chapman called me to reveal that Thames had commissioned a twelve-part series and he invited me to act as technical adviser for the whole run. I would be paid £190 per episode, plus an additional £60 for three days' attendance at the studios per week, which meant I could give up my job with the Hotel and Catering Industry Training Board. I was very grateful to Michael for this incredible opportunity. Then came the magic moment. Michael said, 'I know you have done some writing. Would you be able to give me a story idea on a single page?' Boom! I wasn't going to miss a chance like this and got straight to work.

I presented my story outline to Michael in person the following lunchtime, on board Teddington Studios' floating barge restaurant that was moored along the bank of the river Thames. As we climbed aboard, I noticed we were walking behind two of Thames' biggest stars: Des O'Connor and Freddie Starr, the latter seemingly in a permanent state of performance. As Michael and I looked for a free table in the heaving restaurant, Freddie Starr spotted a man with a plaster cast on his leg, sitting at a table with other Thames execs. The man's crutches were leaning against the chair opposite. As Starr passed, he picked up the man's crutches, threw them into Teddington Lock and carried on walking, taking the vacant chair with him… Michael looked heavenward and suggested we find a table on the other side of the restaurant…

```
DISSOLVE TO:
INT. TEDDINGTON STUDIOS. BARGE RESTAURANT. 1983.

BARRY and MICHAEL are enjoying an ice-cold lager,
courtesy of Thames Television. It is now time to get
down to business.

          MICHAEL
     Were you able to put together a storyline for me?

BARRY takes a single folded page of A4 from his
inside jacket pocket and hands it to MICHAEL.

          BARRY
     It's called 'A Dangerous Breed'. Would you like
     another beer, Michael?

          MICHAEL
     Excellent. Yes please, thank you, Barry.

BARRY goes over to the bar and orders a couple of beers,
while MICHAEL reads the page. As BARRY returns to the
table, MICHAEL puts down his story premise.
```

```
          BARRY
     It's been a long time since I awaited a verdict.
          MICHAEL
        (smiling)
     This is great, Barry. Low key, just as I suggested.
     I'm going to commission you to write this episode.
          BARRY
     Thank you very much, Michael. Cheers.


They clink glasses.
          MICHAEL
     Cheers. You don't have another idea by any chance?


BARRY reaches into his other inside jacket pocket.
          BARRY
        As it happens…
```

I had brought along a second idea, just in case Michael didn't like the first. It turned out that he liked them both. All of a sudden, a 'nobody' like me was enjoying a beer with a television executive, being commissioned to write two episodes of a major drama series. That simply wouldn't happen now and I was beyond grateful to Michael for this lifechanging opportunity. I would be paid £1,300 per script which, when compared to my £9.7.10 a week as a beat bobby twenty-five years earlier, showed me it was clearly more lucrative to write about being a police officer than being one.

Now with my technical adviser hat on, I gave Michael my honest opinion about the proposed title for the series, *Woodentops*. 'Michael, you cannot call the series *Woodentops*. It's derogatory and I will struggle to get any of the actors into real police stations with that title attached.' Michael was a great listener, and he asked me to go away and suggest some options for a title.

I came up with seven ideas for a new title, including *On The Cobbles*, a nod to the East End side streets I had myself policed, which I knew would feature prominently in the series. At the end of my list, I wrote a little pun… 'I hope one of these fits *The Bill*…' And that was the one that Michael chose! He had also liked *On the Cobbles*, which inspired the famous end credits showing the feet of two officers walking down a cobbled street. Looking back now, I realise how much input I had on the programme.

Having had no success with either of my novel submissions to Film Rights Ltd, I was keen to find a new agent to represent me and handle the money side of my burgeoning career as a scriptwriter. There was only one person I wanted in my corner. Having been so instrumental in getting me started as a writer and been the person to suggest I offer my services as a technical adviser, Teresa Howard was now working at Dr Jan Van Loewen Ltd, a literary agency with offices in the UK and USA.

Teresa set up a meeting for me and her boss, Alan Brodie, at their office in Carnaby Street. I remember going up the stairs and seeing all these lovely pictures of famous writers like Terence Rattigan and Noel Coward, whose estates they managed. Not bad company to keep. Alan offered me exclusive representation, with Teresa acting as my agent. With the admin side sorted, I could now focus on writing my first television script.

For my first *The Bill* story, titled 'A Dangerous Breed', I used a few key ingredients from my police career as a basis for my story, from building relationships with snouts, to tracking down stolen goods. Gary Olsen's character of PC Litten was desperate to prove himself to DI Galloway and join the CID. My story would see Litten on attachment to CID as an aide, just like I had been. Where my imagination took over was having Litten investigate the theft of a priceless necklace and, eager to prove himself and claim all the glory, he would encounter the pitfalls of taking anonymous calls from mystery informants.

I was given a six-week deadline to write the first draft of my script. Pam helped me with the formatting and gave me lots of encouragement, as did Teresa, who then submitted the script to Michael. With bated breath, I waited for feedback, which came to me directly by letter on 21 November 1983:

Dear Barry,
Thank you very much for the script.
    I liked it very much. I think it is a very neat story, nicely told. There are one or two small things that need taking care of, but I will ring you and fix up a time to meet and discuss.

'Good on yer', as they say in another place!

Yours sincerely,
MICHAEL CHAPMAN

I hadn't felt a shot of adrenaline like this since my days on Five Squad. I was off and running. I met up again with Michael, who gave me some valuable feedback, before outlining some important changes for the series. As with *Woodentop*, they would shoot the series on videotape, but this time there would be no studio filming at Teddington. Instead, they were planning on creating their own purpose-built police station on location in the East End. This was groundbreaking – nothing like this had ever been attempted in television before.

There would also be some changes to the cast. Mark Wingett, Trudie Goodwin, Gary Olsen and Colin Blumenau would all be retained from *Woodentop* to play the four central uniformed PC characters. The character of Sergeant Wilding was to be replaced by a new sergeant, and instead of Inspector Deeping, Sun Hill Police Station would now have an in-house chief super. DI Galloway would return from *Woodentop*, but actor Robert Pugh had declined the invitation to return. Also joining Galloway in CID would be two newly created detective characters.

Just over four months later, 'A Dangerous Breed' became the first episode of *The Bill* to be shot. Peter Cregeen would be returning to direct a later block of episodes, but for now he was still engaged on another Thames series called *Mitch*, starring John Thaw. In the director's chair for this first episode in production was Chris Hodson, already something of a television veteran, having been directing programmes since the late 1950s.

As technical adviser, I would attend the read-through for every episode, which would take place on the Friday afternoon before shooting began the following Monday. The first ever cast readthrough for *The Bill* took place on 6 April 1984, which is when I got to meet the new additions to the cast.

Cast as Sgt. Bob Cryer was Eric Richard, an experienced character actor who had just worked with Peter Cregeen on *Mitch*. Eric was spotted by casting director Pat O'Connell in a stage play called *Red Saturday*, where he had a clear chemistry with his red-haired co-star, a young actor called John Salthouse. John was a familiar face, having starred opposite Alison

Steadman in the celebrated TV play *Abigail's Party*. John was only 32 when he was cast as DI Roy Galloway, a conscious choice by Michael Chapman, who wanted a reasonably young cast at the heart of the programme.

Another young actor present was Jon Iles, a very tall and handsome man with a pedigree for comedy, cast to play Sun Hill's Detective Constable Mike Dashwood. Rounding out the CID team as Detective Sergeant Ted Roach was Tony Scannell, a fiery Irish actor who had so far specialised in playing villains on television.

These new faces, along with the *Woodentop* returnees, were the original eight regular cast members of *The Bill*. Two actors with considerable theatre credentials had also been cast as semi-regulars: Peter Ellis as Chief Supt. Charles Brownlow and Roger Leach as Sgt. Tom Penny. Neither character had been devised when I wrote 'A Dangerous Breed', so they were not in this episode.

I immediately built up a rapport with John Salthouse, who on learning I was a former detective was very keen to pick my brains. We started talking about boxing and I mentioned that Dick Richardson was one of my heroes. John replied: 'You're not going to believe this, my dad trained Dick Richardson in the Army. When he finished his National Service, Dick came and lived with us, he even shared my bedroom! Dad got Dick a job as a milkman and continued training him until he turned professional.'

For the next three years, I would work very closely with John, who would often call me at home with questions or ideas, he was so committed to the series. I gave John one of my old Flying Squad ties, depicting an eagle, which he proudly added to his costume for extra authenticity. John learned a lot about the police from me, and in turn I learned a lot about the television business from him. It was John who tipped me off that Chris Hodson was known as 'a safe pair of hands', a director who brings everything in on time and within budget. 'He's very dependable.' Reading between the lines, I think John was telling me not to get my hopes up for how dynamic my first episode might look on screen…

On Monday, 9 April, the first day of shooting on *The Bill* got off to a disastrous start. The production team had created Sun Hill station in an abandoned warehouse at Artichoke Hill in the East End. In those days, television production was heavily unionised and because the OB camera team were told they would not be paid for their travel time from Teddington Studios, they refused to leave base early and arrived late. By the time they got on location and set up, precious time had been lost, forcing director Chris Hodson to abandon his shooting script and shoot it on the fly. There was a feeling in the air that some of the team didn't like this new way of making a programme and were willing it not to succeed.

Another new approach in the pursuit of realism was a first for television drama. Unlike *Woodentop*, there would be no rehearsal period on *The Bill*, just the one read-through before a two-week shoot per episode. This was unheard of at the time and, watching *A Dangerous Breed* back now all these years later, I can see that whilst I was still honing my craft as a writer, the cast were also finding their feet on this first episode committed to tape, having not quite worked out how to play their characters yet. The exception to this was Eric Richard, who embodied Bob Cryer immediately. He was born to play that part.

Perhaps wisely, 'A Dangerous Breed' was broadcast halfway through the first series, which opened instead with a Peter Cregeen directed episode called 'It's A Funny Ol' Business – Cops and Robbers', written by McQueen. Peter felt that Sun Hill station needed to be a hive of activity and cast a number of young actors to play supporting characters, including Nula Conwell as WPC Viv Martella, Ashley Gunstock as PC Robin Frank, Robert Hudson as PC 'Yorkie' Smith and Jeff Stewart as PC Reg Hollis. Also cast, initially for just one episode, was seasoned actor Larry Dann as Sgt. Alec Peters. As time went on, all these characters would become more prominent in the series and each actor got plenty of chances to shine. They were all a pleasure to write for.

My first episode to be broadcast for the series was my second script, 'A Friend In Need', which saw Carver accused of stealing a drunk's wallet after helping him home, his good deed backfiring and his short police career already in jeopardy. Michael Chapman was very encouraging and never interfered with my scripts, he would simply tell me if he needed less or more of a particular theme or character. He offered great advice, reminding me to, 'Keep it low key, don't get too dramatic.'

Naturally, we were all very excited to watch 'A Friend In Need' when it was broadcast on 23 October 1984. At home, the Appleton family did so in rather unusual company… joining us in our living room was Geoff McQueen, who had called me up to say his TV was being repaired and that he didn't want to miss my first episode of *his* show… We hadn't previously met, as he was never present for readthroughs and I think he thought I was trying to take over and wanted to suss me out. The fact is, I was available for Michael whenever he needed me, whereas McQueen wasn't.

We made him welcome and after savouring Pam's excellent cooking, we all sat and watched the episode together. The kids cheered when 'By Barry Appleton' appeared on the screen in huge letters and I must admit, I felt a few butterflies myself at that very special moment. I thought 'Flying Squad cop to TV script writer… what a journey!' McQueen just sat and watched the episode very quietly. By the end of the night, I think we both knew we were never going to be best buddies. We were very different people.

Things were really taking off for me. Not only was I now a televised screenwriter, but Teresa had found a publisher for my novel *A Walking Shadow*. Thanks to her diligence, the hardback was published in the UK by Robert Hale on 20 September 1984, to tie in with the first series of *The Bill*. The book never became a bestseller, despite Teresa organising some nice publicity for me. But I was more excited about the possibility of adapting the novel into a television drama, which Teresa was now pitching to different ITV companies. Suddenly everything was happening.

Having got my first two scripts under my belt, my confidence began to grow and I started to feel like I was tailor made to write *The Bill*. Tapping into more of my own experiences as a police officer helped me create more authentic and gritty storylines, which was exactly what Michael was looking for. He continued to encourage me and ultimately commissioned me to write eight of the first twelve episodes, becoming his lead writer.

My next offering was 'It's Not Such A Bad Job After All', where I decided to develop the characters more and explore what made them tick. I started off with June Ackland, who I wrote as being increasingly disillusioned with the job and ready to quit. Trudie Goodwin seized this opportunity, giving a brilliant performance. Ackland is first on the scene when the body of a teenage girl is found in the woods and June finds herself on the receiving end of Galloway's bad temper early on a Sunday morning.

I based this scene on a suicide I had attended myself as a detective. I'll never forget gently opening this young student's suicide note, exactly as John Salthouse does on screen. The girl's note wasn't addressed to anybody, but at the end she had written 'I would like to give my record collection to my friend Jessie'. I found this terribly moving and incorporated a similar gesture into my script. John Salthouse then delivers one of my favourite lines in *The Bill*. Standing over the body he grimly explains, 'There's parents out there, you know… who still think they've got a daughter.'

I then had Bob Cryer take the parents down to the mortuary to identify their daughter, the very same procedure I had performed as a detective. That couple were understandably overcome with emotion, grief and despair at the sight of their beautiful daughter, and I arranged for someone to take them away. What I didn't include in the script was my own emotional experience after they left. As I signed some forms in the office, I noticed that one of the drawers in the mortuary was open. Inside was the body of a baby. What struck me most was that somebody had placed a single red rose in the drawer alongside the dead baby. Even for a hard-nosed cop who had seen many a corpse, that has haunted me ever since.

Galloway discovers that the suicide girl has been embroiled in a life of drugs, prostitution and pornography and, worst of all, was pregnant at the time of her death. He pulls out all the stops to protect her parents from the truth and to catch those responsible. I knew how much harder a case like that would have been for me as a detective had I not had Pam's support, so I decided to introduce an unhappy family backstory for Galloway, with his wife calling the station to complain about him working on a Sunday and neglecting their daughter.

Script editor John Kershaw was initially reluctant to include this and I later learned that McQueen wasn't very happy about these character developments either. Their plan had been to stick strictly to the cases and keep anything about the characters' personal lives a mystery. Luckily for me, Michael Chapman loved my approach, as long as we showed how their personal lives affected them on the job in the station. He encouraged me to continue developing strands for the characters.

On cases like the one at the heart of 'It's Not Such A Bad Job After All', police officers put in a lot of hard graft, working all hours of the day.

You end up drinking too much booze and smoking far too many cigarettes. This episode not only demonstrated that, but also showed that when a promising young officer like Ackland keeps getting all the dirty jobs, they can't help but question why they do it. Then when you get a decent result and everybody comes together, it doesn't feel like such a bad job after all…

This episode was the first time I worked with John Woods, a young director who had worked his way up through the ranks of the children's department at Thames. Having directed classic series like *Rainbow* and *The Sooty Show*, John was now relishing the chance to make his mark on a primetime drama series. In my role as technical adviser, John had me coming down to Artichoke Hill almost daily, asking me 'What would happen if we did this?' I was starting to see my scripts from a director's point of view and John taught me so much about drama.

I was pleased when John was assigned to direct my next script, 'The Drugs Raid', which was my favourite from the first series. This hard-hitting episode saw drug dealers operating on a local estate and the concerned residents demanding action from the police. Galloway mounts a huge raid on a derelict cinema, which was an easy operation for me to bring to life accurately on paper, having been on so many in my police career.

Later in the episode, Galloway goes to court to apply for a search warrant. As John Salthouse enters the courtroom, standing behind him in a brown leather jacket is yours truly. Having made sure that the courtroom was set up correctly for filming, John Woods invited me to make a cameo. Standing with me is my old Five Squad partner Bill Laver, whom I brought along to show what this television lark was all about. The scene ends with the judge signing off Galloway's search warrant, attached to which he subtly adds a handwritten note that reads 'Good luck'. The two men exchange a knowing look and a smile across the crowded courtroom. This was the kind of little detail that only a copper would know about, which helped sell the series as the real deal.

The challenge was to throw in some dramatic licence, and none of my raids ever went as badly as Galloway's. His snout is found wounded at the scene with severe knife wounds, having been sussed and stabbed by the gang leader, who makes his escape in a car fitted with diplomatic plates. The final showdown between Galloway, Brownlow and members of the

Home Office is brilliantly played, with John Salthouse and the perfectly cast Peter Ellis both delivering knockout performances.

I was very keen to add humour into my scripts and to balance out the darker moments of 'The Drugs Raid', I created a character called Maggie, a tramp and habitual thief of tins of salmon. John Woods cast the phenomenal Liz Smith to play Maggie, years before she found fame in *The Royle Family* and *The Vicar of Dibley*. Maggie is well-known to the Sun Hill mob and when filling in her charge sheet, Cryer jokes that Maggie 'must have more tins of salmon than John West!' John Kershaw had reservations about this level of humour, but I explained that banter was a vital part of how police officers communicated with their regulars. With twenty years' experience as a copper, I was hard to argue with.

Next up for me was 'Burning The Books', an episode in which CID are trying to track down a stolen briefcase. The investigation builds to a cat-and-mouse chase between Galloway and an old adversary called Cohen, a dodgy purveyor of illegal pornography magazines. A couple of weeks after the episode was shown, I got a letter from the actor Max Bygraves, who wrote to say he thought the episode was 'the best thing I've seen on television for a long, long time'. It turned out he was a friend of John Blythe, the actor who had played the villainous Cohen. Bygraves finished by asking me to write an episode of *The Bill* for him... 'In fact, why not write me a series!' I was very flattered by this, but I never got around to dreaming up a vehicle for the legendary comedian.

My next adventure was 'Death of a Cracksman', which saw Sgt. Cryer trying to track down old-school safe-cracker Alfie Mullins, who has not returned to prison. This wasn't *Dixon of Dock Green*, but in Bob Cryer we had a wonderful character who knew all the history of Sun Hill and its inhabitants. He knows Alfie of old and, whilst Alfie is not a dangerous man, Bob plays a straight game and wants him back behind bars where he belongs.

Before we started filming, I met Eric Richard regularly for a quiet drink, as he wanted to do as much homework as possible prior to starting work on the series. The results are on screen and an early example of this is in 'Death of a Cracksman', which features a wonderful long lens shot of Eric walking through a crowd of people, telling Colin Blumenau's character of Taffy Edwards all about Alfie Mullins. Surrounded by members of the public, with a few actors planted along the way for Eric to interact with, that superb shot lasts for three minutes and shows how Eric completely owned his character. A true master of his craft.

Once the series began being broadcast, our low-key drinks together went out the window, as *The Bill* turned Eric into a high-profile star. We once met for a drink in a Cambridge pub where, even miles away from the Smoke, Eric was besieged by autograph hunters. Being such a gentleman, he told the crowd they should be asking for *my* autograph instead, explaining I was the writer of the stories they had enjoyed so much. Eric, you're a class act.

'Death of a Cracksman' features three wannabe robbers trying to blow open a safe. They try to enlist Alfie Mullins' help, but he doesn't want to know. During a heated exchange, Alfie trips over on the pavement and dies. All this was shown without a copper being present. Peter Cregeen would later introduce the rule that every scene would be shown from a police point of view; if our characters didn't witness a crime happening, then the viewer wouldn't either. This brilliant idea became *The Bill*'s USP and offered a great challenge for a writer, which in my opinion, ultimately benefited the show.

Peter was in the director's chair for 'The Sweet Smell of Failure', my next episode based on an old Flying Squad case, which was an interesting and complicated investigation. Five Squad had received information from a private investigation agency, hired by a major international perfume company, that criminals were manufacturing fake perfume and selling bottles labelled with this well-known brand. The contents could be any nice smelling concoction, but the bottles had to look perfect to fool the customer – and they did.

We discovered the small glass manufacturer making the fake bottles and, on the day we thought the bottles would be collected, we set up an observation from a care home opposite. The elderly residents, who were supposed to be playing Bingo, were very interested by our presence and kept coming to join us from our vantage point to look through our binoculars. Mid-morning, a van pulled up and we saw the bottles being loaded and signed for. All we had to do now was follow the courier to catch our culprits…

We pursued the van through the streets of London, passing all the famous landmarks of Big Ben and Westminster Abbey, until eventually the courier stopped at its final destination: outside New Scotland Yard! The courier got out and delivered the bottles to reception. When we went inside, we discovered the box was labelled 'FAO The Flying Squad'. Having realised they had been rumbled, someone had been very clever and whoever arranged this clearly had a great sense of humour. The perfume company were still pleased when the fake company closed down their operations, for the time being at least.

This caper formed the basis for 'The Sweet Smell of Failure', where I also had to include a rather unusual request from Michael. Tony Scannell, who played DS Ted Roach, arrived at Artichoke Hill with horrible facial injuries, after apparently trying to stop two men from mugging an old lady. I had to weave in a bit of dialogue referencing his significant black eye which, after the episode was shown, caused a viewer to write in complaining that Scannell's 'make-up' was over the top.

Ted Roach took centre stage in what was planned to be the final episode of the first series, 'The Chief Super's Party'. This episode featured Brownlow's clerk retiring and most of the relief attending a celebratory bash. Roach ignores Galloway's advice about taking it easy on the Scotch and drives home drunk, ploughing his car straight into a residential garden. Knowing his career would be over if caught, the detective flees the scene, leaving his colleagues to pick up the pieces and cover his tracks.

The main flaw in Roach's plan is PC Reg Hollis. Every station has a Reg: a copper who never seems to be doing any actual policing, but does just enough to justify his presence in the job. Craving an even easier life, Hollis would love to become the chief super's new clerk and thinks ringing Brownlow at home to grass on Roach could lead to him winning favour.

I had not originally written Hollis as the station nark, but whilst discussing the casting of this new character with Peter Cregeen in the canteen, John Salthouse pointed out that we already had the perfect man for the job sat a few tables along. John never saw himself as the leading man on the series, but his passion for the series was clear as day and he would often make suggestions which helped give opportunities to other actors in the cast. Jeff Stewart had initially been cast by Peter as one of the young supporting actors to help bring the station to life, but Reg Hollis would become one of the most iconic and long-running characters in *The Bill*.

'The Chief Super's Party' was planned to close the first series on 29 January 1985… But it wasn't shown. Halfway through shooting, an industrial dispute forced production to close down, and the story was shelved, meaning the first series was made up of only eleven completed episodes. Whilst disappointing for all concerned, Michael assured me that the party would go on if we were commissioned for a second series.

Despite not ending on the intended grand finale, my entire life had changed overnight because of *The Bill*. Teresa even told me I was being referred to as Thames' 'Golden Boy'. Most remarkable for me was when I attended the next Writers' Circle event in Cuffley, this time as guest of honour, where I did my best to encourage everyone present that they could make it too. I couldn't believe that a year on from going home to Pam and threatening to give up my dream, I had gone from zero to hero, thanks to Michael Chapman. Little did I know that this was only the beginning…

CHAPTER 13

THE REAL DEAL

Scriptwriting had come naturally to me, which was a miracle I was very grateful for. But after the first series of *The Bill*, I was worried that the balloon might burst and I'd find myself back at square one. I thought the best way to try and prevent that was to just keep writing. To begin my second year as a screenwriter, I decided to retire my second-hand typewriter and invest in a Brother electric model, which came with a small dot matrix memory bank. This meant I could type a sentence and preview it on a small screen then, after correcting any mistakes, the typewriter would print out my sentence onto the paper for me. This was state of the art technology at the time and was going to make a huge difference.

I found I did my best writing at 5am, before anyone else got up. There were so many ideas coming out of my imagination all the time that I was often getting up in the middle of the night to write them down. To help me try and get a better night's sleep, Pam bought me an Olympus voice recorder, so that I could at least make a quiet note of an idea without having to get out of bed. Without Pam, there is no way that I would have ever made it as a writer.

I also owe a lot to Teresa Howard who, despite the Van Loewen agency making a decent percentage from my first year of writing work, was shockingly made redundant during the broadcast of the first series of *The Bill*. Whilst her aim was still to make it as a writer herself, Teresa was a really good agent and I wanted her to continue to represent me, which Alan Brodie accepted. I gave Teresa a loan of £1,000, which she paid back within a year, helping her set up her own literary agency through an Enterprise Allowance Scheme. Teresa Howard Associates was formed in January 1985, with me as her first client and honorary associate.

Teresa felt that *The Bill* was just the beginning and that 'the stars are the limit!' Targeting opportunities outside of Thames for me, Teresa opened new doors almost immediately. In February 1985, I got the chance to write a treatment for producer Richard Bates, son of the famous writer H.E. Bates, outlining a series following the hard-hitting exploits of a small undercover squad of motorbike-riding detectives, codenamed *The Black Rats*. Richard loved the treatment and commissioned me to write a pilot script.

The Black Rats sadly never saw the light of day, nor did my idea for an original drama series commissioned by the BBC called *Bagmen,* which revolved around a crime squad going up against the American underworld. But I was grateful for the opportunity to experiment with new ideas, especially ones that drew on elements of my police career. I was always scouring newspaper articles looking for inspiration and learned so much from reading people's obituaries, which often sparked an idea for a story.

I once read an article suggesting that if a civilian had been awarded the George Medal, this meant their son or daughter could be married in the crypt of Westminster Abbey. I mentioned this to John Woods, the director who had taught me so much about drama on *The Bill*. He said if I wrote it, he'd love to make it. I dreamed up a main character similar to our salmon-thieving tramp played by Liz Smith in 'The Drugs Raid', who was arranging for her daughter to marry at the Abbey. John and I had an awful lot of fun developing this, even though it was another one that didn't go the distance.

My proper return to action once again came from Michael Chapman, who was now producing a second series of another Thames drama successfully born from a *Storyboard* pilot. *Mr. Palfrey of Westminster* starred the renowned Shakespearean actor Alec McCowen as the titular British civil servant, who also operated as a spycatcher. I was the only new writer Michael invited to join the team for this second series and I was very grateful for the chance to broaden my horizons.

My episode 'Spygame' saw Mr. Palfrey investigating an American aerospace engineer suspected by the CIA of acting as a mole for the Soviet Union. When I went to the read-through, I was introduced to the regular cast, including the highly accomplished actress Caroline Blakiston, playing Mr. Palfrey's boss. I noticed that as I shook her hand, she studied me in such detail that I felt like I was there for an audition. After she walked away, the director Gerald Blake joked in my ear, 'She'd eat you for breakfast!'

Mr. Palfrey of Westminster wasn't the only opportunity Michael gave me away from the streets of Sun Hill. He also commissioned me to write a premise for a children's adventure serial, which I called *Quentin's Folly*. As I knew Michael was a Navy man, I drew inspiration from my childhood memories of playing on a Second World War motor torpedo boat, which had got stuck in the river Wye and remained moored there for several years. In my story, a retired detective begins renovating a similar boat, with the help of some local Cub Scouts. Stripping the paint work, the boys discover a swastika and the detective starts tracing the background of the vessel, leading into a world of espionage and adventure. Michael loved it and we were disappointed when it didn't get picked up.

When *The Bill* was recommissioned for a new twelve-part series to air over the winter months, Michael decided to focus on other projects and handed over the producer's chair to Peter Cregeen, who quickly proved himself to be an excellent producer, running the ship with a light hand on the tiller. Having started on *Woodentop*, he already had great relationships with cast and crew and had a clear vision for the show, including the decision that every scene would now only be written from the police point of view.

I was asked to write four new episodes for the series, as well as an updated version of 'The Chief Super's Party', which was going back into production as the series finale. With the financial security of five script commissions in the bank, I decided to step down from my role as technical adviser and recommended that my old friend and former Five Squad comrade Bill Laver take over. Bill was grateful for the opportunity and, as he knew he would have no advising to do on my scripts, he could focus on working with the new writers who were joining the series.

My first story for the second series was 'Suspects', which saw the Sun Hill team investigating an armed robbery. Director Michael Ferguson chose to open the episode with one long continuous shot following the tea trolley as it was pushed around the factory, gradually revealing the various suspects being interviewed by the police about the £50,000 wages snatch. I was thrilled to see my writing being brought to life in such an imaginative way and the actors relished the chance to perform these long scenes like small self-contained pieces of theatre.

At the finale of the episode, Michael and his team executed an even more ambitious sequence: a three-minute shot where one camera followed John Salthouse and Tony Scannell as they left the pub at the end of Artichoke Hill, walked upstairs and into the CID office, before Jon Iles led them down to the cells to interview 'Chalky' White, the wages clerk who is their prime suspect. The actors had constant dialogue throughout this unbroken sequence, at the end of which the camera moved into a final close-up, revealing that Mr. White has died, suffering a heart attack in his cell. To make matters worse, they then discover he was innocent.

Another subplot in 'Suspects' saw WPC Viv Martella investigating a woman who has somehow been pregnant for thirteen months, using a fake baby bump to hide stolen cigarettes. Martella was played by the very talented Nula Conwell, another member of the cast who John Salthouse requested be given more to do. Nula thanked me for writing 'Suspects' for her, but politely asked me to stop writing scenes where Martella was smoking, as she was trying to quit in real life. Nula was brilliant as Viv and she quickly became one of my favourite characters to write for.

By this time, I had built up great friendships with all the actors, which made the second series even more magical for me. Before the read-throughs, we would all meet up in the same pub that featured in 'Suspects'. Most police stations have a pub on the corner, and this was another reason that those early days filming *The Bill* in the East End were so authentic. As soon as I walked into that saloon bar, the cast would start buying me drinks and suggesting story ideas to me. The series had given many of these young actors the chance to get on the property ladder for the first time and they were understandably very keen that I didn't write them out.

I might have given Ashley Gunstock a fright when he read my next script, 'Hostage', which saw a small-time poacher go rogue with a sawn-off shotgun. Ashley's character PC Frank became the first member of *The Bill* cast to be gunned down, shot whilst bravely trying to apprehend the gunman. To the relief of Ashley, and no doubt his bank manager, Frank survived his gunshot wound and would report for duty again later in the series. The gunman then held Sgt. Cryer hostage, where Eric Richard gave an incredible performance that should have earned him a BAFTA nomination.

Whilst I was in my element delivering new scripts, my son Simon was struggling a bit with his French A-Level. He was studying Napoleon and told me he was having problems visualising the Battle of Waterloo. Long before the days of the internet, all he had to guide him were textbooks with a few basic illustrations. I said, 'Never mind. Tomorrow morning, I'll drive us over to Belgium and you can see it all with your own eyes.'

We left early in the morning to get the ferry to Belgium and arrived at Braine-l'Alleud in the afternoon. On a very foggy day, we walked the 227 steps up to the top of the Lion's Mound, the impressive memorial built to commemorate Napoleon's final battle. These days, the Lion's Mound is besieged with tourists, but that day we had it all to ourselves and, as we looked out at the battlefields, Simon started imagining the cavalries charging against cannon fire. Because of the winter mist, all the trees in the distance looked like an army waiting for combat, which added to the eerie atmosphere. We still talk about that incredible trip.

Whilst we were away for our historic excursion, Sacha and Pam had seized the opportunity to play a little trick on me. I love the music of Bob Dylan, but they couldn't stand the sound of him and I soon discovered that my two favourite girls had hidden all my Dylan cassettes. Some people just don't have good taste in music. They also hid all my cigarettes, as Pam was keen for me to quit. Unlike Nula Conwell, I was finding smoking a hard habit to break, especially after being immersed in cigarette smoke for so many years whilst serving on Five Squad.

My earliest days on the beat, especially my first major arrest involving the stolen Ford Consul, inspired my next script for *The Bill*. 'Ringer' was an action-packed episode which opened with a serious traffic incident involving a Cortina, a motorbike, a lorry, a Porsche and a coach filled with passengers. Conscious that this might be an expensive sequence, I called Peter Cregeen to ask whether we could pull off a major accident within the budget. Peter welcomed the challenge and even arranged for Bill Laver to show the main cast a video detailing a real-life traffic accident, so they could play the scenes as realistically as possible.

The production team did me proud with the staging of the accident wreckage, which looked spectacular on screen. For the location, they blocked off an old East End street that was surrounded by derelict buildings and waste ground. The designers and props boys set up the accident the day before filming, leaving all the vehicles in situ overnight. The budget wouldn't stretch for security to guard the accident scene overnight, so when the crew returned the next morning, they discovered that all the wheels of the Porsche had been nicked. Someone had to quickly ring around and source a similar motor so they could replace the stolen parts.

I was conscious that Trudie Goodwin was still not being given many opportunities to shine and so I built my next script around her. 'With Friends Like That…?' sees Ackland struggling to get a statement from a rape victim, thanks to constant interference from a so-called friend. In tandem with this, I had Sgt. Penny recording the inventory of a vanload of stolen lawnmowers. I used Penny to highlight that some coppers, whilst not exactly 'bent', did their fair amount of ducking and diving. When he discovers one lawnmower too many, he decides to help himself to the extra box, hoping no-one will notice. John Kershaw wasn't happy about my warts-and-all approach to the character, but I explained that many police officers are misfits, coming from all walks of life. Bill Laver backed me up in my quest for realism and Tom Penny remained a rough diamond, played superbly by the late, great Roger Leach.

My final script for the second series was an updated version of 'The Chief Super's Party', which went back into production nearly a year after it had been partially shot. The team had their work cut out for them on the continuity front, as some of the actors had lost weight, others had completely different haircuts and Gary Olsen had left the series, but would appear as Dave Litten in scenes shot in 1984. Litten had a larger role in the original script, so I replaced him in the new scenes with PC Muswell, played by new regular Ralph Brown. This situation gave me invaluable insight into some of the challenges that the production team could face and demonstrated how, through creative collaboration, a writer could help the team find solutions to logistical problems.

Something else that helped my writing enormously was a present I found at the bottom of my Christmas stocking that year. Pam got me a copy of William Goldman's book *Adventures in the Screen Trade*. Having written the screenplays for famous movies, including *Butch Cassidy and the Sundance Kid* and *A Bridge Too Far*, Goldman's absolutely brilliant memoir taught me so much about screenwriting. It was the best gift that Pam could have got me and I highly recommend it to any writer wanting to hone their craft.

Pam also gave me an ultimatum that Christmas: 'If you don't give up smoking, I'll leave you.' Naturally, I swore to give up but, just a few days into 1986, I found myself in a quandary. Teresa had got me an interview at the BBC, to pitch a script for *Screen Two*, the new iteration of the iconic *Play for Today* series. I was unusually nervous about this interview, which was to take place at the famous Television Centre in White City. To calm my nerves, I thought I'd get some cigarettes on the way. As I opened a drawer to get my car keys, I spotted a box of matches and quickly nabbed them.

The foyer of Television Centre was a hive of activity and I did my best to look calm and feel like I belonged as I entered this hallowed ground for the first time. After signing in, I sat with three other writers, all waiting to be interviewed for *Screen Two*, quietly rehearsing their story pitch. Mine was for a drama about Buster Crabb, the Royal Navy frogman who disappeared in 1956 during an MI6 reconnaissance of a Soviet cruiser berthed at Portsmouth Dockyard. Despite knowing this was a knock-out idea, I still felt very nervous. I just had enough time for a smoke to help compose myself. As I took the box of matches out of my pocket, I dropped it and propelled the contents across the floor of the foyer. But instead of matches, I was staring at a sea of drawing pins.

I later learned that Pam had just taken down all the Christmas cards at home, which had been pinned to the walls. She had tidied all the pins away in an empty match box, which naturally she thought I would have no further use for, having vowed to give up smoking… It felt like time had stood still, as all the faces in the foyer stared at me, wondering why this prick had just chucked drawing pins all over Television Centre. As I started scooping up the debris, I saw the famous film critic Barry Norman giving me a curious look. I wanted the ground to swallow me up there and then. Perhaps unsurprisingly, I never wrote for *Screen Two*.

Fortunately, as I was still flavour of the month, I had new offers coming in thick and fast. Teresa got me an opening with Television South and I was commissioned to write an episode of their cop drama *C.A.T.S. Eyes*. This spin-off from the highly successful *The Gentle Touch* saw Jill Gascoine reprising her role as former detective Maggie Forbes. I'll never forget meeting Jill at the readthrough; she was so friendly and had the most incredible, bright blue eyes. There was a great family atmosphere on *C.A.T.S. Eyes* and I was very excited to be joining the series.

This glossy, action-packed show was created by Terence Feely, who had written for every series under the sun. When I met Terence, I explained that *C.A.T.S. Eyes* was the first time I was writing for a series shot on film, rather than videotape. He gave me some great advice: 'Think pictures. Never mind the dialogue, just think about making pictures.' I learned a lot from Terence and, thanks to his advice and encouragement, I came up with an episode called 'Passage Hawk', a little nod to the first time I ever went to the races. My dad took me to Cheltenham when I was 17 and I placed my first ever bet on a horse called Passage Hawk, simply because I liked the name. He won the race at 33-to-1!

The plot for 'Passage Hawk' revolved around a South African bank robber, played by Ian McNeice, who is supposedly dying of cancer. When he escapes custody, the chase begins for Maggie and her team of crimefighters, played by Leslie Ash and Tracy Louise Ward. They eventually track him down to the funeral of a prominent African politician, attended by several world leaders. Armed with Terence's advice to 'think pictures', I dreamed up a highly visual sequence where the coffin being laid to rest was fitted with a timed explosive. Cue Jill Gascoine running through the graveyard in slow motion, yelling 'It's a bomb!' followed by an impressive explosion, shot from all angles by director Anthony Simmonds, an award-winning feature filmmaker.

Another huge explosion occurred in the summer of 1986, when *The Bill* sold to Australia. Broadcast by ABC Television in a primetime Saturday night slot, the series became an instant hit. As part of these sales, the writers received a surge of royalties, which were almost as much as our original fees. As I had now written twelve episodes, these residuals meant I got a healthy cash injection without having to do any new work. But this was just the beginning. The series continued to sell all over the world and the money just kept rolling in. I couldn't believe it.

I was so grateful to be able to provide for my family in a way I could never have imagined. I decided we were going to live life to the full. One weekend, flicking through the *Sunday Times*, I stumbled across an advertisement offering 'a unique chance to buy a converted barn'. The property was in Sturmer, a little village in Essex. I showed it to Pam, who thought I was daydreaming, but humoured me by agreeing that we could go on an 'obbo'.

We found Challice's Barn behind a disused railway station at the end of a narrow country lane, beyond which were wheat fields as far as the eye could see. The barn didn't look anything special from the front, but that all changed when the estate agent invited us to follow her through a side door. We entered a high-walled garden that was filled to the brim with colourful plants, surrounding a central pond. It took our breath away.

Through the entrance, we found ourselves in a huge hall, complete with a vaulted gallery. All the wood and stone used in the conversion had been reclaimed, including a magnificent staircase rescued from a Cambridge rectory. A spacious dining room was set behind glass bullion double doors, while the lounge featured an ornate fireplace in an alcove. The large country kitchen looked out over the garden, but only had temporary fittings as the owners had run out of money to complete their renovation.

Upstairs, arched beams ran along a corridor stretching from one end of the barn to the other. The main bedroom came with an en-suite bathroom, featuring a 1930s freestanding bath, with brass fittings apparently from the Savoy hotel. After inspecting three further bedrooms and another bathroom, we discovered a snooker room and a gym, complete with a sauna. These extras were all included in the price. Having grown up in my grandparents' dilapidated house in Monmouth, I couldn't believe I was standing in a place like this. Could I turn this daydream into reality?

DISSOLVE TO:
EXT. CHALLICE'S BARN. STURMER. 1986.

BARRY and PAM walk out into the garden at sunset.
           BARRY

```
So…
          PAM
It's beautiful.  Can we afford it?
          BARRY
Probably not.
          PAM
It needs a great deal of money spent on it.
          BARRY
Remember my favourite saying?
          PAM
Which one was that?   There's been so many.
          BARRY
"Don't let it happen. Make it happen."


PAM hugs BARRY and they kiss.
          BARRY
So, it's a green light?
          PAM
Only if I can have a new kitchen. The one you've
always promised me.
          BARRY
You just got yourself a deal, Mrs Appleton.
```

Thanks to my overnight success as a screenwriter, we were able to buy this dream home. The barn had been constructed by a gentleman called Mike Webb, an incredible craftsman who was about to become our new next-door neighbour. He hadn't used any nails or glue; instead everything was cleverly joined by wooden dowels. Impressed by his handywork, I hired Mike to construct Pam's new kitchen, which included a showpiece central island. As well as fulfilling my promise to Pam, I also furnished Simon with a top of the range computer and Sacha with a brand-new tennis racket to help sweeten the move for my two favourite teenagers.

The Appleton family weren't the only ones moving house in 1986; so too was Sun Hill Police Station. The second series of *The Bill* had ended on a high, with 15 million people tuning in for 'The Chief Super's Party'. But despite having a major hit on our hands, the series was put on hiatus for over a year. The problem was a series of violent protests that erupted during the Wapping dispute. A vicious battle had arisen between Rupert Murdoch, whose new state of the art News International headquarters was based at the bottom of Artichoke Hill, just yards away from our studio, and the printers, who had gone on strike in protest at the move from Fleet Street and resulting mass redundancies.

During the year-long dispute, more than 400 police officers were injured and over 1,000 people arrested. Our empty police station set was requisitioned by the Met, who used it as their base of operations. This made any filming impossible and by the time the dispute was resolved, Thames' lease on the property had expired and the landlord wanted to charge too high a price to renew their agreement. The production team had to find a new Sun Hill.

Meanwhile, I had to find a new agent. Teresa's play *Grock* had earned her great notices at the Chichester Festival Theatre and led to her being offered a Fellowship at Winchester School of Art, which would involve spending a year as a writer-in-residence. This was clearly an opportunity she couldn't decline and she came to stay with us at the barn to tell us that she wouldn't be able to continue representing me. I completely understood and wished her the best of luck. This was just the beginning of a successful writing career for Teresa, who has gone on to become an acclaimed librettist and lyricist specialising in musical theatre and opera.

When Peter Cregeen called me to update me on progress with *The Bill*, I mentioned that I was looking for a new agent. He kindly introduced me to Erika Bond at the William Morris Agency, a massive talent agency originally founded in Hollywood. I signed up with them in December 1986 and I'd like to think Erika had her own 'Passage Hawk' moment by backing me. Before the ink had even dried on the paperwork, Peter Cregeen commissioned me to write five new episodes of *The Bill*.

In January 1987, I was invited to take a look at the new Sun Hill station. Having failed to find a suitable location in the East End, which was being dramatically redeveloped, the production team acquired the former Rootes car factory at 85 Barlby Road, London, W10. Thinking back to my own 'rootes' at Mann's Garage, I liked this connection, even though the new terrain for the series would take some getting used to. We'd swapped

Wapping for Notting Hill and the cobbled streets of the East End for the relative suburbia of West London. It would be a new-look *Bill*.

As a precaution, whilst the production team arranged all the necessary permits for filming around our new patch, I was asked to write a largely station-bound episode as the first to go into production. I came up with 'Double Trouble', which saw a pair of investigators arrive to interrogate the early turn, after an allegation is made that a uniformed copper has pocketed the proceeds from a parking fine. Michael Ferguson was back in the director's chair and arranged for guest actors Julian Holloway and Chris Tranchell, playing the hard-nosed CIB detectives, not to meet the regulars until they shot their scenes, which added a little spice to the drama.

'Double Trouble' would be broadcast midway through the third series, while my first story to be shown was 'Some You Win, Some You Lose', which involved a massive drugs raid on a council estate. Whenever the Flying Squad went on a raid mob-handed like this, anything could happen. No matter how meticulously we planned, there would always be a surprise or two. In 'Some You Win, Some You Lose', the raid quickly escalated into an extremely violent riot, with our heroes being attacked by petrol bombs. Peter Cregeen directed this explosive sequence with aplomb, achieving a fantastic shot of Tony Scannell running along a balcony surrounded by flames.

This big budget set piece, featuring most of the regular cast and many dozens of extras, was shot at night on a council estate. The location had been found by the brilliant production manager Derek Cotty, who would often ring me up and invite me to join him on his recces. Like everyone who worked behind-the-scenes on *The Bill* in the early years, Derek absolutely loved his job and was very dedicated to the programme and making it believable.

Derek invited me to join him to look for potential locations for my next episode, 'Missing Presumed Dead'. One of the benefits of *The Bill* moving to Barlby Road was that it was easier for me to get the train from Sturmer to north-west London. At this time, I was sporting a 1980s bouffant hairstyle and well-groomed beard. One sunny spring morning, I was wearing sunglasses and couldn't help but notice that the guy sitting opposite me on the train kept looking at me over his paper. Eventually, he said, 'Excuse me, you're not Steven Spielberg, are you?' I laughed and said, 'No, I wish I was!'

I wrote 'Missing, Presumed Dead' especially for Eric Richard. The episode opens with CID investigating the scene of a shooting, except there isn't a body, only a couple of bullets and some blood on the pavement. Sound familiar? When Dashwood sends out an alert that they are looking for a Cortina in connection to the shooting, Sgt. Cryer spots one matching the description and gives chase. Driving along a busy road at night, with heavy rain pounding against his windscreen, Cryer is unable to stop as an old lady walks out in front of him. I wanted to explore Cryer's guilt of causing this woman's death and, as always, Eric gave a stunning performance. Eric was one of our first visitors to Challice's Barn, when he came to stay with us one Friday night with his wife, Tina. After dinner, the great man showed his considerable skill on the piano, treating us to a spectacular performance of 'Send in the Clowns', from the Stephen Sondheim musical *A Little Night Music*. Enjoying Eric's company was one of the highlights of working on *The Bill*.

I always felt it important to counterbalance dramatic moments in my scripts with some humour, especially as this was how my colleagues and I used to cope with the demands of the job. Playing on a memory from my spinal injury, I wrote a funny scene in 'Missing, Presumed Dead' where Ted Roach hobbles into the CID office in agony, carrying a rubber ring under his arm. I had been issued with one of these after my operation, supposedly to help with my balance. Roach tells Galloway that he is suffering from 'farmers', a ruse to avoid revealing that he had suffered a vicious and embarrassing assault in a pub the night before.

Using elements from my old cases helped me offer an unrivalled realism to the series, but I still allowed my imagination some space to run wild. Recalling my investigation of Ginger Marks' flat in 1965, I had the Sun Hill coppers performing door-to-door enquiries around the estate overlooking the setting of the mysterious shooting at the start of 'Missing, Presumed Dead'. Rather than discover a phonebook containing the number for the FBI, I created a flat inhabited by an array of stolen exotic animals. The production team managed to source owls, a huge snake and even a couple of alligators.

Another old case inspired my next script, 'Not Without Cause', where Sgt. Penny goes AWOL and cannot be reached on his radio. His colleagues assume he has gone for a swift one down the pub, but he has in fact been shot. An angry landlord has demanded Penny confront a tenant who is keeping cats in her flat against his wishes. Having got no answer, Penny opens the unlocked door, only to set off a booby trap which pulls the trigger of an old revolver, shooting him in the stomach. I had seen a similar trap to this, where a sawn-off shotgun had blasted a hole in a door, thankfully without a policeman on the other side.

'Not Without Cause' was the final episode of the series to be broadcast, but it was not the last to be filmed. That honour fell to 'Overnight Stay', my ambitious story shot largely on location in a real Holiday Inn. The inspiration for this story came as I walked down a hotel corridor and a door opened to reveal a couple having a heated argument. It occurred to me that behind any one of these hotel doors was a potential story waiting to be told. 'Overnight Stay' saw most of the Sun Hill coppers on 24-hour protection duty, keeping an eye on a jury involved in a gangland murder trial. The tension builds when a suspicious package is discovered in one of the corridors, which I based on an old Flying Squad case. We called an officer from the Bomb Squad out to investigate, though in the end he simply strolled up to the package and poked it with a penknife. 'Nah, it's nothing, throw it…'

Once 'Overnight Stay' was 'in the can', the hotel also played host to our end of series wrap party! We had a big bash in the function room, where I got to see all these talented actors in a completely different light. They each went up on stage and performed their own variety act; some were singing, others were dancing. Simon Slater, who had joined the cast to play Inspector Brian Kite, did an absolutely brilliant Magic Circle routine, while Jon Iles brought the house down, playing an American World War Two fighter pilot, complete with leather hat. Pretending to be up in the air in his plane, he flew around the room mowing the rest of the cast down with a loud rat-tat-tat-tat. It was a wonderful way to the celebrate the end of the third series.

When these twelve episodes were shown between September and December 1987, they proved to be our most popular yet. Thames was making serious advertising revenue from their Top 10 hit and set their sights on more editions of *The Bill*. A lot more. If I thought I'd made it as a writer, I'd seen nothing yet…

CHAPTER 14

SHOW ME THE MONEY

In commercial television, the bottom line is king. *The Bill* had become a major money-maker for Thames Television, attracting a large audience of high spenders, the perfect target for advertisers to show off their products to during the precious commercial breaks. The order came down to maximise this by adapting *The Bill* into an ongoing bi-weekly series of half-hour episodes, to be shown at 8pm every Tuesday and Thursday.

One of my life mantras is to 'adapt, adapt, adapt.' For *The Bill* to survive in its new format, we all had to adapt our creative approach to the programme. Peter Cregeen took the helm as executive producer and brought Michael Ferguson and Richard Bramall on board to each produce an episode a week. Before any new material was shot, Peter asked me to create a cutdown version of my episode 'Double Trouble', to help show us if we could make the series work dramatically in a half-hour slot.

I sat down and worked out which scenes could be removed without losing too much character development or drama and still allowed the story to entertain and make sense. I then joined Michael Ferguson in one of the editing suites at Barlby Road to cut the episode down to twenty-four and a half minutes, the programme time to fill a half-hour slot on ITV, with the all-important commercials either side. After cutting half of the scenes, the story still worked and we felt confident that we could make the new format work from a script perspective.

Writing a half-hour script was a new challenge for me and taught me tremendous discipline. There was no time for padding and it forced me to cut my dialogue down to the bone to deliver a fast-paced drama. I found there was still plenty of room for humour too and for my first script I drew inspiration from our old friend the 'Dog Turd'; the easy life merchant coasting towards retirement. Our version of that kind of copper in *The Bill* was Sgt. Alec Peters, brilliantly played by Larry Dann. I thought it would be fun if Peters committed a hilarious and monumental foul up.

As a family, we had recently visited HMS *Belfast*, the famous battleship moored on the Thames near Tower Bridge. As I walked around the deck, I amused myself imagining Alec Peters arresting some sailors. I came up with a story called 'Good Will Visit', in which our hapless sergeant is on the hunt for a platoon who have enjoyed too many drinks at a disco. I quickly fell in love with the new format and thought the possibilities for a writer were endless. However, when I submitted the script, I got a rude awakening.

Our established script editor, John Kershaw, had been unavailable to work on the first batch of half-hour episodes, so Peter Cregeen brought in Ken Ware, who had performed the same duties on the classic *Z Cars*. I was called in to meet Ken, who immediately struck me as being an unhealthy man. When I walked into his office, the first thing he did was stub out a cigarette, of which there were already mounds in his ash tray, and he stuck a nicotine patch on, which I got the impression would be ripped off the second he was alone.

Before I had even sat down, Ken told me he was rejecting my script. He started talking to me as if I had never written for television before, never mind that I had written more episodes of *The Bill* than anyone. I pride myself on being a collaborator, but Ken's abrupt nature was a shock to the system. Perhaps I had been spoilt in my writing career so far, but now the honeymoon period appeared to be over.

Ken and I locked horns for a while, until the reassuring presence of Peter Cregeen helped restore law and order. Ken apologised for upsetting me, explaining that he loved writers and was just trying to be mindful of the budget, something which had never been raised as being an issue before. He then did a U-turn, saying I didn't need to change a word in my script and, to my astonishment, commissioned me to write another six episodes.

Unlike Ken, I'd had faith that Derek Cotty and his talented team could work their usual magic with the budget and, true to form, Derek organised a real squad of Royal Navy officers to make a cameo in the episode, disembarking in the station yard and filing their way into custody. The sequence looked spectacular and, once again, we added authenticity to the screen.

We were encouraged to write two main stories in each half-hour episode, and it was in the second storyline of 'Good Will Visit' that I arguably made my greatest contribution to *The Bill*. As there would now be two units filming episodes in tandem to meet the demands of the schedule, we needed to introduce a few new regular characters to the cast to help share the workload. I created the character of PC Pete Ramsey, played superbly by Nick Reding.

Pete remains a character close to my heart, as there is a little bit of Barry Appleton in him. When Ramsey arrived for his first day at Sun Hill in 'Good Will Visit', I had him park his Porsche in a space reserved for Chief Supt. Brownlow, as a nod to me doing the same with that stolen Ford Consul at City Road Police Station in 1958. Thanks to the success of the series, I was now driving a Porsche, and the production team sourced a very similar model for Ramsey. When Geoff McQueen spotted mine in the car park, he was inspired to buy himself a brand-new, top of the range model.

Where Ramsey and I mainly differed was that he hadn't joined the Met wanting a career as a police officer; he had seen it as a business opportunity, a chance to earn some serious readies by exploiting his position. In 'Good Will Visit', he takes protection money from a dodgy watch seller at the market and then tries to get his Porsche serviced for free. I was asked to tone that behaviour down in later episodes, but once I saw what Nick Reding could do, I just wanted to push the character right to the edge. Nick was such a good actor that I wasn't sure how long *The Bill* would be able to keep him, so I was determined to make the most of him.

Ramsey was flash and wanted to get back into CID, having been forced back into uniform and seconded to Sun Hill as punishment for his conduct. To help Ramsey make a memorable first impression on Ted Roach and the gang, I dusted off an old Flying Squad case from the memory banks. Five Squad pulled over some suspects we believed were selling drugs and when we searched the back of their van, we discovered it was full of sacks. Bill Laver didn't recognise the substance within, but I knew it was saffron, which Pam used in a lot of her recipes. I remember showing off by saying 'it is made from the dried stigma of a crocus.' Bill asked, 'Is it worth anything?' I smiled, 'A little packet from the supermarket will cost you an arm and a leg. These guys are handling a small fortune!' I slotted that into 'Good Will Visit' and made Ramsey a smart-arse, just like I could be at times on the job.

My next script, 'All In Good Faith', opened with a mother telling her young son to put a weapon he had found into the Sun Hill amnesty box. This was a chance to show an interesting piece of procedure, as police officers are required to check each weapon, including any old souvenirs that could still do a lot of damage. Jon Iles added a funny bit of business where Dashwood tries on a knuckleduster from the box and was unable to get it off. 'All In Good Faith' also featured June Ackland on the trail of a bogus gas man ripping off vulnerable pensioners. This storyline was based on a remarkable case from my uniform days at City Road …

```
DISSOLVE TO:
EXT. END OF TERRACE HOUSE. CITY ROAD. 1962.


BARRY approaches a 1930s pebble-dashed house in dire
need of renovation. BARRY walks through the small tidy
garden and rings the front doorbell. There is a slight
pause before the door opens slightly to reveal the
partial face of MRS. SAMPSON, hidden behind the safety
chain.
          BARRY
     Mrs Sampson? I'm PC Appleton from City Road Police
     Station. You dialled 999.


MRS. SAMPSON, 70s, kind-faced, grey-haired, short, takes
the safety chain off and opens the door.
          MRS. SAMPSON
     I have the chain on because you can't be too
     careful around here.
          BARRY
     Very sensible, Mrs Sampson. So, what's the problem?
          MRS. SAMPSON
     This man said he was an inspector for the gas
     board. There were reports of a gas leak in the
     area and he wanted to check my house. I asked for
     some kind of identification.
```

                    BARRY
That's good, Mrs Sampson. Not many people think
of doing that.

                    MRS. SAMPSON
He flashed some kind of card at me. Looked more
like a library card. I didn't trust him. Horrible
little man. I asked, "Don't you need some sort of
apparatus to sniff out gas leaks?"

                    BARRY
And?

                    MRS. SAMPSON
He barged his way in. Tapping the side of his
nose, he said "I don't need any apparatus, lady.
This nose can smell a gas leak half a mile away!"

                    BARRY
Where did he go in the house? You'd better show me.

CUT TO:
INT. END OF TERRACE HOUSE. HALLWAY. LATER.

BARRY follows MRS. SAMPSON into the house. The living
room and kitchen doors are open. BARRY pauses at the
foot of the stairs.

                    BARRY
Did he go upstairs?

                    MRS. SAMPSON
He went everywhere.

                    BARRY
Is anything missing? Your purse, jewellery,
anything like that?

                    MRS. SAMPSON
No. Nothing.

                    BARRY
Are you sure? In two weeks' time you might realise
something has gone.

                    MRS. SAMPSON
Definitely nothing missing. I'm confident about that.

          BARRY
When he left, did you notice which way he went?
Did he have a car or a bicycle? Something that
might help us trace him.

          MRS. SAMPSON
Oh you don't need to trace him, dear. I know
exactly where he is. That's why I called you.

          BARRY
    (confused)
You know where he is?

          MRS. SAMPSON
He asked me where the gas meter was. I told him
it was in the basement. That door there.

MRS. SAMPSON points to a door under the stairs.

          MRS. SAMPSON
He went down the stairs and I locked the door. He
must have thought I was born yesterday…

          BARRY
    (disbelief)
You mean he's down in the basement right now?

          MRS. SAMPSON
He ought to be, he can't get out. Would you like
a cup of tea before you fetch him?
BARRY unlocks the door and switches the light on. A
forlorn HOUSEBREAKER sits halfway down the stairs, with
his head in hands. BARRY shuts the door and locks it,
before putting an arm around MRS. SAMPSON and giving her
a whopping big kiss on the cheek.

          BARRY
    (beaming with pride)
  Two sugars, please.

My next script, 'Caught Red Handed', opens with a husband being taken to
hospital after being stabbed by his wife for giving her soggy breakfast cereal.
This was inspired by another old case from my City Road days. I'd locked a
woman up for attempted murder, but when I went back to the Section House

after my shift, I got a call from the station. The Dog Turd was custody sergeant and he said he was going to let her go because she'd apologised to her husband, who didn't want to press charges... Unbelievably, he gave this couple their kitchen knife back, which she used to stab her husband again when they got home! I repeated this in 'Caught Red Handed', where the husband was stabbed again after burning his wife's toast.

This episode ended with an infamous scene where Jim Carver goes down a manhole to retrieve some drugs, which CID are expecting to be flushed away before they raid a flat. This was lifted straight out of my Flying Squad days, where anytime we knocked on the front door of a suspected drug dealer's home, we'd hear the toilet being flushed. But during the filming of this, a resident inside one of the flats went to the loo and poor Mark Wingett, expecting to receive the prop packet of drugs, collected a handful of shit instead!

Another old case inspired my next episode, 'Country Cousin'. When officers used to come down from a station up north to collect a prisoner, they usually wanted a night out in the West End before they made their return journey. I incorporated this into my script, with Sun Hill CID playing chaperone to a DS from Yorkshire who wanted to enjoy a few drinks before relieving them of their prisoner. Occasionally, roles were reversed, and I would have to go out to the sticks to pick up a prisoner and bring them straight back to London. All kinds of things could happen in these situations, as I learned as a young aide on Christmas Eve 1959...

```
DISSOLVE TO:
INT. CITY ROAD CID OFFICE. CHRISTMAS EVE 1959.


BARRY has just come into the office. There are a smattering
of Christmas decorations and a few empty whisky bottles
from the night before being tidied away by A CLEANER
with a cigarette drooping out of her mouth. DS LIPTON,
30s, tall, short brown hair, olive skin, confident with a
loud voice, stands in the doorway of DI MEREDITH'S office
and waves.
                    LIPTON
          Barry!
```

LIPTON places a firm hand on BARRY's shoulder and smiles. He'd have arguably been better suited as a used car salesman, rather than a detective.

                    LIPTON
          Got a nice little Christmas Eve job lined up for you.

                    BARRY
          Sorry, Sarge. I'm going out on an observation.

DI MEREDITH, 40s, short, dark receding hairline, bushy eyebrows and roughly shaven, stands up. He stubs out his cigarette and holds up a small file of official looking paperwork.

                    MEREDITH
          Forget it, son. This is more urgent.

DI MEREDITH walks over as LIPTON winks at BARRY.

                    MEREDITH
          I want you to go and pick up a prisoner.

                    BARRY
          No problem, guv. Who's going with me?

                    MEREDITH
          No one.

                    BARRY
          What is it? Local?

                    MEREDITH
          I wouldn't normally ask you to do this Barry.
          You're the only single copper I've got over
          Christmas. All us married guys got kids presents
          to wrap, in-laws to entertain. You know.

                    BARRY
          It's okay, I'm on duty anyway. Where am I going?

                    LIPTON
             (stifling a laugh)
          Bristol.

                    BARRY
             (amazed)
             You're joking?

                MEREDITH
This guy has given himself up. He wants to come
home. As you'll be on your own, take some cuffs
with you. There shouldn't be any problems.

DI MEREDITH hands BARRY the paperwork.

                MEREDITH
Thanks, Barry.

BARRY goes back to his desk to collect his jacket, while
he hears DS LIPTON make a phone call.

                LIPTON
        (on the phone)
Good news, we've got someone to collect the Gentle
Giant.
BARRY shrugs it off as another LIPTON wind-up.

CUT TO:
INT. BRISTOL POLICE STATION. CHRISTMAS EVE. NIGHT.

BARRY is having a cup of tea with DS LUTE, 40s, jovial,
red-faced, sporting a handlebar moustache.

                LUTE
How did you get lumbered with this caper then?

                BARRY
Don't ask!

                LUTE
You've got to give this lag his due. A right
old entrepreneur. Standing on a corner in this
weather selling Christmas cards.

BARRY takes another glance at the paperwork.

                BARRY
He stole them from a printers. He's employed
to sweep up in the warehouse. Slung his broom
when nobody was looking. Picked up a carton of
cards and had it on his toes. Why Bristol?

                LUTE
He don't speak. Shakes or nods his head. That's
about it. He's a bloody big bastard though, must

```
be six foot five! He could pick you up and run off
with you!
```

BARRY finishes his tea.

```
          BARRY
A milk train at two in the morning is the only one
you can get me on?
          LUTE
Yep, leaving from Temple Meads. You and the Gentle
Giant got a carriage all to yourself. Fancy a
drink to pass the time? It's Christmas after all…
```

At 2am, I found myself standing on an empty platform at Bristol Temple Meads with this huge prisoner, who never said a word. The train was running late and I was dying for a pee, so I handcuffed the Gentle Giant to a huge, heavy wooden handcart carrying milk churns, which was standing ready for the milk train. 'Behave yourself, I'll be back in a minute…' I was in the gents when, all of a sudden, I heard a steam train screeching to a halt. I quickly got back out to the platform, and I couldn't believe my eyes: the Gentle Giant had pulled this heavy milk cart along the platform, down the slope and onto the tracks, forcing the train to stop. I followed him down onto the tracks and said, 'I thought I told you to behave yourself?' It was a long and silent journey back to London.

One of the reasons that John Salthouse had decided to leave *The Bill* was that he feared the series would be toned down too much in the earlier timeslot. Whilst we'd had to cut out the obvious things like blood, swearing and nudity, I felt the half-hour format was a chance to stretch the actors who had remained with the series even more and give them some challenging new storylines. I had Ted Roach fail his firearms course in 'Hold Fire', Yorkie Smith accused of dealing drugs in 'Caught Red Handed', Viv Martella held hostage in 'The Visit' and a three-part storyline where Bob Cryer deals with the fallout after his son causes the death of a young girl in a road accident. The actors all delivered knockout performances.

The half-hour format also gave me an opportunity to write fast-paced capers more in the spirit of *C.A.T.S. Eyes*. The action-packed 'Paper

Chase' was based on a major Flying Squad case, which sadly remains unsolved to this day. During that investigation, I was crouched beneath a car in a parking garage, monitoring a briefcase which, we hoped, would be picked up by a mystery suspect. It was surprising how many people walked by this briefcase without paying it any attention. Only one passer-by did – a dog stopped and peed on it! That went into the script for 'Paper Chase'.

My family were also very supportive as I hammered out script after script, every three weeks. Sacha and Simon gave me lots of information about computers for my story about hacking called 'Outmoded', which was quite ahead of its time. Pam helped me write one of my all-time favourite episodes, 'Save The Last Dance For Me', which saw Dashwood and Ackland working undercover in a dance studio, overlooking a house that could be offering shelter to a criminal on the run. To help maintain their cover, both detectives end up joining the dance class. Thankfully Jon Iles and Trudie Goodwin knew their way around the dance floor and got to show off some moves. Pam had been a ballroom dancer in her youth and helped me weave some accuracy into the script.

Once again, this episode was inspired by an old case from 1969, when I set up an observation in a dance hall with an undercover WPC. We were watching a house over the road where 'Public Enemy No. 1', the armed robber John McVicar, was believed to be hiding after escaping from prison. I had previously been paired with a female detective from another station to tail McVicar's girlfriend, who worked in the West End, in case she contacted him. A game of cat and mouse ensued, jumping on and off trains on the underground, but she never contacted McVicar while we were following her. When McVicar was eventually caught, he was cradling a shoebox with one hand, with his other reaching up through a hole in the box, holding a loaded gun.

My old cases helped me write nine of the forty-eight episodes of *The Bill* broadcast in 1988, all of which were also repeated every Sunday in an omnibus edition, meaning I would be paid my fee twice. With overseas sales on top, I was pretty much earning triple money for every script I delivered, receiving thousands of pounds every single week. I had been given the chance of a lifetime and decided that if the series was being watched and paid for by the big spenders, I was going to join them. I treated Pam to a VW Golf car and traded my second-hand Porsche in for a new Range Rover. I'd been invited to test drive a Ferrari in the showroom, which was tempting, but I thought Pam would have gone potty if I drove home in a Ferrari.

We also transformed Challice's Barn. The walls were now furnished with paintings and shelves covered in classy ornaments. Our family of pets grew too, with two Irish Wolfhounds, Kelly and Merlin, and four Burmese cats, Dickens, Doyle, Hemingway and Higgins, soon taking up residence. Hemingway cleverly worked out how to open doors by climbing up the bullion glass panels and applying his weight to the door handle. He showed less skill when navigating our furnishings and developed a habit of knocking vases off shelves and leaving smashed ceramic all over the floor!

One day at the barn, I had a visitor. It was Nicky Birch, my former Five Squad comrade, whom I'd shared that memorable horsebox stakeout with many years earlier. Word of my writing success had reached Nicky, who had now swapped the action and danger for the peace and tranquillity of carrying out repairs to his dad's old church and cleaning up the graveyard. Now he was keen for some advice, as he wanted to try submitting a script to *The Bill*. I was more than happy to help and it was great to reminisce on some of our old adventures together. Sadly, I never saw Nicky again, as he died not long afterwards following a short illness.

My other Five Squad partner-in-crime, Bill Laver, had by now moved on from his position as technical adviser on *The Bill*. He was replaced by Wilf Knight, a former Special Branch officer. I never crossed paths with him during my time on the force, but was aware that he had something of a reputation – and not one to boast about. Seeing as I was well up on police procedure and had now written twenty-six episodes of *The Bill*, I felt that Knight had no work to do on my scripts. On one occasion, he felt differently.

In early 1989, I delivered my script for 'In the Frame', which saw DI Burnside set up by a corrupt copper. Frank Burnside, played perfectly by Chris Ellison, was a brilliant character who trod a fine line when it came to the rule book. For reasons best known to Wilf Knight, he told Peter Cregeen that this episode could not be made, as it would jeopardise a real case. Down at Barlby Road, I assured Peter that my script was pure imagination and offered to sign any piece of paper he needed to safeguard the production. I didn't want Knight interfering with my work again and I told him so, in no uncertain terms. I'm sure he got the message, loud and clear.

I wrote thirteen episodes of *The Bill* in 1989, more than any other scriptwriter. I was tremendously disciplined with my writing and I never missed a deadline, although I was up against it a couple of times during this busy period. The most notable was when I was forced to write one of my scripts from a hospital bed. I had been having trouble peeing for some time and went to see a urologist in Bury St Edmunds, who was charmingly called Dr Christmas. He explained that I required a rather 'uncomfortable' procedure on my bladder, which would involve a further three days of convalescence in hospital after the operation. A nightmare for a writer with a deadline to hit.

Dr Christmas pointed out that if I went private, I could have my own room and would be able to set up my electric typewriter and continue my work in peace and without disturbing any other patients. I have always been a great supporter of the NHS, but I must confess that my experience as a private patient was more akin to staying in a five-star hotel. The night before the operation, a nurse came around with a menu! After ordering my meal, I joked, 'Is there a wine list?' To my astonishment, the nurse produced one and I treated myself to a Chardonnay. She clearly had a great sense of humour and presented my bottle of wine in a bedpan full of ice.

The next morning, I had the procedure. I will spare you all the gory details, but it involved a tube going up to my bladder… no prizes for guessing which route it took. 'Uncomfortable' was an understatement. I had to be connected to this tube for three days and, despite the considerable pain, I was able to finish my script.

After my three days of private torture, I couldn't wait for the tube to be removed and I sat in my hospital gown, eagerly awaiting the arrival of my doctor. At 9am on the dot, a very attractive young nurse came in and closed the door. She looked nervous as she told me that she was going to remove the tube herself, as my doctor had been called away to an urgent operation. I remember asking if the removal would be painful, but she couldn't tell me, as it turned out this was her first time performing this procedure.

The nurse knelt down between my legs akimbo, took hold of my John Thomas and began to pull the tube out very slowly. I looked heavenward, 'Eyes Wide Shut'. This moment could have been the denouement of another Kubrick masterpiece. When I opened my eyes, I saw a sea of smiling faces watching from the corridor, including my doctor! They had set this poor young nurse up and were enjoying every moment. By the afternoon, I was up and about and relieved when Pam arrived to take me home. When I told her what had happened, she simply smiled and said, 'This is why you're a writer. You have such a wonderful imagination.'

During my hospital stay, my imagination had helped me write 'Make My Day', a mafia storyline inspired by my first novel *Lets Kill George Raft*. This latest *The Bill* episode introduced Richard Turnham, a new uniform recruit played superbly by Chris Humphreys, who was perfect for the opening undercover scenes where he posed as a hitman: 'The only people who could have given you references are six feet under.'

I am also proud to have created the clarinet-playing Detective Sergeant Alastair Greig, played by Andrew Mackintosh. Greig arrived when Burnside is short of manpower, but is quick to point out that he has a limited schedule, thanks to an upcoming gig with the Met band in Hamburg. Unimpressed, Frank replies, 'A gig? I'll give you a gig… My office!' I had known police officers like Greig and, once again, my experience helped me create interesting characters grounded in realism.

My days as a CID aide inspired my story 'Sun Hill – Fort Apache', where a gunman infiltrates the station, posing as a bogus inspector, in order to retrieve an accomplice from the cells. I based this character on Tony Diamond, a detective I worked with at City Road. He had a very military bearing, always wearing a collar and tie under an impressive British Warm overcoat, with an umbrella over his arm. A strange game he played was to park his BMW outside a police station off our patch. 'Watch this, I'm going to go and sign the books.' I would then watch in disbelief as he marched up to the front desk and conduct a fake inspection. 'I want the Crime book and the Lost Property book. Now!' Tony would sign all these books with an illegible signature. He was a very odd bloke; instead of a detective, he should really have been an actor.

The cast of *The Bill* were such a talented bunch and every single one of them gave an award-winning performance in my favourite story 'Don't Like Mondays'. The incredible Nick Reding had decided to move on after a year of playing Ramsey. The decision was made to kill him off and I, as his creator, was asked to do the deed. To be honest, I felt uncomfortable about this as I loved the character and could have written for him forever. Killing off main characters would later become a regular trick used by producers to get bums on seats, but it hadn't yet been done on *The Bill*. I decided that if Ramsey had to die, he would go out as a hero.

The episode sees Taffy and Yorkie responding to a disturbance in a bank caused by a customer, who they recognise on arrival as the wife of DC Tosh Lines. I had already established that the Lines family were having financial problems and now Mrs Lines, with her five kids in tow, is unable to draw money out of her account. While Yorkie attempts to settle the situation, Taffy calls the station and suggests that Tosh get down there. All of a sudden, armed gunmen storm the bank and a hostage situation unfolds.

When I wrote the script, I had Taffy and Yorkie on their knees, held at gunpoint, with Tosh's kids playing in the bank, thinking it was all a game and not understanding the situation. But during the shoot, director Antonia Bird chose to follow the children as they weaved between actors Colin Blumenau and Robert Hudson, hands behind their heads, surrounded by shotguns. That was our first problem. Next came the moment when Ramsey was gunned down. Having already saved Ackland from being shot outside the bank, Ramsey tries to prevent a desperate Tosh from running inside to his family. One of the robbers opens fire and Ramsey gets both barrels. While performing his death scene, Nick Reding writhed in agonising pain, his uniform covered in blood.

Peter Cregeen always presented the final cut of every episode to his boss, Lloyd Shirley, who was Thames' Head of Drama. Lloyd was a Canadian who had served in the marines before becoming a television producer. I'd heard that he frightened some people, as he could be a taskmaster, but I always had a good relationship with him. But after watching 'Don't Like

Mondays', Lloyd turned to Peter and me and said, 'This is an outstanding episode. But it is too violent and cannot be broadcast before the watershed. You need to remake it.'

Unfortunately, because of the way the episode had been shot, there was no way to simply trim out the violence. Antonia Bird was not invited back to direct the reshoot, and she would never direct for *The Bill* again, which was a shame as she was a talented director. The responsibility for the remake fell to Terry Marcel, a feature film director who had a pedigree for action.

Terry had already delivered something of a miracle on my ambitious script 'Somewhere by Chance', which featured a deranged soldier threatening to blow up a packed shopping precinct with a rocket launcher. That script could have bankrupted Thames in another director's hands, but Terry managed to shoot most of the episode on a Sunday, when Brent Cross shopping centre was closed. Terry was a huge asset to *The Bill* and he inspired incredible performances from all the actors.

I was paid to perform an urgent rewrite, reducing the bloodshed and leaving Ramsey's fate open-ended. Terry Marcel's version of 'Don't Like Mondays' is a masterpiece, it's fast-paced and exciting, without being too violent. Even though Ramsey was still gunned down whilst saving Tosh's life, the production team gave him an ambiguous exit, in the hope that they might be able to entice Nick back one day, which in the end never happened. I could have written an entire series for Ramsey and I was going to miss the character. But all good things must come to an end and, as the decade drew to a close, I too set my sights on new horizons…

CHAPTER 15

MOVING TARGETS

The 1980s had seen my life completely transform. Having started the decade as an exhausted former cop running a pub, I finished the decade as a very successful television scriptwriter. I was now able to provide a life for my family beyond our wildest dreams. I felt reinvigorated with the same energy I'd soaked up in the 1960s, where everything felt possible. My target for the 1990s was to devise my own television series and, thanks to my success on *The Bill*, new doors were opening for me at Thames Television. Impressed by my work on 'Don't Like Mondays', Lloyd Shirley invited me to pitch my idea for an original comedy drama.

I was quickly commissioned to write a pilot for *Two Drummers Drumming*, the adventures of two young tearaways who had been nicked for housebreaking. They ended up doing community service and the series would have seen them gradually cleaning up their act, saving up enough money to restore an old American car that had been abandoned on their council estate. It was an aspirational, coming-of-age story and would have been a great vehicle for two young actors.

Lloyd Shirley loved the script and Thames bought it. At that point, a writer signs a contract that means the television company not only owns your idea, but it can feel like they are holding onto a piece of your soul too. I was gutted when Thames decommissioned the *Storyboard* series in 1990, meaning that they didn't shoot a pilot for *Two Drummers Drumming*. But as Thames didn't want me to take the idea to a rival broadcaster, their option over the series was renewed in 1991, and again in 1992.

Another script Thames paid for over and over was called *Borderlines*, a series I devised that would have seen the Flying Squad team up with Interpol to solve major international crimes across Europe. Then there was *Waiting in the Rain*, a drama about different generations of a family all born and bred on a rundown council estate. The world changes around them, but life on the crumbling old estate remains the same and I saw great dramatic possibilities of this endless cycle. Thames did too, but again this was another Barry Appleton drama that never lived off the page.

I thought I'd hit the bullseye with *Running Scared*, a compelling drama about a prison visitor who helps criminals as they prepare for life beyond the gates upon release back out into the wild. After writing a fifty-minute pilot, Thames commissioned me to write the synopses for twelve more episodes, with the aim of selling the series internationally. *Running Scared* ended up languishing in development hell for years, complicated even further when Thames lost their franchise in 1992. Another one bites the dust.

In television, it always helps to have friends in high places and I was very lucky when Peter Cregeen left *The Bill* in 1989 to become Head of Series at the BBC. He invited me to develop a pilot for a new police procedural drama series, *The Registry*. We decided to build a series around a forensic scientist and I based the main character on a real pathologist I had worked with at the Met, who was operating privately as a freelancer. Peter and I worked closely on the development of this series, and I arranged for us to visit the police pathology department at Vauxhall for research. It was such a good concept, but it was another one died a death. A few years later, after Peter had left the BBC, Nigel McCrery created a little series called *Silent Witness*… So close, yet so far!

The BBC was also the new manor for another former Sun Hill senior officer. In 1991, Michael Ferguson was producing *EastEnders* and invited me to develop a pilot for one of his stars, Michael Melia, who was about to leave after playing Queen Vic landlord and former copper Eddie Royle. We brainstormed a gritty crime drama for Melia, a terrific actor who later landed a starring role in *Dangerfield*, but this was a further shot that missed the target.

Yet another former *The Bill* producer, Geraint Morris, had also joined the BBC and was assigned to oversee the development of my situation comedy *Oddballs*, which followed two police officers in a rehabilitation centre who, for one reason or another, never want to leave. I was commissioned to write a pilot and storylines for the next five episodes, which would have been entirely studio-bound. I had so many ideas for hilarity and pathos,

I felt *Oddballs* could have run and run. Despite encouraging feedback from Geraint, I never got a chance to become the next John Sullivan.

As recompense, Geraint offered me the chance to write an episode of *Casualty*, but instead I enlisted with the other emergency services smash hit of the day. *London's Burning* was a red-hot Sunday night extravaganza, following a brave team of firefighters from Blackwall fire station's Blue Watch. The combination of likeable characters, outstanding production values and breathtaking stunts meant that the London Weekend Television show was pulling in over 18 million viewers.

I met producer Paul Knight and story consultant Anita Bronson at the famous LWT studios, overlooking the South Bank of the Thames. They explained that the main location used for the series was a working fire station, Dockhead in Bermondsey, where real-life personnel would double up as extras when off-duty and assist with the filming of the spectacular shouts that had made *London's Burning* compulsive viewing. To help inspire me and provide a flavour of life on Blue Watch, they asked if I was willing to shadow the team at Dockhead for a few days… You bet I was!

I reported to Dockhead Fire Station, where five officers were cleaning and checking their equipment. All eyes turned to the stranger in town as I walked through the huge garage doors, silhouetted by the glare of the morning sun. The leader of the motley crew ready to put me through my paces was George, a muscular man sporting a shaved head and designer stubble. He was a proper cockney and a great guy. He introduced me to the team and gave me an in-depth safety briefing, followed by a tour of the station. After kitting me out in a spare uniform, the guys invited me to join them for a game of basketball, which they played in between call-outs to maintain their energy.

I was working up a sweat when a loud bell started ringing. The firefighters quickly sprung into action and within seconds they were all wearing their heavy protective equipment. I did my best to keep up with them and boarded one of the impressive fire engines. I was still trying to fasten all my gear as we sped through the streets of London, weaving in and around the traffic that had stood still at the sound of our deafening siren.

After a few minutes, we came to a halt in the middle of a road next to a car that had caught fire. A small group of onlookers had gathered and watched as the team jumped out and put the mighty hose to work, spraying around the engine until the flames died down and all that remained was the charcoal shell of a car.

Our next shout was a huge fire on the third floor of a small block of flats. It was an astonishing sight, with flames fanning wildly out of broken windows. The building had already been evacuated and the police had set up an exclusion zone, herding all the shocked residents away from the immediate area. I watched as these skilled firefighters manned the pump ladder and shot a high-pressure jet of water into the heart of the blaze. We were there for most of the night, until the boys eventually had the fire under control. The amount of damage caused by a fire is staggering and, when you see it up close, you appreciate how dangerous an element it is and how brave the men and women who fight it are.

When I reported for duty early the next morning, George had arranged a little surprise for me. I was whisked off to the local training centre and put through my paces, experiencing some of the training that all firefighters must endure. I had to crawl through a purpose-built revolving tunnel, in complete darkness, where I had to overcome all kinds of obstacles blocking my path until I found my way out. Next, I was treated to a dose of tear gas in a small room, which I'd already experienced during my police training. I think I impressed George with my stoicism and I came away with even more respect for firefighters and their endurance.

My imagination was now ablaze with ideas for my *London's Burning* script, which featured all the usual action, plus something different for the regular cast to get their teeth into. I introduced a side hustle for Colin Parrish, the probationer played by Steve North. Having a few financial problems, he starts selling off cheap smoke alarms and tries to persuade his colleagues to buy one off him. This backfires when they attend a house fire and the badly burned occupants recognise Parrish as the man who sold them their smoke alarm, which failed to work.

Anita and Paul were excited about my script, but just as we were about to go into production, the Smoke Detectors Act was passed in July 1991, meaning the government were now committed to providing and fitting smoke detectors in all new dwellings. This made my storyline out of date overnight and my script went up in flames. I was invited to pitch another script, but I was unable to turn around a new script to meet their deadline, as I had already been engaged for another well-established series.

Former *The Bill* script editor Ken Ware had commissioned me to write for *Van der Valk*, Thames' classic crime series set in Amsterdam. Barry Foster had originally starred as the titular detective for three series in the 1970s and had now returned to the role for a mini-series in 1991. I was asked to write one of three new episodes for the next series, with Anthony Simmons, who had directed my *C.A.T.S. Eyes* episode 'Passage Hawk', in the director's chair. With Lloyd Shirley overseeing the production as executive producer, I had a good feeling about *Van der Valk* and was excited to finally get my name on a new show.

Ken Ware arranged for me to go on a research trip to Amsterdam and meet a Dutch police officer, who would show me the sights and fill me in on local police procedure. I arranged for Pam, posing as my secretary, to join me for the trip. We were very excited… until we got to the airport and found our flight had been cancelled due to weather conditions. We managed to get on the next available flight three hours later but, despite calling Thames from a payphone at the airport to let them know of the delay, by the time we got to Amsterdam, the Dutch police officer had given up waiting and we arrived with no one to greet us.

I got no help from the airport police, so I rang my old friend Martin Grieves, who arranged for us to meet a friend of his stationed at The Hague. Later that evening, this charming Dutch superintendent took us out for an incredible twenty-four-course meal at an Indonesian restaurant! As enjoyable as this feast was, I still came away with little information about police procedure in Amsterdam. Afterwards I said to Pam, 'Let's forget about *Van der Valk* and enjoy ourselves.' I booked us into a new hotel and for three days we saw the sights, partied like kids and had a wonderful time.

On our return, I wrote a script that saw Van der Valk investigating a diamond heist and the murder of a retired judge. Considering the lack of assistance I'd received on the ground in Amsterdam, I thought I delivered a pretty good script, incorporating some of the locations we visited, including the Grand Hotel Krasnapolsky in Dam Square and the Restaurant Luden. Remembering Terence Feely's advice on *C.A.T.S. Eyes*, I had 'thought pictures' and packed my screenplay full of visuals that I knew Anthony Simmons would enjoy capturing on 35mm.

When I went down to Teddington Studios for a meeting about one of my pilots, I popped into producer Chris Burt's office to find out when my *Van der Valk* would be shown. I was taken aback when he said, 'I liked your story, but not the way you told it.' He then revealed that the episode had been rewritten and that I would receive a 'based on a story by Barry Appleton' credit. I went to see Ken Ware in his office, who suggested that I take my name off the episode's credits. I took his advice. When the episode was shown in February 1992, the title had been changed to the cliché-ridden 'The Ties That Bind', but the storyline and most of my dialogue remained the same. When the credits rolled, they claimed 'Screenplay by Kenneth Ware'. That's show business for you.

The Nineties might have got off to a frustrating start, but I never lost perspective on the fact I was being well paid to do what I loved. The phone was ringing all the time, with different producers coming to me for ideas, which I never took for granted. Most screenwriters have drawers full of scripts that have never seen the light of day and I used to explain to friends, 'Just because you haven't seen my name on the box for a while, it doesn't mean I haven't been busily typing away.'

Despite a list of near misses, there was still one old faithful in my corner. After Peter Cregeen left *The Bill*, Michael Chapman had returned to the captain's chair to steer *The Bill* into a new decade. Encouraging as always, Michael continued to commission me to write new scripts and I penned a further nine Sun Hill adventures. But even with my old friend and mentor back at the helm, for me *The Bill* had now sailed a long way from home.

When the lease at Barlby Road ran out after three years, the production had been forced to move once again, eventually finding a repurposed warehouse in Merton, South London. These new premises were vast, with purpose-built courtroom and hospital sets, as well as a much larger police station to incorporate an increased team of three units filming episodes continuously. I felt like a stranger walking around this huge complex, a stark contrast to the Artichoke Hill days, when I could just pop in for a chat with anyone like one of the family. Now I had to book an appointment and wait in a corporate reception area. This wasn't *The Bill* I remembered.

I'll never forget walking through the new 'flight deck' where all the production team had their offices. Passing a sea of fresh faces, I got a rude awakening when I walked by two junior members of the team who were putting scripts together. By coincidence, one of them was stapling together copies of my latest script, 'When Did You Last See Your Father'. As I passed, I heard the title being read out, followed by: 'What a stupid title!' I pedalled back and introduced myself to this red-faced youngster, explaining that my story was named after and inspired by a famous painting depicting a young boy being interrogated by the Roundheads during the English Civil War. After finishing my history lesson, I walked away feeling a bit of a dinosaur.

In 1992, I heard that my old friend Jon Iles would be leaving *The Bill* after eight years' service as DC Mike Dashwood. I felt this was a huge loss for the series, as Dashwood's grammar school presence made him the perfect foil for the likes of Burnside and Roach. He was a terrific character to write for and Jon played him brilliantly. In hindsight, I should have written a spinoff series for him, with Dashwood joining Special Branch. I decided to give Jon a starring role in 'Going Soft', my fiftieth episode for *The Bill*, which also felt like the perfect milestone for me to walk away from Sun Hill.

I am proud of my work on *The Bill*, especially to have played a part in launching the series. It changed my life and, thanks to the international sales and repeats, I would continue to earn royalties for many years. Many of my scripts were adapted into novelisations and also translated for two international police dramas: *Bureau Kruislaan* in the Netherlands and *Die Wache* in Germany. The series was a gift that kept giving and I remain grateful to Michael, Peter and everyone else who gave me a chance to follow my dream.

My time at Sun Hill had been a fairytale, but removing the safety net of my old stomping ground made me more determined than ever to try and land myself a new crime drama. I hoped a new agent might do the trick and I joined the prestigious MBA literary agency, where Diana Tyler wasted no time in setting up some lucrative opportunities for me. In 1993, I was the man picked to drive *The Sweeney* back onto the small screen.

Rather than a direct sequel, LWT were looking for an action-led, hard-edged series with a modern audience in mind, presenting life on the squad from a different angle. Instead of a Regan figure, I created DI Judith Cassidy, a single mother who was having a challenging time juggling both the job and her domestic life. The series was called *Eagles* – another nickname for the Flying Squad – and I was commissioned to write a pilot for the first episode, 'Cashback'. I received glowing feedback from Sarah Wilson, Controller of Drama at LWT, but sadly ITV didn't commission us. They don't know what they missed!

It was soon time to reload as Diana quickly got me a new opportunity across the border, when I was invited to write a feature-length screenplay for *Taggart*. Scottish Television's highly successful crime drama had a similar history to *The Bill*, having started as a one-off pilot back in 1983. That was where the shows differed, as *Taggart* was a big-budget glossy affair, shot on film and delivering a murder mystery wrapped in pure entertainment. Each story was told across three fifty-minute episodes, which would also be combined for a feature-length omnibus repeat.

Each new grisly murder on the streets of Glasgow was investigated by DCI Jim Taggart, a hard-nosed, whisky-drinking copper of the old school. This dedicated but cynical copper was brilliantly brought to life by the celebrated Scottish actor Mark McManus. His sidekicks were DS Mike Jardine, a mild-mannered tee-total Christian, played by James MacPherson, and the efficient no-nonsense Jackie Reid, played by Blythe Duff.

Scottish Television was a meticulously organised company and I felt like I was working for a Hollywood studio. Rather than me relying on trains or taking on a gruelling six-hour drive up to their studio for meetings, they arranged for me to fly. As I lived about twenty minutes from Stansted Airport, I would leave home at 8am and catch a flight to Glasgow, arriving in the studio for 10am in time for breakfast. They then assigned my own personal chauffeur to drive me around Glasgow, showing me different locations to help fuel my imagination. I would then be back home by 7pm in time to have dinner with Pam. This was more like it!

I was commissioned to write a *Taggart* called 'Death Benefits' which involved the auctioning of life insurances, setting up a series of bizarre murders. We were very lucky to have Tip Tipping on the team, an accomplished stunt performer who could also play small parts. I already knew Tip from *The Bill*, where he played a villain who steals a rare and valuable bird's egg in my episode 'Sun Hill – Fort Apache'. For 'Death Benefits', Tip performed a spectacular stunt where he was forced off a motorcycle, sending him flying off a wharf and into the water below. I was extremely sad when Tip was tragically killed performing a parachute stunt for the BBC series *999* just a few weeks later. He was a really nice guy.

One of the victims in 'Death Benefits' was the local vicar, who selflessly cashes in his life insurance policy to be able to pay for repairs to his church bells. Unfortunately for him, his good deed led to him plummeting to his death from a great height. The inspiration for this subplot came from St Mary's, our local church in Sturmer. This fourteenth-century place of worship was in desperate need of repair and after Pam and I joined the Church Parish council, the vicar, Michael Hewitt, gave his blessing for me to carry out some minor repairs, which brought me even closer to God.

As well as inspiring my first *Taggart* script, St. Mary's also saw me making a brief return to playing detective. The church can be found at the end of a long, picturesque driveway called Church Walk, just off the main road in Sturmer. Behind the church is Grandville Manor House, a huge building which had for a long time been derelict, until a wideboy from London moved in and started breeding horses there. One day, without permission, he put up palatial gates at the entrance to Church Walk, locked with a chain, which blocked the right of way from the main road to the church and its graveyard. This once prevented a funeral procession from being able to bury their dead, until a bolt cutter came to the rescue.

Word about this wideboy's selfish behaviour quickly spread among the community, who soon started turning up to services in their droves in support of the church. We began a fundraiser to go towards repairing the fourteenth-century clock tower and I auctioned off signed copies of my old *The Bill* scripts. As a result, the fundraising was so successful that not only could we fully repair the tower, but also the church bells, which had not rung for decades. Michael ensured that those glorious bells rang loud and proud, making it impossible for the wideboy to enjoy any more Sunday lie-ins.

Things escalated when the wideboy took Michael to court, where we had to prove that the church had right of way, as if the name 'Church Walk' wasn't enough of a clue… I returned to CID mode and started gathering evidence, interviewing all the oldest residents of the village, taking statements that confirmed the church had always held the right of way. Eventually, the wideboy agreed to leave his gates open and my final case was closed.

The reinvigorated St. Mary's then gave me an idea for another *Taggart* script. Because Michael's services were now thriving, the church was visited by a group of former American soldiers, who had been stationed at the nearby airbase during the Second World War. I was fascinated by all these old war horses, who rocked up in their original leather jackets from the 1940s. I turned to Pam and said, 'I've got to write these boys into *Taggart*...'

I wrote an outline for a story where all these GI Joe veterans came together for a VE anniversary. I pictured the opening sequence taking place at night in an aircraft hangar, still housing a few original Dakota planes. I then imagined Jim Taggart and his team attending the celebrations, with the men dressed in period uniforms and the women dancing to Glenn Miller in their vintage dresses. Then one of the veterans is found dead and, in true *Taggart* style, the old soldiers are each murdered one by one as the story unfolds. I pitched it to producer Robert Love, who thought it was a great idea, but it was too expensive even for their budget.

Robert did quickly commission my next script, 'Death Without Dishonour', where Taggart and his team must protect the witnesses involved in a trial between two warring taxi firms. I loved writing for the series, I felt like I could use my imagination more than I had on *The Bill*. I particularly enjoyed writing dialogue for the titular detective, who could be savage to his colleagues. I discovered that the actor who played him could treat some of his co-stars with similar hostility. At the read-through for 'Death Benefits', it had become clear to me that Mark McManus and Harriet Buchan, who played Jim's long-suffering wife Jean, didn't see eye to eye. Mark could be terribly rude to Harriet, which inspired me to write several blazing rows between them in 'Death Without Dishonour'.

Mark was a brilliant actor, but it has been well documented that he was plagued by a serious drink problem. When I joined the show, his mother had recently died and in the space of a year he also lost his brother and two sisters. Mark's drinking 'mates' did him no favours and he started hitting the bottle badly. During the filming of 'Death Without Dishonour', he went missing for several days. Because of his untimely absences, I was paid to rewrite my script and reassign Mark's lines to his co-stars.

The poor man was eventually found, his so-called friends having abandoned him. The production team were very supportive and managed to get him back on set the next morning. Somehow, he managed to successfully complete his scenes in the episode. Robert Love never threatened Mark with the sack, but he was very concerned for his welfare. Mark vowed to dry out and went to an Australian clinic for a break, promising to return sober.

My next episode, 'Prayer For The Dead', saw Taggart and the team investigating the murders of two young girls. But shortly before production of the episode began, Mark's wife Marion died of cancer. It was the final blow for the poor man, who had lost so many of his loved ones over a two-year period. In the middle of the night, I got the phone call from producer John Temple that I had been dreading. 'Barry you better get up here. Mark is in hospital and he's not coming out.' Mark died on 6 June 1994, aged 59.

A crisis meeting was held where we had to put our sadness temporarily on hold and work out how to salvage 'Prayer For The Dead'. Mark had managed to complete a handful of his scenes for the episode, where he looked gravely ill. Because the idea of cutting him out of his final appearance was unthinkable, it was down to me to rewrite the script to factor in what he had already shot, whilst also explaining his absence from the rest of the episode.

The obvious solution would have been for Iain Anders' character of Chief Superintendent Jack McVitie to step in to handle more office scenes. But McVitie was already in hospital, having suffered a heart attack triggered by an argument with Taggart, who had now been made up to cover his guv'nor. Mark McManus had shot the scenes where he explained McVitie's heart attack and his promotion, but hadn't shot the argument or any scenes of him running the department.

The only solution was to have Taggart suddenly go out to attend a senior management course and give his dialogue to other characters. I can't say I am proud of the episode, though at least Mark had shot the final scene of the episode where Taggart and McVitie make amends. The pair share a laugh before Jim leaves the office and Mark McManus is seen walking away through a rippled glass door, leaving the screen for the very last time. A sad ending.

My final script for *Taggart*, called 'Legends', revolved around a Sixties rock group called The Adders. After one of their records is re-released, the lead guitarist is found dead and, you've guessed it, he's been 'murrrderrred!' The story was based on Janis Joplin, the iconic American rock star who died from a heroin overdose. Her second album was released just months later and topped the billboards charts, making a lot of money for her estate. Jardine and Reid find themselves investigating the mirky world of sex, drugs and rock'n'roll! The responsibility of carrying the series seemed to lift the performances of James Macpherson and Blythe Duff and, despite the sadness we all felt about losing Mark McManus, 'Legends' remains my favourite *Taggart* story.

I had been commissioned to write *Legends* before Mark's untimely death and I certainly didn't expect the series to continue beyond this. But to my surprise, I was invited to a meeting at STV where Robert Love and the team brainstormed a strategy of how *Taggart* could continue. I remember someone said: 'If James Bond can get away with different actors leading the franchise, so can *Taggart*.' I personally wanted to write a drama, rather than a 'brand', which was another word that kept cropping up. Even though 'Legends' had turned out well, I felt *Taggart* without Mark McManus wasn't something I wanted to write for anymore. I am very proud of my work on the series, which earned me an award from the Writers Guild when *Taggart* won 'Best Original Drama Series'.

With my new status as an award-winning scriptwriter, Diana Tyler found it even easier to open new doors for me. In the summer of 1995, I was commissioned by Yorkshire Television to write a two-hour TV movie as part of their *Circles of Deceit* espionage series. This primetime drama followed John Neil, a former SAS operative reluctantly recruited by MI5 to work as a special agent. In a strange way, this script took my television career full circle, as playing the Guiness-drinking, Walther PPK-wielding John Neil was none other than Dennis Waterman, some twenty years on from when I'd shown him the ropes on Five Squad and he'd drunk me under the table during his preparation for *The Sweeney*.

Dennis had already played the character of John Neil in a one-off TV movie in 1993, which had performed well enough in the ratings to warrant a follow-up series. My two-hour screenplay was called 'Dark Secrets' and opened with an armed robbery, inspired by a scene from my favourite movie *Bullitt*. The rest of the high-octane story sees Neil investigating a former SAS colleague who is considered a threat to national security after stealing important government documents during the robbery.

I always enjoyed writing strong roles for women and director Nick Laughland assembled an impressive cast including Holly Aird, Adjoa Andoh, Kate Buffery, Pippa Guard and Melanie Hill. The villain of the piece was a ruthlessly ambitious MP played by Corin Redgrave and I couldn't believe a member of that illustrious acting dynasty was reading my dialogue.

When 'Dark Secrets' aired on 27 December 1995, it was watched by over 9 million viewers… but I wasn't one of them. Despite finally hitting the bullseye and reaching new heights in my scriptwriting career, I had already left it for dead.

CHAPTER 16

A NEW CHAPTER

I will never forget the buzz I felt when, whilst renewing my passport in 1984, I got to list my occupation as 'Writer'. What a moment for an ex-cop. Our first destination with my spruced-up identification was Cyprus and, as soon as we arrived, we fell in love with the country. We adored the incredible food, friendly people and easy way of life. We were particularly attracted to Paphos, a city on the south-west coast brimming with culture and breathtaking ruins hailing from ancient Greece. We visited this special place over and over, every time feeling relaxed, healthy and even more in love.

Our next signpost to Cyprus came via Sacha who, whilst studying Maths and French at university in Manchester, was sharing digs with three Cypriot girls: Maria, Monica and Marilena. They challenged Sacha to learn how to speak Greek and she quickly mastered the basics of the language. During one of their term breaks, Sacha brought Maria back to Sturmer to meet us. As we sat enjoying a glass of wine, Pam explained that we would be going back to Paphos soon for another holiday. Maria insisted that we introduce ourselves to her parents during our trip.

Petros and Christalla Charalambides had originally lived up in the north of the island, but like thousands of others, they'd had to abandon their homes and flee in the middle of the night to escape the Turkish invasion of 1974. With baby Maria in their arms and very few possessions, they made it to Paphos, where they literally lived on the beach, surviving only on the fish that Petros was able to catch. After starting their lives again from scratch, Petros went on to become the biggest road contractor in Paphos.

We met Petros and Christalla at their home near Paphos harbour. Their house was traditionally Cypriot, adorned with religious icons and dozens of family photographs decorating every wall. All the extended Charalambides family were there to meet us too and immediately these kind people made us welcome. They had prepared so much food, it could have been Christmas day. Joining us for this extravagant feast was one of Petros' friends called Christakis, nicknamed 'Douggie', a Soho-born former mini cab driver. As Petros didn't speak a word of English, Douggie kindly did all the translation for us, delivered in his classic cockney accent.

This enjoyable evening proved to be the start of many long and close friendships. By the end of the holiday, we had been introduced to an even wider circle of the community, who all similarly treated Pam and me like family. The night before we were due to fly home, Petros and Christalla expressed, via our cockney translator, a warm enthusiasm for us to come and live in their country. I found this an irresistible idea.

Two weeks later, I was standing in our kitchen at Challice's Barn, thoughtfully leaning against the table and looking outside at a dark and dismal sky. The pouring rain had been a constant for three long, damp days. I found myself daydreaming of Cyprus…

```
DISSOLVE TO:
INT. KITCHEN. CHALLICE'S BARN. 1995.


PAM is about to prepare lunch when she notices BARRY
staring outside. After putting an arm around BARRY and
laying her head on his shoulder, they silently watch
the ghastly weather outside. Eventually, PAM whispers
in BARRY's ear.
                    PAM
     A drachma for your thoughts?


BARRY turns to look at PAM. He manages a weak smile. PAM
offers a knowing look.
                    PAM
     You know it rains in Cyprus as well? It can pour
     down cats and dogs and be very, very cold. That
     Mount Olympus you were challenging me to race up
     even gets snow in the winter!
```

> BARRY

Remember when we first met? We promised ourselves that one day we would live in the sun. I think that day has come.

PAM returns to her salad ingredients.

> PAM
> (laughing)

You are a complete nutcase!

BARRY turns to face PAM.

> BARRY
> (smiling)

You're a bigger nutcase for marrying me.

> PAM

Cuffley to Sturmer was a huge move, Barry. But at least I could drive over and see my friends when I felt like it. Cyprus is a different proposition!

> BARRY

You wouldn't have to worry about that. You'd have a job stopping them coming over every five minutes.

> PAM

What about your writing?

> BARRY

I've written so many scripts now I've lost count. I've done more than I could ever have hoped. I just want to be with you now. Follow our dreams.

> PAM

What about Simon and Sacha?

> BARRY

They've left home!

> PAM

The dogs and the cats?

> BARRY

We'll take them with us.

> PAM

What about this lovely house? I have such wonderful memories here.

A NEW CHAPTER

If Pam had wished for us to stay in Sturmer, then I would have respected her decision. But we soon found ourselves thinking about our first magical fortnight together in Majorca and how, whilst holding each other afloat in the cool Balearic waves, we had vowed to one day live by the sea. Thirty years on, we chose to make that promise to each other come true.

After agreeing to spend the rest of our lives in Cyprus, we decided to do something special to mark the occasion. After the next Sunday service at St. Mary's, Michael Hewitt conducted a special ceremony for us, where Pam and I renewed our marriage vows. It felt like the perfect way to mark the end of our time in Sturmer and thank God for bringing us together. Everyone who attended church that morning was invited to stay for our ceremony, then join us for drinks and food at Challice's Barn.

We knew people who had bought a second property abroad to use as a holiday home, but we weren't going do this, it was all or nothing. Everything had to go, except our beloved pets, all of whom we were determined to take with us. I had to say goodbye to the Mercedes and sell off all our antique furniture, which wouldn't have been suitable in Cyprus. If we were going to burn our bridges, we had to do it properly, even if it meant letting some valuable items go cheap. After a rather protracted process, we sold Challice's Barn and made the big move to Cyprus in September 1995.

We rented a villa in an upmarket area called Kamares, just outside Paphos. Our first mission was to have fencing put up for our pets, who would have to spend time in quarantine. The fencing was a slightly alien concept to our Cypriot neighbours, who let their pets roam the roads. When the time came to collect our four-legged friends from the airport, we had to wait a couple of hours for a vet to arrive and examine them.

We'd ordered two huge crates for Kelly and Merlin, our two Irish Wolfhounds, to travel in. But it wasn't until we went to collect them that I discovered just how huge these crates were. I then realised we had a problem. I had borrowed a double-cabin truck from Petros, but it clearly wasn't going to be big enough for these two enormous crates. The only way I could try to make it work was to keep the tailgate down, but I had no rope to tie them on with. After Pam secured the cat boxes on the back seat, she voiced her concerns about the crates on the back. I reassured her, 'As long as I drive carefully, they will be fine…' Bad move, Appleton.

As soon as I drove out of the airport and came to the first roundabout, one of the crates slid off and broke open. Merlin made a run for it and this big cream buffoon, who was supposed to be kept in quarantine for a further week at the villa, made straight for the sea! I rushed over to the airport's police station, where there seemed to be a great panic on, with officers rushing around taking rifles with telescopic sights out of lockers. It looked like they were preparing to respond to an invasion, with radios blaring non-stop.

No one was taking any notice of me, but I managed to grab the attention of a female officer. 'Please help me. I've lost my dog!' She stopped abruptly and, in broken English, asked me, 'What type of dog?' I did my best to describe Merlin and she immediately yelled out across the room. Immediately the panic calmed down. It turned out they had received a report that Merlin had entered a restricted area on the island, hence all the panic.

I was given permission to go in and retrieve my dear friend, but I never mentioned that Merlin was supposed to be in quarantine and thankfully they never joined the dots as to why I had just been at the airport in the first place. I'll never forget the sight of this daft dog happily amusing himself, paddling in the sea. Perhaps he was considering swimming back to Ireland? Merlin was a gentle giant and when he saw me, he ran over, stood up tall with his paws on top of my shoulders and started licking me to death.

Meanwhile, Pam had been frantically waiting by the side of the truck and managed to find some string to tie Kelly's crate to the truck. We parked the cats in their boxes on the side of the road while we tried to comfort Merlin, who was by now rather excited by all the commotion. I put him on the back seat and, after a while, he finally laid down. I took a deep breath and started the long journey back to Paphos. We hadn't got far when Pam screamed 'Stop!' I screeched to a halt. 'What's the matter?' She looked at me aghast. 'We've left the cats behind!' Thankfully our favourite felines were still at the side of the road, meowing their hearts out! Not my finest hour…

This adventure confirmed that Paphos was no place for a flash car. I needed something practical and I soon became the proud owner of a big second-hand truck. We also learned that there was only one petrol station in the whole of Paphos, right in the middle of the town. This was closed on Sunday, meaning on Fridays and Saturdays there would always be long queues of frustrated drivers, all hoping to fill up. During our first experience of joining a somewhat disorderly queue, I turned to Pam. Before I uttered a word, she smiled and said, 'I know. Adapt, adapt, adapt…'

After getting off to such a hairy start, I was delighted to be invited out fishing with Petros, Douggie and four more Cypriot friends. They kindly picked me up and took me to a small harbour, where we boarded a beautiful twin-engine boat. The guys had all the diving gear you could think of, but I didn't have any. I soon discovered that this wasn't required, as once we were out at sea, I was informed that I would be taking over the steering. I'd never driven a boat before, but no one else seemed worried by this…

Every 100 yards or so, a diver armed with a spear gun would go over the side and I had to work out where I had dropped each of them off by using points on the land. It was all very ad-hoc and these guys had clearly never heard of a 'buddy' system, preferring to go on their own solo missions. I sailed towards the Akamas Peninsula, an outstanding beauty spot, and after dropping the last man off, I was to turn off the engine and wait for twenty minutes before turning around and picking up each diver in reverse order. I laid back with my hands cupped behind my head and closed my eyes. It took me a moment to realise that this wasn't a dream; this was my new life. I thought back to my days hurtling around the M25 riding shotgun with Bill Parsons and wondered what my former comrades would think if they could see me now…

After soaking up this feeling of bliss, I began my return journey and safely collected all the divers, who between them had caught lots of fish, mostly grouper, a deep seawater fish and a staple of the Mediterranean diet. I handed the wheel over to a more experienced seadog and we sailed into a deserted bay, where a small white sandy beach looked particularly inviting. A fire was lit, the fish were scaled, gutted and cooked, and we washed them down with a couple of bottles of local wine. I had found paradise.

This joyous excursion would become my new regular weekend activity all through the summer. I embraced my role as ship's captain and enjoyed learning about the tides and docking procedures. I got to be quite good at it, but I soon encountered a completely different kettle of fish. One of the divers had a larger boat with an upper deck, moored in the main harbour, which he used for tourist trips. One day, he suggested we take his vast vessel out for our next fishing expedition. The idea of me navigating this massive and very expensive boat out of the harbour was very daunting, but thankfully he took over the wheel for this.

My passengers fished with spearguns, even though this was illegal. At the end of each voyage, as soon as we pulled alongside the harbour, my job was to climb onto the wharf with the fish hidden in a black plastic bag, run to my truck and drive away. After years on the Flying Squad, I had learned how to get in and out of vehicles very quickly without anyone noticing, only now I felt a different kind of adrenaline doing it without a warrant card. I would then drive to a friendly taverna, enjoy a coffee and wait for the rest of the crew while the fish was prepared for cooking.

But on one particular morning, we happened to sail into the harbour at the same time a big Russian trawler was about to dock. The police were waiting to check for illegals coming off the trawler and as I ran along the wharf with my black binbag of fish, little did I know I was heading straight into the middle of an operation. An undercover policeman spotted me and, assuming I'd just jumped off the trawler, signalled to another cop to stop me. Remembering these guys were armed, I stopped immediately, dropped the fish and put my hands in the air. As I was only wearing a t-shirt and shorts, with no identification papers on me, I was in big trouble!

The next thing I knew, my fishing buddies had grabbed me and were trying to pull me away from the police. A crowd gathered to witness this tug of war, with lots of arguing from both sides. Thankfully, one of our divers knew the officer in charge and it all got resolved, much to my huge relief. But our bag of fish mysteriously disappeared, and I can hazard a guess which side of the law were enjoying it for supper that night…

Another near miss came when my good friend Vassos Kyriacou, former road manager to Meat Loaf and a talented watercolour artist, offered to take me up in his plane. Pam and I were keen to move out of our expensive rental as soon as possible, so Vassos suggested that the best way for me to look for our forever home was from the air. On a quiet Sunday morning, we headed over to Paphos airport, but when I saw the plane that Vassos was planning on taking me up in, I felt a shiver up my tender spine…

This old aircraft was the very definition of a bone rattler; the only way to start her up was by cranking a rusty starting handle on the side of the engine. On the runway, Vassos challenged me to try and start this old relic up, which was certainly a workout. My reward for ferociously turning this ancient handle was to be consumed by a ball of smoke from under the engine!

These thick grey plumes were spotted from the control tower and, before we knew it, an army of fire engines were heading towards us. When the firemen opened the engine compartment, the cause of the smoke turned out to be an old bird's nest. As a result of our runway barbecue, all the flights were transferred to Larnaca airport as a precaution. Us two daredevils saved our flight for another day and quietly skulked off to the nearest taverna with our tails between our legs.

Rather than buy an existing property, I had a vision of building something special for Pam and I to live in for the rest of our lives. We didn't mind whereabouts, as long as we could see the sea. One afternoon I was out in the truck, taking in the fragrance of the countryside and enjoying Neil Diamond with my faithful companion Merlin. After looking around for plots of land, I spotted a goat track which I thought would be a good shortcut back home. I drove down the track and suddenly, I realised I was going uphill.

When I reached the top, I got out of the truck with Merlin and we stood on this hillside, looking out at a breathtaking view. There was nothing between us and the deep blue Mediterranean Sea, glistening in the sunshine. It looked like you could just walk straight out to it. I turned around and discovered a plot of land with a 'For Sale' sign. I continued along the track until I arrived back in the quaint little village of Tala and found a phone box. I set up a meeting with the developer and couldn't wait to show Pam…

```
DISSOLVE TO:
EXT. HILLSIDE. CYPRUS. 1997.
```

The sun is not yet at its hottest and there is a gentle breeze. BARRY and PAM are standing in the countryside and looking out at the pin-sharp blue horizon. Parked on the goat track below is the developer's SALESMAN, enjoying a smoke, leaning against his BMW.

PAM suddenly jumps and wraps her arms around BARRY

>PAM
>
>I just saw a snake!

>BARRY
>
>Never mind that! What d'you think?

>PAM
>
>It could have been poisonous!

>BARRY
>
>We're here to make a decision, never mind the snake!

>PAM
>
>I hate snakes! Tell it to go away.

>BARRY
>
>It's a Whip snake. They're harmless.

>PAM
>
>How come all of a sudden you're an expert on snakes?

>BARRY
>
>I read up about them for a script. If it was dangerous, I'd grab it by the throat and have severe words with it. See you're safe with me. C'mon. Isn't this the best plot we've seen?

>PAM
>
>If it wasn't for the snakes.

>BARRY
>
>Forget about the bloody snakes!

                    PAM
        Yes. I admit the view is beautiful. Will I have a
        suitably beautiful kitchen?
                    BARRY
        We will design it ourselves. Imagine a swimming
        pool surrounded by palm trees. A customised
        barbecue. An incredible garden…

PAM smiles at BARRY.

                    PAM
        "Don't wait for it to happen. Make it happen."
                    BARRY
        I love you so much. You know I would never go
        against your wishes. We'll only do this as a
        team. Together.

They seal it with a kiss.

Pam and I designed the plans for our new home together, which we decided to name Villa Chloe, after our first beloved Siamese cat. To avoid me becoming 'the man in the shed' outside, we planned to have a basement that would contain a workshop for my tools, as well as an office and a utility room where all the pets could have their meals.

On the ground floor would be our main living and dining rooms, connected to a nice kitchen for Pam to work her magic in, with an outdoor conservatory area at the back for us to sit and eat our dinner in the evenings. We would have two bathrooms, essential for every happy marriage, and upstairs would be two guest rooms and then our bedroom, which would have arched windows and patio doors leading out to our own balcony with a beautiful sea view. All three floors would be connected by a spiral staircase.

Surrounding the villa would be space to grow our own fresh fruit and at the back, we would have a tiered garden with Mediterranean plants and palm trees, all overlooking our own swimming pool set against a backdrop of the bright blue horizon. Heaven on Earth! Petros recommended a local developer and ensured that we got the best price for all the work and materials. It was very exciting watching our dream home get built from the ground up and I used to leave the builders a crate of booze whenever we visited the site.

Once the main build was complete, I got to dust off my inner artist, last seen watching his fireplace being sledgehammered to the ground by Elton John's mate. I started doing lots of bricklaying and greatly enjoyed getting my hands dirty with a bag of ready-mix concrete. Our plot is surrounded by wild countryside and I loved going out and finding rocks to use as I built several stone arches for the garden. It was great going back to nature again, especially after so many years working in the smoke. I felt reborn.

At the time, our only neighbour for miles around was the local goat herder who, every morning and evening, used to come along with a herd of about a hundred goats. I used to go and sit with this old boy while his goats grazed. He couldn't speak English and I couldn't speak Greek, but somehow we formed a friendship. We used to exchange gifts; I'd give him a bottle of Scotch and he'd bring me a bottle of wine. Sometimes we would open the front door and there would be a basket of eggs for us.

One day, Pam and I came back from the supermarket and we spotted the farmer's wife, who was also quite elderly. She was trying to herd the goats back up the track, but one of them was in labour. She was desperately trying to catch this goat that was running around in the middle of giving birth. We got out the truck and helped her catch this goat and Pam helped her deliver the kid, while I got the rest of the herd organised. I loved our new life.

Down the road from our villa, we discovered a taverna run by a gentleman called Vrasidas. This was to become our favourite local haunt. Here we got to experience quintessential Cypriot food, including the most delicious meze, with dish after dish coming until we said no more! We would leave loaded with a box of leftovers, as well as fresh eggs and homegrown fruit, all given away in the act of friendship. We would return the compliment, bringing over a basket full of fresh lemons and peaches grown in our little 'orchard'.

Sometimes we'd go for a stroll through Paphos at sunset, where we were always struck by how the tables outside the restaurants would all be laid out with cutlery and serviettes, ready for the next day. There was no trace of theft, vandalism or petty crime, just constant signs that everyone respected each other. Nobody locked their doors and the local bank was completely open plan inside, meaning you could just walk in, sit down and talk directly to the manager with no barrier in between. You could actually see the cashiers opening the safe right there in the same room. I was a long way from City Road now.

When I walked into one taverna in Paphos, I experienced a classic case of 'Of all the gin joints in all the towns in all the world…' In the corner of this tiny little bar was a television and I couldn't believe it when I heard a familiar theme tune… It was a repeat of *The Bill*. I ordered myself a beer and sat down to watch the start of the episode for old times' sake and I nearly fell off my stool when the words 'Country Cousin – By Barry Appleton' appeared on the screen.

All the memories of my old life came flooding back and I found it quite moving. But I was puzzled to see that some of the scenes had been cut out. I then remembered that the episode featured several key scenes set in a Cypriot nightclub and the taverna showing the repeat was on the Greek side of the island. Because the nightclub scenes had a Turkish flag in the background, the channel had edited all those scenes out, meaning the second half of the episode didn't make any sense at all.

By now I hadn't written a single word of dialogue for nearly two years. After *Circles of Deceit*, I realised I had spent most of the last decade indoors at a desk and once we'd decided to move to Cyprus, I was quite content to leave my writing career behind me. I had been very successful and achieved far more than I ever set out to do. I had also been lucky enough to earn a living that had given Pam and me this chance to enjoy a retirement in the sun. But seeing my name back on screen stirred something inside me. Perhaps I could have one final stab at writing my own series?

Diana Tyler at MBA had continued to represent me, handling any approaches and ensuring that any residuals made their way over to me. We even invited Diana and her husband to visit us while they were holidaying in Cyprus and, after drinks at Villa Chloe, we took them out for a meal at Vrasidas Taverna. I told Diana that I'd had an idea for creating a crime drama following the investigations of a Greek Cypriot detective. She took a copy of my treatment away with her and I suggested it might be a good vehicle for Peter Polycarpou, an actor of Greek-Cypriot descent, then best known for his role in the sitcom *Birds of a Feather*. Diana rang Peter's agent and arranged for the four of us to have a meeting back in London. But this was as far as that idea went, as Peter and I didn't sing off the same hymn sheet, so I returned to paradise.

An actor I was more in tune with was John Salthouse, who was one of the first people to come out and visit us at Villa Chloe. John has a fantastic energy and we had a great time together, and he particularly enjoyed bombing around the sandy terrain in my old second-hand truck. We once brainstormed an idea for a movie project together. I had researched a mineral that could theoretically be used to power batteries, decades before electric cars became a reality. That idea never got out of second gear, but by the time John visited us in Cyprus, he had hit the back of the net by producing and starring in the highly successful football drama *Dream Team*, which ran on Sky for ten years.

Despite my best-laid plans, I soon discovered that a writer never truly retires. One morning, an elderly English gentleman came to Villa Chloe. With a lovely smile, he introduced himself as Mike Steele, Chairman of 'Stage One', a successful amateur theatrical group based in Paphos. Made up primarily of ex-pats, they performed four three-night productions a year from Emba Theatre, a converted cinema.

Having learned that a 'retired' English scriptwriter was now living in Paphos, Mike tracked me down and came to ask if I would consider writing their Christmas play for 1997. There was no money involved, as everyone took part for the sheer love of it, but it didn't take long for me to decide. This was a form of writing that I had never thought about before and I couldn't resist finding out if I had what it takes to be a playwright. 'Once more unto the breach, dear friends, once more…'

CHAPTER 17

OUTSIDE THE BOX

With an intended ex-pat audience firmly in my mind, I came up with a play called *No Room At The Pub*, a farce set in a Saloon Bar late at night on Christmas Eve. I thought it would be fun to throw together a merry band of misfits, including a butcher, an Elvis impersonator, an elderly policeman and a grumpy Santa Claus who have all been working right up to the wire on the night before Christmas. Also in the pub was a married man who was trying to break off his affair with a young girl, who is pregnant with his child. After he abandons her in the pub, the young girl gives birth, with the policeman, Elvis impersonator and Santa Claus becoming the three wise men, surrounded by a holy mist.

No Room At The Pub was performed for three nights in December 1997. The actors all loved working on it, especially after learning I had written for *The Bill* and *Taggart*, which meant they treated me like a celebrity throughout all the rehearsals. They all gave excellent performances, while behind the scenes all the crew did a great job making the sets and costumes. For these retired ex-pats who hailed from all walks of life, being part of this theatre was now their main passion and between them, they produced a production that any professional would have been proud of.

I had completely underestimated how popular Stage One was and got a shock on the first night, when we arrived at the Emba Theatre to discover it was packed, with some of the audience having to sit on the stairs in the aisles. At the end, the show got a standing ovation and there were cries of 'Author! Author!' Pam nudged me, 'Go on. They want you on stage with them to take a bow!' I reluctantly walked down the stairs to loud clapping, which I couldn't believe. After a decade of having my work enjoyed by millions all over the world, taking a bow with the cast on that stage was another experience altogether. It might not have been the West End, but that wonderful moment still gives me tingles.

When we went back for the second performance, something unintentionally funny happened. During the quick change before the final three wise men scene, the smoke machine was put on stage as usual to surround the actors with a holy mist. But at this special moment, one of the backstage boys decided to nip outside for a crafty fag. Without thinking, he opened the stage door at the back of the building and in came a gust of wind, just as the curtains opened for the grand finale. All the dry ice from the smoke machine was blown off the stage and straight out into the audience. There literally wasn't a dry eye in the house!

I loved every minute of this marvellous experience and when Mike Steele asked me to write the next Christmas play, I jumped at the chance. In December 1998, Stage One put on a production of *Millie*, an original play named after my mum, who came out to stay with us for Christmas and see the show. My new comedy told the story of Miles, his cartoon muse Millie, his mistress Judith, his ex-wives Stella and Marcia, his daughters Joella and Jayne, and a young lady called Laura… eat your heart out Ray Cooney! The show was directed by Jan Clarke and her talented team created the production from start to finish in just six weeks, performing a knock-out show. I was also thrilled when Stage One started handing out acting awards, voted for by their membership, which they named 'the MILLIE awards'.

For the Christmas show of 1999, I wrote a play called *Dreamers*, inspired by *Casablanca*, which remains one of my all-time favourite films. Set on New Year's Eve, *Dreamers* followed a young man called Eddie who wants transit papers for travel. Rather than trying to get to Lisbon as in *Casablanca*, Eddie just wants to make it into the millennium. The play takes place in Eddie's imagination and, as with most dreams, the most unbelievable things happen to him. Featuring an eccentric cast of characters, we crammed the show full of 1940s fashion, music and nostalgia, which the ex-pat audience lapped up in their droves.

Casablanca is the kind of romantic thriller I wish I had dreamt up. Writing a movie and seeing my name on a big screen had always been my greatest fantasy as a scribe, perhaps fuelled by happy memories of going to Saturday morning pictures as a kid. Whilst I had written several feature-length screenplays for television, my words had never made the great leap from the box onto celluloid. But then, out of the blue, I got a phone call from Andros Achilleos, the man behind the best fish and chip shop in Paphos, as well as several restaurants along the seafront. He was ringing to tell me that he wanted to make a movie.

My curiosity piqued, Pam and I agreed to meet Andros and his wife Brenda for dinner. He explained that he had bought lots of second-hand film equipment over the years. The next day, he proudly showed me his warehouse, which was filled to the rafters with top-notch camera equipment that he had started renting out to foreign movie companies who wanted to shoot in Cyprus.

Andros had made a few small films himself and obviously had ambitions to be the next Steven Spielberg. Eventually, he asked me what he had been building up to all along… 'Will you write me a script?' Because I had just been in *Casablanca* mode for Stage One, and found Andros' enthusiasm infectious, I agreed and began to let my imagination run wild.

My greatest desire was to create a crime thriller, mixed with a touch of the spaghetti western, another of my favourite genres. One of my cinematic heroes is Clint Eastwood and I loved his repertoire of wandering gunfighters with no name. He was so good at seemingly doing nothing and perhaps his most memorable gunslinger was Blondie in *The Good, The Bad and the Ugly*, where he needed barely any dialogue – just the glint of the sun in his eyes, before throwing back his cape, twisting his cheroot to the other side of his mouth and rapidly drawing his Colt 1851 Navy from its holster. None of those bandits ever stood a chance as Clint regularly dished up even more dead bodies than an episode of *Taggart*!

I knew that Cyprus would make the perfect setting for paying homage to the spaghetti western, with plenty of dry and dusty landscapes, covered in glorious sunshine nearly all the year around. The country had also seen its fair share of violence in recent years, courtesy of the very bloody conflict between the Greek Cypriots and the Turkish Cypriots in 1974, which had forced our friends Petros and Christalla to abandon their home and run for their lives.

Many villages in the countryside were evacuated overnight and there are still quite a few that remain deserted to this day. I thought one of these 'ghost towns' might make an ideal setting for our movie, so Andros picked me up in his SUV and drove me out to look for locations to inspire my story. We came across a deserted Turkish village, where the only inhabitants were hundreds of goats living in the long-abandoned houses. They were looking out at us from upstairs, downstairs, even over the balconies. We tried to drive down the main street and were surrounded by more goats, curious to investigate the strangers in town.

This recce helped inspire the screenplay for *East of Wild Goat Rocks*. My main character was a young woman called Elena, who hailed from a Cypriot village that had been a stronghold of an underground nationalist movement of Greek Cypriots, who were dedicated to ending British colonial rule in Cyprus. Seemingly secluded from the outside world, the inhabitants still had bitter memories of the atrocities carried out by British soldiers. Twenty graves in the cemetery are populated by victims, including Elena's uncle. But after she marries an Englishman, Elena is disowned by her parents and made an outcast from her Cypriot home.

Having been happily married and living in England for fifteen years, Elena's world is turned upside down when she is summoned back to Cyprus to identify a body. The corpse turns out to be her husband Gavin, who has been found on a beach with a gunshot wound to the back of the head. How and why he came to be in Cyprus is a complete mystery to Elena, who vows to find her husband's killers. To add some spice, I made the lead detective one of Elena's former lovers and I also threw a corrupt priest into the mix for good measure. All these ingredients helped create an exciting story, which we now had to work out how to bring to life.

Andros was able to raise some funds by leasing out an empty premises on the sea front, while Pam and Brenda tried to find sponsorship for the film. Some offered to support by providing transport for filming, while others would kindly provide catering at no cost. But no-one wanted to part with any cash, meaning we would have to make our epic thriller on a shoestring budget. I thought this would pose a big problem when trying to hire a cast and crew, who would not be paid unless the film made any money.

To my astonishment, when Andros put an advertisement in the local paper looking for actors and a crew to volunteer to make a film, the response was staggering. We held auditions in a cinema, where I gave the actors a fairly short audition script to perform. It didn't seem to matter to any of our willing volunteers whether they were paid or not – everyone was excited to be involved and live out a fantasy that they might become a movie star. Andros' offer of free fish and chips proved a great incentive too. We soon had our cast assembled, including Antonia Kayariannis, who was to play Elena.

In television, everything is meticulously planned weeks in advance by a production manager and a dedicated team handling contracts, permits, locations, call sheets etc. Our production of *East of Wild Goat Rocks* was another world entirely, where I never knew what was going to happen from one day to the next. I'd see something and say to Andros: 'Let's put that in!' Or people would pass by while we were shooting, from guys on horseback or a farmer herding goats, and we'd go up to them and say, 'Would you like to be in our movie?' We made things up on the spot and I changed the script as we went along.

This felt like pioneering filmmaking at its best and I found this new form of creativity exhilarating. However, it soon became clear that our merry band of volunteers didn't share the same level of enthusiasm. We had about sixty people offering their time and services for us on the first day. Then gradually, as the weeks went by, the crew got smaller and smaller. The core team became Andros on his Super 16mm film camera, his wife Brenda with the boom microphone, Pam manning the clapper board and me slipping into co-director mode to help Andros.

I had never considered directing before, even though it is perhaps the next natural step for a writer to take. I certainly got the taste for it making *East of Wild Goat Rocks* and a scene I desperately wanted to bring to life was a shoot-out between three men in the main square of the abandoned Turkish village. Reminded of my days on *C.A.T.S. Eyes*, I had definitely been thinking pictures when I wrote this scene and I knew that if we shot in the early evening, the low sun would cast long shadows behind our actors. The main challenge would be how to get rid of the goats but, to our great surprise, when we arrived there weren't any to be seen anywhere. Perfect! The stage was set for this dramatic scene, in which one of our characters would lose their life…

DISSOLVE TO:
EXT. WILD GOAT ROCKS DESERT. DAY 3. 1810

A long time ago, these three men were comrades in arms.
Now times had changed, but not for some... PETROS, 50s,
cold, ruthless, casually dressed, moves into a position
forcing TASSOS, 50s, a humble shepherd, to face the
evening sun. TASSOS raises his shotgun in defiance as he
squints into the glare. ZENIOS, once a trusted friend of
TASSOS, circles him from the other direction.

        TASSOS
These killings were a mistake, they've put us all
in danger. Don't you see, we're old men fighting
old battles. Nobody cares anymore. We should have
moved on, but you came back and made it personal.

ZENIOS suddenly rushes forward and snatches the shotgun
from TASSOS' hand.

        ZENIOS
Sorry, my friend. I did warn you.

TASSOS just stands, naked without his gun, offering no
resistance.

        TASSOS
Killing for a cause is one thing, killing for
pleasure is another. I'll see you in hell, Petros.

PETROS levels the gun at TASSOS' head and smiles.

        PETROS
Goodbye my friend. You've outgrown your usefulness.

The bullet hits TASSOS in the centre of the head. He
drops to his knees, then topples forward into the dust.

The 'actor' playing the farmer who was about to meet his maker was
also called Tassos, who in real life was a local taxi driver. To make
this sequence look as realistic as possible, Andros and I fitted him up
with a condom full of chicken's blood, taped to his chest. Andros then
attached a tiny explosive charge, made up of gunpowder from a shotgun

cartridge. We connected a wire that we hid under his costume, which ran down his back to the nearest building. This would be detonated on 'Action' and, hopefully, Tassos would appear to have been blown away Eastwood style...

As I did up Tassos' shirt to hide the blood-filled condom, I joked, 'I hope you're insured, Tassos?' He looked me in the eyes and said, 'I can't get insurance. I've got a bad heart.' I panicked and ran straight over to Andros, who was setting up the camera, and exclaimed, 'We can't do this, he's got a bad heart!' Tassos called out, claiming he was only joking and insisted that he wanted to do his stunt... I'm still not sure he was telling the truth.

Come the moment 'Action' was called, the small charge exploded, chicken's blood sprayed everywhere and Tassos went straight down like a sack of spuds... He stayed there, completely still. Fearing the worst, Andros and I rushed over to him. We turned him over and he wasn't moving. After a moment, he opened his eyes and said, 'I'm waiting for you to say cut!' Pam suggested we call it a day and open a bottle of wine. 'I think we need something stronger...' I replied with a puff of the cheeks.

The following day, we were back at the same location to shoot more material. We didn't make the film in story order and so Tassos was back from the dead, performing new scenes that would take place earlier in the film. Thankfully, the goats had returned, which was good news as we needed them for our first scene, where Tassos' character would be sitting on a boulder amongst the goats, looking forlorn. We then see a concerned Elena make her way through the goats to place a comforting arm around him. Antonia gave such a brilliant performance and the camera loved her as much as we did – she had such a photogenic face.

By the time we got all the equipment set up and were ready to shoot this scene, Pam suddenly said, 'Wait a minute, where have the goats gone?' None of us had noticed that all the divas had got bored and ambled off to fresh pastures. We needed them desperately to make the scene work, so everyone who was able started rounding up the goats and doing their best to encourage them back 'on set'. This was not an easy task, but we managed to coax enough back in our direction to make the sequence work.

After this scene was successfully in the can, we realised that Nick, one of the actors required for the next scene, was missing. Brenda pointed out that he had been helping round up the goats near a ravine… We headed over to where he was last seen and heard distress calls for help. Nick had lost his footing and fallen into the deepest part of the ravine. We made frantic phone calls and an air ambulance came out and rescued Nick, who had broken his thigh. Despite his ordeal and being hospitalised for a short time, Nick was keen as mustard to return and finished filming his scenes a few weeks later, where Andros ensured that there was always something in the foreground to mask his plastered leg.

Perhaps because of our misadventures in guerilla filmmaking, by the last week of filming there were only us two married couples left behind the scenes, plus Antonia as Elena, who thankfully stayed to the bitter end. For our final scene, we had got permission to shoot in the belly of the main hospital, where the mortuary was situated. This was for the important scene where Elena would identify the body of her husband, Gavin. Under the white sheet lying on the slab was yours truly, doing my best not to giggle. After filming, Andros yelled a triumphant, 'That's a wrap!'

I wasn't involved in the post-production of the film, although I did get to see some of the rushes, which looked very good. The biggest problem was the sound, perhaps unsurprisingly with us amateurs who had just been trying our best. An awful lot of the film's sound would need to be re-dubbed and Andros fixed up a booth to record the dialogue in. However, by this point our leading lady Antonia had now moved back to the UK, meaning Andros had to find somebody else locally to dub her entire performance, which was a real shame. These are just some of the complications when trying to make a movie without a budget.

The lack of money inevitably meant that Andros had to prioritise paid projects and ultimately *East of Wild Goat Rocks* was never completed. Despite failing to see my name on the big screen, my foray into filmmaking was one of the most incredible experiences of my life. I had an unbelievable amount of fun, made friendships for life and nobody died – even if Tassos and Nick gave us a couple of frights along the way!

Pam felt that my screenplay was some of my best work and suggested that I adapt the script into a novel, which allowed me to expand each of my characters and conjure up sequences that Andros and I would never have been able to capture without a proper budget. I greatly enjoyed working on the novel, which was eventually released by an independent publisher and I requested that all my residuals go to charity.

Having finally scratched my filmmaking itch, I could now get back to enjoying my retirement and spending more time with my family, which had now grown. Pam and I were thrilled when we became grandparents to Simon's children, Phoebe, Zoe and Matilda. We were also delighted when Sacha moved permanently to Cyprus, where she became a successful tennis coach. We have all enjoyed exploring this great country together and found one of our favourite lunchtime spots at Viklari, also known as the Last Castle, which stands on the edge of a clifftop along the Akamas peninsula. The view is spectacular.

Close by is the Lara Bay Turtle Reserve, a conservation area for these amazing creatures to breed and nest every year. As a family, we have been lucky enough to witness the special moment when the baby turtles hatch. The sight of these tiny lifeforms taking their first steps and making their journey across the beach and into the sea is one of the most joyous sights to behold on God's earth. Another Cyprus miracle.

Driving to Lara Bay was always an adventure, as the road would often be blocked by an unusual obstacle... A donkey, who for years lived nearby and appeared to have ordained himself as guardian of the Akamas. He would block the road and it would be up to him whether or not you would be allowed to pass. If he liked you, he would stick his head in through the window for a pat and a stroke. If he really liked you, he would throw in his special windscreen service, licking the dust off the front of the truck. He was a real character.

Pam and I had now been dubbed honorary Cypriots; the Greek name for Barry is 'Paris', while my own Goddess became known simply as 'Beautiful Pam'. We both even started to look Greek, sporting Mediterranean tans after spending ten months of the year outside, usually eating breakfast, lunch and dinner out in the fresh air. Pam's cooking also went to the next level and in 2004, she was particularly excited about the prospect of Cyprus joining the EU. She wrote to *BBC Good Food Guide* to explain that us ex-pats thought it was a great idea and, to her delight, the magazine responded to say that they would like to feature us in an article. Pam pulled out all the stops and created a fantastic Mediterranean feast using local ingredients and a merry band of us were photographed enjoying this magnificent spread out on the terrace at Villa Chloe.

But as our years living the good life trickled by, our family began to shrink again. First, we had to say goodbye to our beloved Merlin, who passed away after a short illness. I mourned the loss of our great friend deeply and missed the sight of him at the dining room table, where even though he was sat on the floor, his great height meant that his head would be level with ours, as if he was joining us for dinner. He was always welcome. Not long after this, the rest of our pets all went to heaven as well. They had all settled down very well in Cyprus and lived a good age. But slowly, one-by-one, these reminders of days gone by were leaving us.

Then in March 2007, I got a phone call from my sister Susan, informing me that our mother was gravely ill in hospital. Pam and I managed to get back to the UK in time to see her and talk to her. The next day, she passed away, aged 85. During the twenty-eight years she lived without my dad, we had adopted a series of dogs to keep her company. Taking them out for walks had helped introduce Millie to meet new people and she made lots of friends. Whenever she baked Welsh cakes, which were her seminal dish, her neighbours would all follow the scent and scoff them up.

Even though she was a very friendly person who would talk to anybody, my mum remained a very private person in my eyes. She rarely revealed much about her feelings, which strong women of her generation tended not to do. Despite this, we shared a mutual love of jazz and I treasure the memories of us listening to music together whenever she came to stay with us in Cyprus.

After losing my mum and all our pets in such a short space of time, Pam and I certainly needed cheering up. Sensing this, Sacha surprised us with a pair of tickets, treating us to an evening of music at the historic Kourion theatre in Limassol, where Jacques Loussier and his trio were to perform a special one-off concert as part of an international music festival in July 2008. I had followed this talented musician's career for many years and the chance to see his famous band performing live in Cyprus was a moment to savour.

The ancient Greco-Roman amphitheatre stands against a magnificent ocean backdrop, giving the impression that the stage connects to the sea. We were advised to bring a cushion to place on top of the seating, made of large stones dating back to the second century. As Pam and I ran our fingers along these ancient monuments, we could almost feel the history beneath us. It was a warm evening with a slight breeze and the huge moon illuminated the beautiful calm sea.

As the venue began to fill, I became deeply embarrassed. We were amongst an audience made up mostly of British tourists, complete with T-shirts, shorts and flip flops. Pam and I thought we were doing much better in our smart-casual gear, but we were soon completely upstaged by a French contingent, who arrived in immaculate evening wear. Sacré bleu!

I soon forgot all about my embarrassment when the famous trio walked onto the curved stone stage, a grand piano, a set of drums and a bass guitar awaiting them. Loussier waved to his appreciative audience and the place erupted with tremendous applause. As the musicians sat on their stools, ready to entertain us, a hush descended across this hallowed ground. The opening notes of Ravel's *Bolero* were then tapped out on a small cymbal, commencing a truly magical evening.

I looked across at my beautiful wife, her eyes lit by the moonlight, and we shared a kiss before cuddling up and enjoying a night of breathtaking music. I would replay this majestic moment in my mind over and over again in the dark days ahead, when my old friend fate made an unexpected return. Only this time, he wasn't on my side.

CHAPTER 18

TOGETHER WE MADE IT HAPPEN

Having come to terms with recent family bereavements, I turned my attention to a series of DIY jobs around the villa. I have always tried to maintain my fitness and whilst the thought of laying a new patio might seem alien to most 70-year-olds, I was as willing to get stuck in with the old ready-mix concrete as ever before. I'm often reminded of an old favourite saying, which as time goes by has been altered and attributed to the likes of George Bernard Shaw, Oscar Wilde and other intellectuals… 'The tragedy of youth is that it's wasted on the young.'

This time, I could not defy my age and whilst laying the patio, I sprained my back. Pam took me to see our doctor, who upon reading about my old spinal injury in my notes, booked me in to have an X-ray. There is no mucking about with the health service in Cyprus and I got an appointment straight away at a clinic just a couple of streets away.

I was then called back for a further scan, as they wanted to double check their findings. It was at this point that the consultant sat Pam and I down to deliver some grave news. They had found tumours on my ribs, which they feared were secondary. I was booked in for a next-day appointment with a specialist in Nicosia, who carried out further tests. The evidence was damning; I was diagnosed with advanced prostate cancer, which had spread to my bones. I required immediate treatment. Pam's eyes filled with tears. She told the consultant that she would love and look after me, before giving me a big hug. Suddenly, it felt like my world was crumbling down around me. 'Oh, I believe in yesterday…'

For my treatment, neither chemotherapy nor radiotherapy were recommended. Instead, I was put on Zometa for my bone cancer and received a hormone injection in my stomach every fortnight for my prostate cancer. To be honest, I can't remember being in any pain and had

I not sprained my back, no-one would have ever known I was ill, least of all me.

A short time into my treatment, Pam suggested we take a short cruise around the Greek islands to take our minds off things. This would mean putting my treatment on hold, which was a potential problem, as some of the drugs being used on me were still on trial. But we decided to let tomorrow look after itself; for now we just wanted to get away and enjoy ourselves while we were able.

We hadn't been on a cruise since our twenty-fifth wedding anniversary back in October 1990. That trip began at the Fontainebleau Miami Beach, a famous hotel that has been used as a location in many iconic movies over the years, from *Goldfinger* to *Scarface*. On our silver anniversary, there was a knock on the door of our hotel room. I answered and a waiter pushed a trolley into the room loaded with Champagne, smoked salmon and all kind of goodies. 'I think you have made a mistake,' I said. The waiter pointed at an envelope on the trolley that read 'Barry and Pam Appleton'. With a smile, he replied: 'I think somebody loves you!' Simon and Sacha had done us proud with this lovely surprise.

We then climbed aboard our ship at Fort Lauderdale and set sail for the Caribbean. We got dressed to impress for dinner, where I had paid extra so we could have a table for two. But when we took our seats, we discovered our romantic setting was on top of a table of eight, at the head of which was a wideboy behaving like a total control freak, organising what everyone in his orbit was going to eat, drink and seemingly think. Pam gave me a knowing look, meaning that when this Del Boy character suggested we join his table, we were already prepared to abandon ship.

I will talk to anybody, but the idea of being marooned at dinner every evening for the next two weeks with this wannabe raconteur was out of the question. We had enough professional entertainers on board to listen to whenever we wanted, including some incredible cabaret acts. The head waiter moved us next to three other couples, all of whom turned out to be great company.

There was so much to take in over the following fortnight. We spent time exploring most of the Caribbean islands, even venturing underwater in a small submarine to look at ancient wrecks. We also hired a helicopter to take us around Saint Martin, flown by a Vietnam veteran who had plenty of interesting war stories. This once in a lifetime trip had been a dream holiday for Pam and me, renewing our love and living like a couple of mad teenagers once more. The idea of feeling like that again during my cancer treatment was very appealing.

We went to a travel agent to book our new cruise, but when we attempted to pay on a debit card, the payment was declined. Luckily, we had another card that did work, and we were able to book our escape and have something to look forward to. Later that day, I tried to use the debit card and it was declined again. When Pam tried to ring the bank to report the issue, she discovered that the line was dead.

Since moving to Cyprus, we had been forced to bank offshore due to new regulations preventing ex-pats from using banks based back in England. Our financial advisor had recommended using a bank based on the Isle of Man, which had since been taken over by an Icelandic company with no banking experience, who had gone bust overnight. Most of our savings were wiped out in a flash. Many months later, the Isle of Man government offered us compensation, but the amount we received was nothing compared to what we had lost.

In order to be able to pay for our cruise, I turned to an old friend. When I first started writing for *The Bill*, Michael Chapman arranged for me to join the Writers Guild. He took me to a meeting and suggested that I sign up to their pension scheme, meaning a percentage of each of my script fees would be matched by the television company and paid into my pension. This turned out to be a shrewd move and, in our hour of need, I cashed in my pension to make sure that Pam and I could survive and enjoy a break. Once again, thank you Michael Chapman.

As distressing as it was to lose our life savings, especially on top of my cancer diagnosis, all I wanted to do was focus on being with Pam. Our attitude has always been that there was nothing we couldn't face together and we have forever felt grateful that God brought us together and given us this extraordinary life, full of love. Our cruise around the Greek islands was tranquil and peaceful; waking up every morning to a balmy breeze and crystal blue sea was good for the soul. We sailed at night and each day of our voyage would take us to a new island to explore. We appreciated the beautiful food and pleasant company of our fellow passengers, making many new friends along the way. We never shared our problems with anyone, as that has never been our style.

On our return, I went back to the cancer clinic in Paphos and came away with a carrier bag full of different medications. I was still feeling fit, doing light weights and going swimming every day. That all changed as soon as I started taking the drugs in my goodie bag; I felt extremely tired and my face went grey. We'd go out for dinner, but halfway through the meal I'd have to sneak outside for a nap in the car. Another of the side effects was feeling very unsteady on my feet. Once I started the cancer treatment, the doctors kept adding more drugs to counteract the side effects of the first batch, which in turn had their own side effects. They then added more to counteract the side effect of those.

Despite the drugs making me feel dreadful, I think the Oncology Centre in Nicosia must be one of the best cancer hospitals in the world. But what was most distressing was seeing how many young people were in there, kids and teenagers who shouldn't have been living with cancer. We would all sit together in a circle, each connected to wires delivering our medication. It was funny when the nurse came around with a clipboard to take a register and confirm all our details. When she called my name out and I put my hand up, she looked at her clipboard in a puzzled manner. 'Is this your correct date of birth?' she asked. I nodded. '1939? That means you are 70?! You don't look anywhere near 70!' All the kids started cheering, which made me smile.

I really enjoyed the company of all these young people, I felt like we were all part of a special club and it was nice to have this beacon of light in such a dark period of my life. I also found the bravery of all these delightful kids, who were just trying to make the best of their situation, very inspirational. They all gave me a great incentive to try and do the same. But just before I left the Oncology Centre, my consultant told me they had found something on my liver and that I needed to return a few days later for further tests. 'It might be nothing, but we don't want to take a chance.' Within moments of feeling more positive about my treatment, I felt like an eagle who'd just had its wings clipped. If the cancer had spread to my liver, that was it, end of story.

As I drove back from Nicosia, I reflected on my life, uncertain about how much time I had left. What was I going to tell Pam about this latest body blow? I desperately needed a one-to-one with my maker. I pulled off the motorway and headed to an old church I knew, just outside a village. Old churches are lovingly restored back in the UK, whereas in Cyprus they simply build new ones, the size of cathedrals, and abandon the old crumbling ruins. Locals who have been christened or married in these old churches still visit them and light candles for their loved ones.

This old empty church wasn't much bigger than a double garage, with only the lingering smell of burnt-out candles to greet me. Particles of floating dust disturbed by my entrance were illuminated by the shafts of technicolour sunlight, shining through the old stained-glass windows. Solemn saints adorned the natural stone walls, waiting to be kissed and worshipped. I lit a candle and knelt in prayer to the Father…

When I got home and told Pam that the cancer might have spread to my liver, she hugged me. 'Whatever the news when we go back to the Oncology centre, we will take it as it comes.'

DISSOLVE TO:
INT. ONCOLOGY CENTRE. 2010.

BARRY and PAM sit holding hands, preparing themselves for the worst. Opposite them, the CONSULTANT, 30s, tall, dark and handsome, puts BARRY's test results to one side and looks over his half-moon glasses with a reassuring smile.

              CONSULTANT
  Cheer up. You have a typical Cypriot complaint.

BARRY and PAM looks at each other in amazement.

              BARRY
  It's not the cancer?

              CONSULTANT
  You have a fatty liver. Do you drink the dreaded local fire water?

              BARRY
  Zivania? Occasionally.

                PAM
    "It's a man's drink!"
                BARRY
        (jokingly)
    It's forced on me.
                PAM
        (sarcastic)
    Oh yeah!
                CONSULTANT
    Believed to be the panacea of all ills. It's
    great for cleaning floors, washing windscreens,
    scrubbing toilets and aching joints. Not so good
    during cancer treatment. My advice, if you need to
    drink, a glass of red wine will be more beneficial.
        (Rising to his feet).
    Have a nice day.

As well as hiding my bottles of the dreaded Zivania, a Cypriot pomace brandy, Sacha did plenty of reading about my cancer. She spoke to her friend Caroline, a qualified herbalist and naturopath, who recommended that I drink Essiac tea, a herbal blend originally used by Chippewa Indians as a form of cancer treatment. Pam helped brew up the tea for me, which we bottled, and I drank a cup every night. Within a week, the grey look that my medication had given me disappeared, and gradually my energy came back. It got to the point where I no longer felt sick and I confided in my family that I felt like a fraud, despite living with advanced cancer.

Just as I started to feel like we were getting our lives back on track, my old friend fate delivered another cruel blow. I noticed that Pam had developed a slight slur in her voice, which she dismissed when I questioned it. The following week, when we went to Vrasidas Taverna, Pam stumbled and fell over. We all rushed to help her up and she joked that she wasn't drunk. I knew that something wasn't right with my soul mate, but she wouldn't accept that there was anything wrong. Over time, the slur in her speech got worse, but she refused to go to the doctor.

When we went back to the UK to visit Simon and his family, I confided in him about my concern for Pam's health. Simon finally managed to persuade his mum to book an appointment and back in Cyprus, her doctor began to run some tests, during which time she also found that she couldn't swallow food properly. We went to see a number of consultants, who carried out even more tests, including electric shock treatment.

When I went back two days later to collect the latest test results, the receptionist told me that the doctor wanted to see me. He sat me down and explained that Pam had Motor Neurone Disease, a condition for which there is still no known cure. There was nothing we could do. I gathered as much information about her condition as I could and then sat down to explain it all to her.

We were devastated.

Pam and I made a tacit agreement that we would go together, and I gave up all my cancer treatment to look after her, as I could not afford to be away from home travelling to the Oncology centre. I was put on palliative care and threw away all the drugs I had been prescribed and only took the herbal supplements.

Pam kept a diary at this time, explaining how her body was feeling. With each page, as the months went by, her handwriting rapidly deteriorated, until it eventually became a series of scrawls. Pam had always been very good at crosswords and sudoku puzzles, but now she was unable to enjoy these hobbies. She got worse and worse in a matter of weeks and soon lost control of all her muscles through this terrible disease. Seeing my best friend in such distress was unbearably upsetting and painful.

I offered to set up a bed downstairs to make it easier for Pam to get around, but she insisted that she wanted to sleep in her own bed, by my side, overlooking the view from our balcony in the dream home we had built for ourselves. With Sacha's help, I carried my beloved wife up to bed every night. As she was no longer able to go outside, I vowed to bring the garden to her and I brought in fresh flowers every day, grown in the lovely garden we had designed and created together.

Eventually, Pam was no longer able to eat, but I still cooked her a proper meal every night, delivered on a tray to her in bed, as I still wanted us to enjoy the experience of a candlelit dinner together, as we had always done. Afterwards, we would hold hands and pray. I remember looking into her eyes and quoting one of my favourite sonnets from the Bard:

TOGETHER WE MADE IT HAPPEN

To me, fair friend, you never can be old
For as you were when first your eye I eyed
Such seems your beauty still

Our love for each other is so profound, as is our enormous gratitude to God for our life together and nearly fifty years of marriage. But no words can adequately express the anguish we suffered together during this time of darkness. Just months after her diagnosis, Pam left us on 5 February 2014. She was 76.

I didn't want the service at Pam's funeral to be prolonged, so I arranged for it to be conducted at her graveside, in the sunshine and fresh air. Nobody was allowed to dress in black and we all wore a red rose, which we then placed on Pam's coffin. After the vicar's sermon, I asked Simon to read the eulogy. Instead of a speech, Simon read the last verse of 'The Highwayman', an inspirational folk song written by Jimmy Webb about a group of people from the past, one of whom has died and lived again…

I'll fly a starship
Across the universe divide
Until I reach the other side
I'll find a place to rest my spirit if I can
Perhaps I may become a Highwayman again
Or I may simply be a single drop of rain
But I will remain
And I'll be back again
And again, and again and again.

Simon chose this song as he knew how much the words mean to me. He read it beautifully and did us all proud.

Cremation is not an option in Cyprus, so everybody gets buried. There is a little graveyard where we live, but we could not bury Pam there as we were informed it is for Cypriots only. It wasn't until the day before her funeral that we found out Pam's final resting place would be a lovely plot at the main cemetery in town, surrounded by lots of trees and nature. I had her tombstone engraved with the words 'Together we made it happen'.

Having withdrawn from my cancer treatment, I then set all my affairs in order and expected to be joining Pam in that beautiful cemetery before long. Sacha had other ideas. Having moved in to help me care for her mum, Sacha now made it her mission to improve my health. She transformed my diet, ensuring I ate a lot more vegetables and cut out nearly all processed food. She then introduced a spring clean of my body; a strict two-week nutritional detox that helps clean out the 'zombie' cells that linger in our bodies as we get older. Sacha then introduced a different kind of omega 3 supplement, combined with olive oil, and also support for my gut, immune system and general health. Gradually my energy levels increased and I continued to feel better and stronger.

I have always believed in the power of prayer and this, combined with Sacha's love and ongoing nutritional guidance, has meant that somehow I am still here. My cancer is currently 'static' and apparently not doing anything at the moment. I'm sure that sometime in the future it will bite me in the arse but, for now, I am grateful for every day. Thank you, God, for this latest miracle and thank you Sacha, for giving up your life to look after your old dad. I love you and I am grateful.

I have also been lucky to have great friends like Vassos, Vrasidas, Andros and his nephew Leandros, who I first met when we made *East of Wild Goat Rocks*, all of whom have been great support. They all dropped everything when Pam died and helped me through the toughest time of my life. They also helped me when I was in danger of becoming a recluse and backing away from the world beyond Villa Chloe. Those friends have become family.

Something that has always made me sad, especially since losing Pam, is the number of people I encounter who are estranged from their families. I have met people who literally don't know where their own children are in the world. I am a big believer in the family dynamic, perhaps because of how I had grown up during the war, with my parents largely absent while they both doing their bit for 'King and Country'. It has become increasingly important for me to keep my family together.

My sister Susan and her husband Dave are always great company when they come over to visit and I make sure I ring Susan every week for a chat. My son Simon, who now runs his own successful company and annual boardgames festival, visits me several times a year with his partner Sarah. And all my grown-up grandchildren have also been over here with their boyfriends too. For my 85th birthday, I treated them all to a lovely meal at a local taverna and I loved sitting at the head of the table, listening to all these young people talk about their hopes and dreams.

Sacha has been phenomenal at keeping me going and helping me find the positives in life. She suggested that we start adopting rescue dogs and provide a home for feral cats. Before long, Villa Chloe found its voice again and I very much enjoy taking the dogs for a walk. I still do my two-week detox twice a year and have done my best to stay active, manage my diet and maintain my fitness. I go swimming most days and enjoy pottering in the garden.

I also try to focus on living in the moment and enjoying the little things in life, from listening to my favourite music, to watching programmes like *Bangers & Cash* and *Wheeler Dealers*, both of which remind me of happy days working at Mann's Garage and racing around the skid track in Monmouth. I am still trying to improve my Italian cooking and my 'weapon of choice' these days is either a Chianti Reserva or a Merlot, neither of which require a holster.

There are not many of us 'Old Bill' left now. I was sad when Nipper Read passed away in 2020, at the grand old age of 95. I last saw him when he was on holiday in Paphos with his wife Pat, a former WPC who I had worked with way back on G Division. Nipper and I met up for a coffee and talked about the old days, then went for a meal with Pat and Pam. Nipper was a great copper and a really nice man, I liked him a lot.

I have kept in touch with a few of my old comrades in arms who are still standing. Dave Dixon is now enjoying retirement after serving as head of the Anti-Terrorism Squad. Bill Laver, my other partner in crime prevention, is also enjoying retirement and like me is still amazed by the ongoing appeal of *The Bill*. Both he and Bob Robinson, former head of the Flying Squad, have been out to see me in Cyprus and we continue to chat regularly and remind each other of some of the extraordinary cases we worked on. We all went through a lot together and I am happy to still be in touch with these brave and brilliant men.

I also occasionally hear from my old colleagues at Sun Hill. In 2017, I got a phone call from a very familiar voice. It was John Salthouse. 'You won't believe this, Barry, but we're back!' John revealed that the Drama Channel in the UK were going to start repeating *The Bill* from the beginning. 'Bring on the repeat fees, my son!' The royalties duly started to come in, which were a big surprise and, whilst a fraction of what they had been in our 1980s heyday, I was very thankful for them.

These repeats helped introduce our old stories to a new generation of fans, who had not been born when the likes of Ackland, Carver, Cryer and Hollis were first walking the beat back in 1984. I was then amazed when I was asked to be interviewed by Oliver Crocker, a television historian, for his two *Witness Statements* books about *The Bill*, which gave me an excuse to revisit all my old episodes. Suddenly, I felt back in the game.

A very important person who helped me become a screenwriter in the first place was Teresa Howard, my first agent. I had lost touch with Teresa when we moved to Cyprus, but in July 2024, I heard she was attending a film festival in Greece. With a bit of help, I managed to get her phone number and I gave her a call for the first time in twenty years. 'Teresa, it's Barry'. 'BARRY?!' I couldn't believe how happy she was to hear from me.

Teresa changed the rest of her trip and came to stay with us in Villa Chloe for a few days. She was devastated to hear about Pam, and we both had a good cry. Having this emotional reunion, forty years after she had opened so many doors for me as a writer, was a truly special experience. Looking back on our 1980s partnership, which was transformative for us both, we realised just how magical a time it had been and what a fairytale my writing career was.

The television industry is completely different now and today a writer starting out would have far more hoops to jump through before getting their break. Programmes are now produced by committee and the days of people like Michael Chapman and Peter Cregeen giving an untested writer a chance to write for a major drama series are sadly no more. It reminded me just how lucky I had been.

It still amazes me when I think about my life; the boy from the Welsh valleys who ended up chasing armed villains around the streets of London and investigating some of the biggest crimes of the twentieth century. And perhaps even more incredible that I made the leap from Flying Squad cop to small screen scribe. I also appreciate that I am lucky to still be here and so, keen to give something back, I have started attending writers' circles here in Cyprus, giving talks to new and established writers, sharing my experiences and hopefully offering some useful advice.

Also important for me is to try and be a faithful servant to God in thought and prayer and closely follow His way with whatever time I have left. I was sometimes reckless in my youth and could easily have turned out to be one of the bad guys. God has done so many wonderful things for me, helping me work out how far I can go and occasionally remind me where the lines are along the way. He has shown me the true path, through love, and I have been grateful for His forgiveness throughout my life.

Writing this book has been an incredible journey for an old man and given me a new lease of life. I could not have completed this book without the support of Sacha and Simon, nor without Oliver Crocker, who became my right-hand man and helped draw out my memories, find all the corroborating evidence and make sense of the many unbelievable things that have happened in my life so far. I also couldn't have done any of it without Pam.

I have done my best to make the most of every single moment over the last ten years since Pam died. However, the truth is I still miss her terribly; she is and will always be my rock. As Kris Kristofferson famously sang, 'Loving her was easier than anything I'll ever do again…' When we got married, we became as one and I faithfully believe that Pam's life did not end at that open grave. She continues to live on, one way or another, by my side and I know she is still with me. Pam is my judgement; she helps me make decisions and she certainly continues to help me with my cooking. I still light those candles on the dinner table for Pam, every single night. I look forward to being reunited with my soulmate once again. But for now, we still have work to do.

Together, we'll make it happen.

ACKNOWLEDGEMENTS

I would like to thank my daughter Sacha and my son Simon for all their love, support and input.

I would also like to thank my ghost, Oliver Crocker, who created an engaging autobiography; high on action and entertainment whilst perfectly capturing the magical moments of my life, adding a touch of good humour and pathos along the way. Nobody could have done it better.

We would both like to thank Teresa Howard for sharing her personal archive with us and giving such support and encouragement and Amy Jordan at Pen & Sword for believing in the project and Matthew Potts, Jon Wilkinson and Rosie Crofts for their support and input.

We are also grateful to Michael Allen and Sheldon Kosky from the Potters Bar Museum, Ralph Brown, Peter Sandwith from Stage One and Nigel Wilson for allowing their photographs to be reproduced with permission.

We would also like to thank Andros Achilleos, Kim Bowers, Rob Cook, Peter Cregeen, Tessa Crocker, Rebecca Deeprose, Dave Dixon, George Fairbrother, Johnny Fleming, Chris Humphreys, Jon Iles, Edward Kellett, Bill Laver, David Lipton, Nick Reding, Eric Richard, Bob Robinson, Natalie Roles, John Salthouse, Edward Smith at the Metropolitan Police Museum, Patrick Stratford, James Thompson and Peter Walsingham for providing advice, information and support.

And above all, I would like to thank Pam – for sprinkling some good luck gold dust on us when we needed it.

Dear Reader,

We hope you have enjoyed this book, but why not share your views on social media? You can also follow our pages to see more about our other products: facebook.com/penandswordbooks or follow us on X @penswordbooks

You can also view our products at www.pen-and-sword.co.uk (UK and ROW) or www.penandswordbooks.com (North America).

To keep up to date with our latest releases and online catalogues, please sign up to our newsletter at: www.pen-and-sword.co.uk/newsletter

If you would like a printed catalogue with our latest books, then please email: enquiries@pen-and-sword.co.uk or telephone: 01226 734555 (UK and ROW) or email: uspen-and-sword@casematepublishers.com or telephone: (610) 853-9131 (North America).

We respect your privacy and we will only use personal information to send you information about our products.

Thank you!